P9-EDG-008

COLUMBIA BRANCH
RECEIVED
DEC 22 2018

NO LONGER PROPERTY OF
SEATTLE PUBLIC LIBRARY

FRENCH GRILL

FRENCH

GRILL

125
REFINED & RUSTIC
RECIPES

Susan Herrmann Loomis

The Countryman Press
A division of W. W. Norton & Company
Independent Publishers Since 1923

Page 226: A variation of the Sablés recipe was published in *French Farmhouse Cookbook*.
Pages 276 and 279: On Rue Tatin's Tender Tart Pastry and Vanilla Sugar have been
published in each of my previous books.

Copyright © 2018 by Susan Herrmann Loomis
Photographs © 2018 by Francis Hammond

All rights reserved
Printed in China

For information about permission to reproduce selections from this book,
write to Permissions, The Countryman Press, 500 Fifth Avenue, New York, NY 10110

For information about special discounts for bulk purchases, please contact
W. W. Norton Special Sales at specialsales@wwnorton.com or 800-233-4830

Manufacturing through Imago
Book design by Nick Caruso Design
Production manager: Devon Zahn

The Countryman Press
www.countrymanpress.com

A division of W. W. Norton & Company, Inc.
500 Fifth Avenue, New York, NY 10110
www.wwnorton.com

978-1-68268-084-1

10 9 8 7 6 5 4 3 2 1

I dedicate this book to Family
(Mom, Dad, Joe, Fiona, Jeff, John, Mary, Kate, Ellen, Lena, Karen, Brinn).
They get you started; they keep you going.

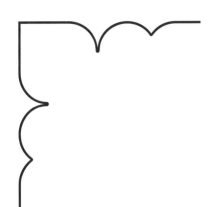

CONTENTS

Acknowledgments 10

Introduction 13

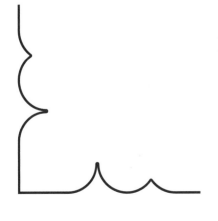

"O! for a muse of fire, that would ascend
The brightest heaven of invention!"

—WILLIAM SHAKESPEARE

ACKNOWLEDGMENTS

Though I am responsible for everything in this book, I could never do anything like this without the help and inspiration of many, near and far. Part of the beauty of a project like this, aside from learning how to dance around flaming whiskey, tip coals without any falling on your foot, and trying to avoid looking like Cave Girl by the end of a grilling evening, is the people who come forward. To that end, many thanks are in order:

Thank you, Bruno Verjus of Table restaurant, Chef Eric Trochon of Semilla and Freddy's, Chef Bertrand Simon of *Le Monde* newspaper, my handyman Christophe Guégan, and my dear and darling friend Astrid Bonnafont-Serre. Each of you contributed a nugget or more of vital information that set me on this particular grilling path with stability, excitement, and an abundance of ideas that have made it such a wonderful project and have resulted in what I hope is a wonderful work!

Research is a huge part of writing a book. A wise friend once told me that I would always end up doing 10,000 more hours of research than I would ever use, and she was right. One has to read, read, and ask, ask so much to digest and figure out the hows and the whys. I've researched and read, and I want to thank my old friend and colleague Steve Raichlen, grill maestro extraordinaire, for his books and all of his very classy and world-wise grilling wisdom; Jamie Purviance, for his amazing work and multitude of books; and Meathead Goldwyn, for his book and blog. You've each written and explained so much about the technical aspects of grilling and have done it so well and thoroughly that I don't have to. *Thank you.* I've absorbed your wisdom. Dear reader and cook, I direct you to these three fine grill experts for tips and tricks on how to set up your grilling universe.

Thanks to Lindsay Kinder for cheerfully keeping my business going during this process; thanks to sweet Helen Liang and brave Carolyn Johnson for reading through the manuscript (Carolyn while on a Doctors Without Borders ship off the coast of Libya).

Thanks go to my team of US recipe testers, particularly Kelly Lytle, who always says "Sure!" even when she's asked to test coconut ice cream; Shannon Lemon, who stops at nothing, is happily surprised at everything, and keeps me smiling; and Sandy Kitchen, Robin Currie, Rochelle Rush, Christine Dutton, Kim Wiley, Marion Pruitt, and Vivian Savaris. You're terrific and your comments and wisdom have made everything better. I also want to thank testers in extremis, Karen Kaplan, Cathy Arkle, and Deborah Ritchkin. My group of lifesavers.

As for music, which is so important to life, the artists that helped me through this book include Simon & Garfunkel, Erik Satie, Ottmar Liebert, and occasionally Country Joe & the Fish.

My friends are now accustomed to my various projects, and I must salute them for joining in once again, having patience (wine and appetizers help—turn to Carmelized Dates Stuffed with Almonds, Sweet and Salty Grilled Almonds, and Smoky Olives!), even when dishes were in their "early stages of development," and generally adding their two centimes to the whole affair: Ellen Cole and Michael Daum, Christian Laporte for his special support, Rod Hildebrandt and Matthew Meehan, Christian and Nadine Devisme, Betty and Louis Garcia, Baptiste and Mathilde Bourdon, Nathalie Souchet and Arnaud Héridon, Edith and Bernard Leroy, Lena Sodergren, Salah and Dalila Boufercha, Michel and Chantal Amsalem, Elisabeth Hyde, Randy and Chris Shuman, François Xavier and Inès Priollaud, Bernadette Gohel, Therese Leduc, and the unforgettable "Overs," Nelleke Geel and Sabine Baak, who keep me going.

Thank you to my next-door neighbor, Mr. Stéphane Coutard, the butcher. Always there, always ready to help with gorgeous meats, advice, and recipes. "Slow" is his byword.

Thank you, Bruno Richomme, the fishmonger. Always there, always ready to help with gorgeous seafood of all kinds. As Herodotus said, "Neither snow nor rain nor heat nor gloom of night stays these fish mongers from the swift completion of their appointed rounds."

Thank you, Baptiste—I talk about you all the time because you nourish me, my family, and my friends on a daily basis. Without people like you, life and our plates would be a sad affair.

Now, for Francis Hammond, photographer: a huge, big thank you for the photos, for the great photo sessions, and for the seriously silly jokes that doubled us over time after time. You're an artist and a pleasure to work with. Anytime, Francis Francis. Anytime.

Thank you to my magical agent Jane Dystel, for endless encouragement, patience, and sincerity, and Miriam Goderich, for her enthusiasm and excellence. Thank you to my fantastic editor Ann Treistman, and to Aurora Bell for keeping all the strands untangled. Thank you, too, to the promotion team of Devorah Backman, Maya Bayan, and Chloe Rose for getting the word out to the world about *French Grill*.

Last, but first, there is Fiona, my darling daughter, who gracefully lived through this entire project with me on an intimate basis. She is usually vegan, always vegetarian, and extremely tolerant as she watched me grill pound after pound of meat and seafood, then sat down to eat around them. She inspired me because she has a fine palate and a fine mind, and she helped out always, as she always has.

And thank you to my wonderful son, Joe, whose first contribution was lighting the coals on my kitchen stove. I'm not sure how he does it, but his encouragement, ideas, and support from across the miles are as immediate as if he were here every day.

Finally, but not finally at all, I thank my brother, Jeff. A consummate grill chef, he came, he oversaw, he contributed his vast knowledge and a panoply of accessories that have made my grilling life easy and professional.

Lucky me.

INTRODUCTION

French Barbecue. This is an oxymoron, *non? Mais non!* The French invented barbecue. You didn't know that? Well, here is what happened. Way back when, the Gauls were racing through lush forests in what is now Brittany, Normandy, and the Loire Valley, hunting wild boar, deer, and fleet-footed rabbits. They were also raising their own brand of pig. When they weren't doing that they were spearing and netting wonders from the sea.

They would return to the village, build a huge fire, and split whatever animal they had from *la barbe à la queue,* literally the "beard" or head to the tail, for roasting. Thus, the technique and the word *barbecue* were invented.

We think of the Gauls as barbarians, which is exactly what the Romans thought when they came and, eventually, conquered them. Perhaps the Romans thought this because the Gauls didn't wear white robes and eat lying down, but they shouldn't have. The Gauls were incredible craftsmen and creative cooks. They understood salting and curing, sausage making, and cooking meats until they were crisp on the outside, red on the inside, just the way we like them today. They used herbs and different woods for flavoring, and they made bacon. They set mussels and clams on a bed of pine needles over the coals, nestling oysters under and around them, and skewered fish either whole or in pieces, charring them just until their juices began to drip. And they made frothy beer from grains and honey, as well as wine.

Nothing has really changed. The French are still great barbecuers, though they are only now beginning to celebrate their traditional skill. Why, just this evening, the first time it's been warm since last fall, I rode through town and inhaled the mouth-watering aroma of food on the grill. Let me be specific: of *meat* on the grill. The French *love* to grill meat, and the minute the skies dry up and the sun comes out even slightly, they're building fires and watching them turn to red-hot coals as the meat sits at room temperature, ready for its hot fate.

The Gallic skill with meat has left its trace in many things, not the least of which is the amazing panoply of sausages found in every butcher shop in the land. On any given day I can go to my neighborhood butcher and find *saucisson à l'ail,* a garlicky, fat pork sausage that sizzles so gratifyingly over the coals; *Jésu de Morteau,* which are fat, smoky pork sausages from the Jura, a department in eastern France; skinny *chipolatas* that come in dozens of flavors from curry to thyme; *le chistera* from the Basque country that combines pork, beef, and a fair sprinkling of red pepper; and paprika-red chorizo from the Maghreb region of North Africa. Come summer, my butcher cannot make "brochettes"—skewers threaded with meat, bell peppers, and onions—fast enough.

We have a lot to thank the Gauls for (Hermès bags, for instance; the Gauls were the precursors of France's fine leather workers), with grilling at the top of the list. The Gauls had an endless supply of wood, they had fire, they had meat, they had appetites, and because they were on the way to becoming the French we know today, they had palates and style.

Grilling didn't stop with the Gauls; it evolved. Fast-forward to the Middle Ages, when fires were now burning in huge stone hearths or in outbuildings. Grilling was still common, but stewing had crept in and food was being cooked in closed pots with herbs and vegetables, still over an open fire. Wood was the fuel, slow grilling the method.

The French have had centuries to refine their barbecuing, and they're still working on it, using tried and true methods, copying others, and inventing still others. They've borrowed the gas grill from the United States, the *plancha* from Spain, and the *méchoui* method from North Africa. Call it what you like; it's all barbecue, and it's being done in homes and gardens throughout the country.

GRILLING SEASON

The aroma of grilled foods begins to waft through the air in France with the first fine weather, which can be as early as March, when those warm, rogue weekends dawn after a long winter. The butcher hasn't yet had time to make brochettes, but it doesn't matter. Any protein will do for the early grill chef.

Grilling becomes de rigueur by May. Then, flowers in the gardens and parks of France are bursting into bloom and everyone with a backyard grill—most French people who live in the "country," defined as any place within a half an hour of a major city—begins to dust off their grilling equipment. By May, stores have stocked up on charcoal, briquettes, grilling accoutrements, and grills, and the butchers are really paying attention. Once the temperature crests 70°F, they begin to say farewell to the meats of winter (joints, tails, cheeks) in favor of grill meats (steaks, ribs, loins, and every possible part of the fowl).

I've mentioned that the French barbecue chef is meat oriented. Chef Simon, the resident chef of the center-left newspaper *Le Monde,* who supplies recipes to its readers, says, "The preponderance of meat on the French barbecue no doubt relates to the alpha male who shows off in front of his children ['and everyone else,' I say!], and wants to make the most of all the time he spent lighting the fire." Personally, I think the preponderance of meat on the grill is due to Gallic-ness ingrained in the DNA of every French man (maybe every man?). This is changing, thanks in part to people like Chef Simon who challenge the

French barbecue alpha male to add vegetables and fruits to his repertoire.

IT'S NOT A WOMAN'S JOB

And make no mistake, in France it is always "him" at the grill. Seriously, grilling can be a messy business, and in France, where roles are still quite defined, well, I've found myself in some pretty funny situations related to the gender gap of a woman grilling while men sit alongside to watch. First, greeting guests with my long grilling gloves on and smudges of charcoal on my face has made everyone, including me, split with laughter. I'm so involved in what I'm doing that I don't realize what I look like.

I can't count the times we had friends over for dinner, and while I was outside supervising the grill,

so were all of the men, hovering, suggesting, practically grabbing the tongs out of my hand. Fortunately, my friends are used to me taking charge, and, after some delicate dancing and making sure that all egos were intact, I took back the tongs and had the last laugh when they cut into the perfectly grilled *côte de boeuf* (Grilled Beef Chop, page 127), the succulent rabbit with bacon (Rabbit with Mustard and Crisp Bacon, page 83), the tender asparagus (Grilled Asparagus, page 174). Oh my, but challenging the established order is a tricky thing.

GAS OR COAL

I've always grilled over coals, though I knew I needed a gas grill to write this book (plus, it seemed like a great new culinary toy to have). I invested in a gorgeous Weber gas grill with three big, fat burners. It has pride of place next to my Weber charcoal grill and isn't far from my kitchen fireplace. I was so excited to have it so that I could be like my friends in the US, who are constantly stepping outside to grill something. The simplicity of it has always amazed me.

And it has been exciting. How great it is to light up a gas grill outside, prepare everything inside, and go back out to cook it. There's no muss, no kitchen fuss, and no heat inside on a blistery day. It's the outdoor kitchen that everyone in France used to have in the old days, not always by choice but by prudence, when cooking was done over the fire and houses were built of wood and thatched with straw.

But cooking over gas has also been disappointing. I somehow thought that grilling on a gas grill would result in smoky food. It doesn't. I know. I'm the only person who didn't know that before I tried it. Of course with a certain amount of manipulation, you can make smoky food over gas—it's a process that involves pans of wet wood chips set over gas burners. I didn't do anything like that for this book because it just isn't the way I want to cook, or show you how to cook, or the way the French cook. It feels like too much manipulation and not like the natural, lovely, wonderful cooking that issues from the soul.

So, as I developed, tested, and retested recipes for this book, I inevitably found myself building a fire in the big Weber charcoal grill. Fire has been, and still is, the thrill of grilling for me. It is also the way the French grill. No one I know here has a gas grill. When I got mine it was like a scene from 1950s France when the first tractors arrived—everyone wanted to see it. They'd come just for that and stand outside in the courtyard to ooh and aah. "*Quel engine!*" they'd say. "What a machine." Then they'd go home and cook over wood.

All of this is to say that I've tested most of the recipes on the charcoal grill and many of them on the gas grill too. They've all been tested in the US, most of them on gas grills. Almost everything will turn out the same, except the kiss of wood smoke. Timing and temperature are all almost exactly the same on both grill types, and that's what's most important to me. There is a caveat—some recipes in this book have to be done on the charcoal grill to get the real flavor and effect.

INGREDIENTS FOR THE GRILL

Pretend that you are French, and think local and seasonal when you're searching for ingredients. Local and seasonal ingredients give you the best flavor, are the most economical because there is little waste, and have a carbon footprint that is negligible. You'll love the feeling of putting your money directly into the hands of the person who produced your food, too. It not only gets you the best there is, but it assures their livelihood both in the present and the future.

ORGANIC OR NOT ORGANIC

After singing the organic hymn forever, I've come to favor something we call *culture raisonée,* or smart farming. When a grower follows this system, she or he treats crops for problems only when needed to survive. This is smart, because a crop that fails isn't good for anything or anyone. Farmers need an income to continue; to ensure they have one, a smart farmer will treat the specific cause of a specific problem (think antibiotics for pneumonia). So my suggestion is to think local first, then organic, and always think seasonal.

GETTING OUT OF THE WAY OF INGREDIENTS

This is my mantra and the mantra of all French chefs. The Gauls invented the notion of getting out of the way of their ingredients, and then everyone forgot it until the Renaissance. After the Middle Ages, out went the heavy, spicy sauces and in came fanciful yet simpler preparations, where ingredients came first. Then Auguste Escoffier (1846–1935) came on the scene. He lightened up sauces as he reorganized the kitchen, further honoring the ingredients. Fast-forward to nouvelle cuisine and Michel Guerard, the first minimalist chef to blend the idea of haute cuisine with that of small portions, fine ingredients, and simplicity. While all of this was going on, Mamie was in the kitchen preparing her cocottes and rotis, jardinieres and salads using meats from the animals she raised and vegetables and fruits she'd just picked from her garden or orchard, all with skill but little fanfare.

What does all this have to do with a book about grilling? Everything, because all food is first about ingredients. These developments, notions, and practices lay the case for simplicity, excellent ingredients, and straightforward preparations. They also lay the case for subtlety.

FLAVOR

There is a temptation to muddy the waters when it comes to adding too much flavor to a dish. Occasionally I'll get a recipe back from a US tester and he or she will say, "We loved this, but what about adding more . . . lemon juice, hot pepper, avocado, black pepper, zest . . ." I've already tested and approved the recipe, mind you, so I understand what is happening. To begin with, ingredients in the US sometimes miss a shade of flavor that their French counterparts have. In addition, the French way is to be subtle, to let the ingredient shine, to enhance a dish rather than bury it with flavor. So keep this in mind, then spice things up to suit your palate!

SMOKING FOODS

Using the barbecue to smoke foods isn't a French notion. As such, when creating the recipes for this book, I did not do any *serious* smoking. Instead, I adopted the French style: Give foods the "kiss of smoke," which will enhance flavor, not bury it. I like to use grapevine cuttings or small, dry branches from my apple and pear trees. I don't soak them—I just put them on the fire about five minutes before I smoke whatever I'm cooking. Flames leap then die down, and delicate smoke is left to lightly flavor foods and make them perfect. You can also buy all the wood you need, or you can get it from your neighbors. Just make sure that you're not burning any resinous branches—they don't give good flavor to foods.

TWO-STEP COOKING

I've tried to keep the recipes in this book simple, straightforward, and doable. To this end, I've made every effort to avoid what I call two-step cooking, where part of the cooking process is done in the kitchen, the rest on the grill. I like to grill for so many reasons, and one of them is that it's all outside. It's fantastic! However, there are times when some two-step cooking is necessary, but you won't have to do it much, I promise!

These experts admire, respect, and want the heat of the flame, and they stand back and let it slowly do its work, taming its heat. I've learned to do the same. That's why pork chops grilled à la Française take 20 minutes, rabbit takes an hour, chicken takes an hour and a half, skinny little carrots take 8 minutes, and asparagus—that ultimate quick cooker—takes a full 7 minutes. There isn't a rush to sear, to blacken, or to carbonize, but instead a desire to get the fullness of flavor. I'm not saying the recipes in this book take hours, but many things grill longer than you'd think, and the results are . . . *ooh la la!*

PLEASURE

Grilling slowly doesn't mean there isn't dark, crispy yumminess in the results of the recipes here, from grilled onions to bacon-wrapped cod, to that marvelous rabbit that turns oh-so-slowly over the coals to emerge crisp and juicy (a rabbit on the grill, juicy? Amazing!). There is so much flavor and texture that develops as foods cook slowly, which is what makes foods from the *French Grill* so particularly delicious!

Although food is nourishment, in France it's also pleasure. There is pleasure in the memory of past dishes, in anticipating those in the future. There is much pleasure in planning for and preparing meals, and then there is the ultimate pleasure of sitting down to enjoy what's been prepared.

Grilling takes food a step higher on the pleasure scale because, from the moment the coals are lit, the elemental aroma of smoke tempts and makes people hungry. For the past months and months, every meal we've eaten has come from the grill, and I've seen the pleasure in everyone as they anticipate what's to come. I've discovered, too, immense pleasure in preparing and eating dishes from the grill. Grilling calls upon many instincts and sensual pleasures; it's so compelling, and the results are simply delectable.

FIRE

Grilling is about fire, and it's straightforward and elemental. As Chef Bruno Verjus from Table restaurant in Paris says, "Grilling is the real cooking, it's about the use of heat." He grills over gas flames in his restaurant, everything from paper-thin ramps to whole birds that turn, turn, and turn before getting a final flame just before being served.

Eric Trochon, chef of Semilla and Freddy's in Paris, has a similar feeling about grilling, though he insists on charcoal and fire. "Grilling is primitive," he says. "What interests me about it is the fire, the real fire."

My butcher, a true meat expert, wraps meat or poultry destined for the grill, then fixes you with his eyes. "Don't cook this too hot," he says with deliberation. "It needs tiiiimme."

PAYING ATTENTION

There is something else about grilling. It insists on your total attention. You can have the finest equipment, the most expensive wood or charcoal, the best grilling outfits, but then you can muff it up if you don't pay attention. I'll say right now that the French grill simply. They rarely have fancy equipment. Their style is more to slice a barrel in half and put a grill in it, or make a brick fireplace outdoors and lay a grill in it, or even sweep back the gravel in a courtyard, build a temporary affair, and set a grill on *that*—then proceed to cook the most wonderful dishes. When grilling, I've learned from the French to keep it basic and simple, to pay strict attention, and to thoroughly enjoy the process.

THE RECIPES

Each recipe in this collection includes cooking times. Some include cooking temperatures. All include carefully weighed and measured ingredients, and each gives you a list of specific equipment you'll need and a level of difficulty to expect (which rarely exceeds simple). This is the least I can do for you. And it is really all I can do for you, aside from opening up the world of French grilling. As with much cooking, but even more so here, grilling is a matter of intuition and aroma. Everything about grilling depends on everything else, and the elemental-ness of it can drive you crazy if you're anxious and inattentive.

So while you follow the recipes, pay attention, use your intuition, and focus. Make sure your guests are happy so they aren't distracting you from your task. Invite enough people so they have someone to talk with while you're grilling, and serve them delicious things to occupy their attention.

The recipes here have been tested multiple times in my kitchen, then retested in US kitchens. I can tell you that the times and temperatures listed in each recipe were accurate for me and for the testers. But I

can't control your variables. When working with fire, I can barely control mine.

For instance, I give you the recipe Drunken Lobster (page 105), which should result in the finest lobster you'll ever eat. But what if you're in Maine, it's below zero, and your wet tea towel freezes solid when you walk out to the porch to check the grill? Well, the size of fire and cooking time I give you in this book isn't necessarily going to mean much in that situation. You'll have to figure it out.

So all I can do is tell you to be vigilant, because the variables are many—a strong wind, a rain storm, a hot day, a freezing day, small lump charcoal, large lump charcoal, brands of briquettes, logs, chips, vines, cuttings, barbecue styles—well, I could go on, but you get the idea that there are a million variables that affect the results of grilling.

RECIPE TECHNICALITIES

The recipes are written with the *mise-en-place* (which literally means "putting things in place" and, in cooking terms, means doing all the work of chopping, slicing, and weighing amounts before the cooking begins) worked into the ingredient list. Before you use a recipe, read through it and do everything outlined on the ingredient list. For instance, when a recipe says "one medium onion, diced," dice the onion before proceeding to the next ingredient on the list and, by the time you get to the first cooking step, all your ingredients will be ready to grill.

I've specified building fires that leave room for foods to cook away from the coals, so that they have heat but not fire. This is important, and I hope you'll follow my directions.

Every recipe includes one or many *astuces*. What is an astuce? It's a tip and a trick. The astuces in the recipes are me giving you tips and tricks to make things easier, more clear, more efficient. Life in France requires millions of astuces to get by; I think cooking does too.

ESSENTIALS FOR THE FRENCH GRILL

- Grill(s)—Both charcoal and gas if you have space

- Combustible materials—I like to use a blend of lump charcoal (which burns hot and quickly, and lends a lovely, light smokiness to foods) and briquettes (I prefer Weber brand because they are made with sustainable wood and potato starch and no petroleum products); I sometimes build a wood fire with actual logs, particularly if I'm grilling in the chimney

TOOLS

- Chimney starter—the best tool ever invented for the grill chef/cook

- Flat, rectangular plate or platter to hold oil and salt for rolling vegetables, fruits, and everything else in oil before grilling

- Drip pans, for putting on the barbecue to catch fats as they fall

- Grill brush, preferably metal

- Grill pan—the perforated, metal variety; nonstick is ideal

- Heavy-duty, heatproof gloves

- Instant-read thermometer

- Kitchen twine—which won't burn away, I promise!

- Long metal skewers

- Long tongs (16 inches; 40 cm or more)

- Lots of rags

- Mesh screen—nonstick, rollable

- Multiple timers

- Newspaper—for starting the fire

- Pastry brushes (not silicone; they don't work!)*

- Plancha, or a flat griddle or grill—you can also use a cast-iron skillet

- Rotisserie for the barbecue (amazing tool)

- Tasting spoons

- Trussing skewers

*You have to be willing to sacrifice your pastry brushes, as the bristles may get damaged if you're brushing on sauces over a hot fire. It's a sacrifice for the greater good, since pastry brushes with real bristles are a necessity. The silicon varieties glop or drip sauces all over the place.

FUN HAVES

- Aluminum charcoal holders, for corralling the briquettes/wood on either side of the barbecue

- Small charcoal grill, for taking on trips so you always have a grill at hand

HOW TO BUILD A FIRE

As I've grilled, I've developed a fire-building system based on efficiency and success. It's simple and it works. If you follow these directions, you'll have success every time.

Loosely crumple two sheets (you don't need more) of yesterday's newspaper. Put them, along with a natural fire starter without petroleum products in it, such as small "pods" made of wood shavings and food grade wax, under the chimney. Holding the fire starter in place, quickly set the chimney down in the center of your charcoal grill so the starter doesn't fall out.

Fill the chimney with a mix of briquettes and charcoal (about two-thirds briquettes to one-third charcoal), and light the paper and the natural fire starter with a match or a lighter stick.

Stick around to be sure the paper and the fire starter are burning. When you're sure that all is alight, you can get back in the kitchen to prepare whatever you're going to grill.

Depending on the fuel you've used, the coals should be red-hot inside the chimney in 20 minutes. You'll be amazed at how easy this is. I am, every time; I have so many memories of my wonderful father cursing politely at the barbecue and dousing it with fire starter fluid that smelled like the inside of a poison factory as he struggled to get a good fire lit.

Wearing long, thick, protective gloves, tip out the burning coals from the chimney into your barbecue. Depending on how much you'll be cooking, you may want to add more briquettes and charcoal. Spread out the red-hot coals, and then top them (without burying them) completely with new briquettes and charcoal. Let these burn until they are red and dusted with ash before cooking.

Proceed with your recipe.

Rule of thumb: Briquettes stay hotter longer; lump charcoal gives more smoke flavor. I use a mix.

Sometimes you'll have lots of leftover coals. Here is what you do: Cover the grill and close all the openings. The next time you're going to build a fire, dust these off and use them. They will still have lots of burn time in them.

GRILL CLEANING AND UPKEEP

It's vital to keep the grill clean. The best way to do this is through heat, using a sturdy metal brush, then either a lightly oiled rag or a half a lemon (which cleans off any grease). If you don't want to "waste" a lemon, use a cloth dampened with white vinegar to remove grease.

Brush the grill firmly with a wire brush before building the fire. There is controversy in the US about using metal grill brushes because the bristles can break off and get lodged in food, becoming dangerous. The solution is to brush the grill, then rub it briskly with a lightly oiled rag, which removes any errant bristles. Rubbing it with the half lemon or vinegared rag is further assurance against loose bristles. Set the grill over the hot coals. The heat will burn off anything that may be left on the grill.

Clean the grill during grilling, between foods. For instance, when the chicken is cooked and you want to move on to the asparagus, quickly brush the grill, rub it briskly with the lightly oiled cloth, then proceed.

When all the grilling is done, give a quick brush to the grill and a quick wipe with the cloth, and then put it to bed. The next time you're going to grill you can clean it thoroughly.

INSTINCT, INTUITION, AND SAFETY

There are two other very important necessities to fine grilling: instinct and intuition. They come into play for grilling more than for any other type of cooking because grilling is immediate. Things happen quickly when you grill. You're working with fire, after all, and you have to play with the heat to make it all work. As you go through these recipes, you'll develop both instinct and intuition, which will make you an expert, safe grill chef/cook. You will learn that if flames start to shoot up under foods, you need to move them. When you think you need to turn some-thing, you will turn it. If you misjudged, you will turn it back. If your fire isn't hot enough, you'll know to add coals, wait until they're hot, and proceed with cooking. If your fire is too hot, you'll learn that the lid is like a damper—use it to reduce heat by putting it on, closing the vents, and waiting until the coals calm. Then, once the coals have cooled, open up vents and proceed.

Here are a few other gems:

- Use timers.

- Always have gloves at hand.

- Use long tongs.

- Don't go inside the house and start to write the Great American Novel while grilling—you need to stay close to the grill.

HEALTH AND GRILLING

Grilled foods are healthy, right? Yes, they are. Super healthy. But as with any cooking method or food you eat, you have to pay attention to the details. I've outlined some basic information that will keep you grilling healthily.

Place meats on the grill so that fats don't fall directly on the coals or gas grill element, because when they do, they cause the formation of potential cancer-causing substances. The most talked about are polycyclic aromatic hydrocarbons (PAHs) and heterocyclic amines (HCAs). PAHs can form when fat from meat falls directly on coals or a grill element. HCAs form when animal protein is subjected to high heat (not just grilling, but frying, sautéing, and broiling, too). There is no *definitive proof* that either PAHs or HCAs cause cancer, but there are suggestions that they might.

OTHER HEALTHY TIPS

- When you build a fire in the barbecue, make sure to leave part of the grill free, and not directly over the coals, so that you can move foods if there is a flare-up.

- Avoid petroleum products (fire starters, briquettes that are held together with paraffin, etc.).

- Avoid an abundance of fatty, meaty foods.

- Move the coals to either side of the grill and put a drip pan between them.

- Grill fatty meats *in the center of the grill* to begin with. The fat will drip in the grill pan and not on the coals, and the food will turn golden, with time, just the way you want it to.

- For meat that needs quick cooking and browning that only direct contact with heat from the coals can give, first cook the meat in the center of the grill over the drip pan, then put it briefly over the coals and turn it frequently. If there is a flare-up, remove the meat from over the coals until the flames die down.

- On a gas grill, use the two outer elements for heat and cook over the center element.

- Make your own marinade so you know what is in it. Use olive, canola, or nut oils.

- Cook over lower, rather than higher, temperatures. (This is the French way, except in the case of a few foods.)

- Turn meats frequently when they are grilling over high heat.

HERE IS WHAT I MEAN WHEN I SAY . . .

Allow me to point out a few vital elements of the *mise en place* of a recipe so that your eyes won't glaze over as you read them time after time. They are absolutes, vital to the success of a recipe, and I think once you've read them here, you'll remember them forever!

When I call for the following ingredients, this is what I mean:

CLOVE GARLIC: Unspoken is the need to remove the green germ when necessary. This is the nascent garlic plant wanting to grow, and while it won't hurt you, it can be tough and bitter. To remove it, cut the clove down the middle, and then extract and discard the germ.

FRESH BAY LEAF: Unspoken is the variety, *Laurus nobilis,* from the European bay tree. Use this and not the leaf from the California bay tree, *Umbellularia californica,* which has a strong and, to me, unpleasant flavor. If you don't have access to fresh bay leaves, use dried, from Turkey.

OLIVE OIL: Always use extra virgin. It is the first pressing of the olive, the purest oil, sometimes referred to as the juice of the olive. There are many different qualities of extra virgin olive oil. Use the best as a condiment and use a less best, but still delicious, for cooking.

PIMENT D'ESPELETTE: This *very* special pepper is grown only in and around the Basque town of Espelette, near the French and Spanish border. It is richly flavored with a slight kick, and it enhances everything it touches.

RECIPES

"There is no good cooking if,
from the very start,
it isn't made out of friendship for
he or she who will eat it."

—PAUL BOCUSE

CHAPTER 1

APPETIZERS (AMUSE~BOUCHES)

"The apéritif is the evening prayer of the French."

—PAUL MORAND, ARTIST, DIPLOMAT, WRITER

SWEET AND SALTY GRILLED
ALMONDS

GRILLED CHICKEN LIVERS AND ONIONS

CARAMELIZED DATES STUFFED
WITH ALMONDS

SMOKY OLIVES

GRILLED OYSTERS WITH POMMEAU

GRILLED BREAD WITH SMASHED
TOMATOES

SMOKY GUACAMOLE

GRILLED SHIITAKES

CUTE LITTLE MUSHROOMS
ON THE GRILL

Appetizers, or amuse-bouches, are one of my favorite parts of the meal. One reason is because they're small bites, and you can be creative when you both think about and make them. The other reason is because they are served when guests first arrive. Everyone is brushing off their day, shaking out their fatigue, and entering into the spirit of the evening. Anyone who enters grumpy, tired, and out of sorts quickly relaxes and becomes their real self when presented with appetizers like the ones to follow.

SUGGESTED BEVERAGES

Apéritifs are technically drinks, although we refer to the presupper moment as the apéritif, too. I like to serve the same thing to everyone because it establishes a feel to the moment, and everyone is sharing the same experience. But I am here to tell you that I have a group of friends who don't always agree with me! When I am invited into their homes there is always wine, be it white, red, and rosé, and champagne. There might be whiskey, orange juice, pastis, Porto, and champagne. Oddly enough, there is rarely beer. In France, beer is what you drink at the café on a beautiful sunny afternoon, sitting in the shade, quenching your thirst.

Despite what my French friends do, I hold with my philosophy to create an ambiance and a feeling of togetherness by deciding what there is to drink. But if you want to be like the French, offer as much variety among apéritifs as you want.

SWEET AND SALTY GRILLED ALMONDS

AMANDES GRILLÉES SUCRE SALÉES

Makes 2 cups (300 g)

You make this recipe in a quick minute, preferably on the gas grill, then keep just slightly warm and ready to serve to guests the second they walk in the door. I make them when the grill is heated but before I cook dinner. They're a perfect solution for an appetizer. Serve these alongside rosé in the summer, champagne any time of year, or as I did recently, with glasses of chilled pastis to ward off the intense heat of a mid-summer evening.

~~~~~~~~~~~~~~~~~~~~~~~~~~~~~~~~~~

SPECIAL EQUIPMENT: *Grill pan, wooden spatula*

PREPARATION AND GRILLING TIME: *8 minutes*

DIFFICULTY LEVEL: *Simple*

2 cups (300 g) raw almonds

2 teaspoons olive oil

1½ teaspoons fleur de sel or fine sea salt

2 tablespoons sugar

2 teaspoons fresh thyme leaves

ASTUCES: You'll need to supervise the almonds toward the end, as they can burn quickly. And when you strew the sugar, don't worry—what doesn't stick to the almonds will burn off the grill.

PLACE THE ALMONDS IN A LARGE BOWL

and drizzle them with the oil. Toss the almonds, preferably with your hands, until they are coated with the oil. If you think you need a bit more, add a bit—but not too much. Strew in the fleur de sel and toss thoroughly.

Heat all three burners of the gas grill with the grill pan sitting on it. When the grill is hot, place the almonds on it and let them brown, covered, for 3 minutes. Stir them, cover, and cook until their color deepens, an additional 2 minutes. Strew them with the sugar as evenly as you can, stir them, and cook, stirring from time to time until they pop and are quite golden, an additional 3 to 4 minutes. The sugar that doesn't stick to the almonds may send up some curls of smoke; don't be concerned.

When the almonds are toasted, transfer them to a large, heatproof bowl. Add the thyme leaves, toss them, then pour them out onto a plate or platter to cool evenly. As soon as you hear your guests arrive, transfer them to a serving bowl and watch them disappear. (Actually, don't watch. You've got grilling to do!)

GRILLED CHICKEN LIVERS AND ONIONS

FOIES DE VOLAILLES AUX OIGNONS

Serves 4 for a generous appetizer

When I buy a whole chicken at the butcher or the market, the liver is still where it was meant to be; that is, inside the chicken. This makes it challenging to find chicken livers, but every now and then I can order them either from the butcher or from a local chicken grower if they've had a particularly heavy week of chicken breast demand. If so, they keep and sell the chicken livers separately.

The chicken liver trend in France right now is brochettes of livers and hearts. Hearts are tough to find (see above re: livers), so I decided to replace them with baby onions that are just a bit larger than a chicken heart. The combination is gorgeous. This is technically an appetizer, but I predict that if you serve this with a glass of Languedoc red in front of the fireplace, you can skip the first course and head right into the main part of the meal.

~~~~~~~~~~~~~~~~~~~~~~~~~~~~~~~

SPECIAL EQUIPMENT: *4 long skewers (optional), grill pan (optional), tongs*

PREPARATION AND GRILLING TIME: *30 minutes macerating time; 15 minutes preparation and grilling time*

DIFFICULTY LEVEL: *Simple*

---

2 tablespoons olive oil

Generous ½ teaspoon freshly ground nutmeg

12 chicken livers (about 10 ounces; 300 g total), chilled, trimmed, and cut in half crosswise

10 smallish spring onions, trimmed and cut in half

20 sprigs (or more) fresh thyme, rinsed and patted dry

Coarse sea salt and freshly ground black pepper

PLACE THE OIL AND NUTMEG IN A MEDIUM bowl and whisk together quickly and thoroughly. Add the livers, onions, and thyme and fold them all together. Set aside for at least 30 minutes, and up to 1 hour, refrigerated. You can also do this the night before you plan to grill the liver and onions. If you do this, make sure to remove them from the refrigerator at least an hour before you plan to grill them.

Build a medium-size fire in the barbecue.

When the coals are red and dusted with ash, spread them in a tight, single layer, leaving a perimeter of grill with no coals under it; they need to emit concentrated heat. Set the grill over the coals.

To make the brochettes, begin with an onion, and alternate on the skewer with the pieces of chicken livers, making sure as you skewer the livers that they include some thyme sprigs. You may need to be creative about skewering the livers; you want to avoid having parts of the livers dangling off the skewer, so go ahead

continued

ASTUCES: I call for chilled livers because they are easier to trim, cut in pieces, and thread on skewers. I like to cook these on skewers because they're easier to handle and rather dramatic to serve. Depending on the size of the livers and the onions, you may prefer to grill these, separated, on a generously oiled grill pan.

and skewer each piece in several spots if need be. Season the livers and onions with a generous scatter of salt and pepper.

Place the skewers over the coals and cook them until the livers are browned on one side, about 1½ minutes. Turn them and repeat. Cover and cook for 1½ minutes, then turn, cover, and cook for an additional 1½ minutes for a total grilling time of 4½ minutes. Remove from the grill. Season with more salt and pepper and serve immediately.

CARAMELIZED DATES STUFFED WITH ALMONDS

DATTES CARAMÉLISÉES FARCIES AUX AMANDES

Serves 8

Oh my. You will adore these, not only because they're unusual and so scrumptious that they almost defy description, but because they're no effort to make. I love these with the very light veil of smoke they get from charcoal, but if all you have is a gas grill, make them on that. I wait until guests have a glass in their hands to grill these. They're so quick that everyone can enjoy them while the rest of the meal is being prepared.

SPECIAL EQUIPMENT: *Grill pan, long tongs*

PREPARATION AND GRILLING TIME: *5 to 6 minutes*

DIFFICULTY LEVEL: *Simple*

24 dates, preferably Deglet Noor variety, with pit

24 almonds, lightly toasted

1 to 2 teaspoons olive oil

Fleur de sel

ASTUCES: When you pit the dates, don't cut them all the way in half—they need to stay attached so the almond can be tucked inside them. Be sure to tell your guests that there is an almond in the date and not a pit, and that they can pop the whole appetizer in their mouth. The rule of thumb I use is three dates per guest. Anyone could and would eat more, of course! While Medjool dates are gorgeously honey-like, they're almost too rich for this recipe. I prefer a smaller date like Deglet Noor, which is less rich and caramelizes beautifully.

SLIT THE DATES DOWN THEIR LENGTH BUT don't cut them in half. Remove the pit and replace it with an almond. Fold the date over the almond to enclose it. Gently toss the dates in the oil, making sure that no almonds fall out while you do. If they do, tuck them back where they belong!

Build a medium-size fire in the barbecue.

When the coals are red and dusted with ash, spread them in a tight, single layer, leaving a perimeter of grill with no coals under it; they need to emit concentrated heat. Set the grill over the coals and set a grill pan on the grill.

When the grill pan is hot, place the dates on it and grill them, keeping them moving at all times, until they are deep golden on the outside, which will happen more quickly than you thought possible. Make sure they are very hot and caramelized evenly; the whole operation will take 1 to 2 minutes, though this will depend on the size of your fire.

Transfer them to a small bowl, shower them with fleur de sel, shake them up a little bit to spread the salt around, and serve.

SMOKY OLIVES

OLIVES FUMÉES

2 cups (320 g)

I love olives, and the variety available in France is astounding. My favorite is the Picholine from Provence, the fennel-scented green olive that is so meaty and "olive" tasting. There are several other varieties of green olives available to you, be they from France, Italy, or Spain. Each has its own distinctive flavor, and all turn smoky and delicious on the grill in no time. Try these at your next barbecue—they're a cinch to make.

SPECIAL EQUIPMENT: *Olive or cherry pitter, grill pan, grapevine or other wood cuttings or chips, long tongs*

PREPARATION AND GRILLING TIME: *About 15 minutes, including pitting*

DIFFICULTY LEVEL: *Simple*

---

2 cups (320 g) top-quality green olives such as the Picholine or Castelvetrano variety, with pits, pitted

2 to 3 teaspoons olive oil

2 teaspoons fresh thyme leaves

ASTUCES: I call for olives with the pits because they are much higher quality than pre-pitted olives. When you're serving these as an appetizer, you don't need to pit the olives. When serving them as a side dish like Steak with Smoky Olives (page 128), pit them first.

MIX THE OLIVES WITH THE OLIVE OIL UNTIL they are thoroughly coated.

Light a medium-size fire in the barbecue. When the coals are red and dusted with ash, spread them in a tight, single layer, leaving a perimeter of grill with no coals under it; they need to emit concentrated heat. Set the grill over the coals. Set a grill pan on the grill.

When the grill pan is hot, slip a few wood chips or grapevine cuttings through the rungs of the grill, or lift the grill slightly and put them on the coals, then lower the grill and place the olives on it. Grill, stirring them constantly on the grill pan, until they are golden in spots on the outside and have softened, which will take 3 to 4 minutes.

Transfer them to a serving bowl and fold the thyme into the olives. Serve immediately.

GRILLED OYSTERS WITH POMMEAU

LES HUÎTRES GRILLÉES AU POMMEAU

Serves 4 to 6

This is the simplest delight in winter, when oysters are at their firm, briny best. Pommeau, a very local Norman apéritif, is made of apple juice and Calvados that age in an oak barrel. It has always been made on the Norman farm, but things are more formal today. To merit the name and the AOP (Appellation d'Origine Protégée), Pommeau must be made within a specific part of Normandy. That said, I have friends just outside official Pommeau territory who make it. Their version looks, tastes, and feels just like Pommeau, but they're not allowed to call it that because of the territorial guidelines. I use it in cooking, sip it in front of the fire on a winter evening, or serve it with an ice cube in summer, and call it simply apéritif Normand.

This is a late fall and winter dish, because oysters are at their best in the months with the letter "r" in them. This seasonal reference isn't just an affectation; it has to do with the period when oysters spawn, when the water warms in late spring through summer.

I have a fireplace in the kitchen, so I don't have to get cold to make these oysters. But I would brave the cold if that's what it took to make them, because they're gorgeous. So pluck up your courage, put on a coat, pour yourself a glass of Pommeau (some of which you'll use on the oysters, so make sure you have enough in it), and have fun.

SPECIAL EQUIPMENT: *Grapevine or other wood cuttings or chips, long tongs, oyster glove or heavy towel, oyster knife*

PREPARATION AND GRILLING TIME: *5 to 7 minutes*

DIFFICULTY: *Simple*

---

2 dozen medium oysters, shells scrubbed clean

1 to 2 tablespoons (15 to 30 g) unsalted butter, melted

2 to 4 tablespoons Pommeau or dry sherry, heated slightly

BUILD A MEDIUM-SIZE FIRE IN THE BARBECUE, or light up the gas grill with all three burners. When the coals are red and dusted with ash, spread them in a tight, single layer, leaving a perimeter of grill with no coals under it; they need to emit concentrated heat. Set the grill over the coals.

When the grill is hot, add some grapevine cuttings or the wood of your choice, and let it flame up. Then set the oysters—cupped side down—on the grill, balancing them so they sit upright. Close the grill, leaving the vents open, and cook until the oysters open, which should take about 5 minutes. Look at the oysters carefully—sometimes they just open a bit. Don't wait for them to open wide—they'll be overcooked.

continued

ASTUCES: If you cannot find Pommeau, then use sherry in this recipe. Be sure to set the oysters cupped shell down so when they open, their juice doesn't spill out. The size oyster you use depends on your own taste. I adore small oysters; there used to be a category called *boudeuses* in France, tiny little things that were the perfect size. That category is gone, so I just take the smallest oyster I can find so that I can enjoy it in one, ultra-crisp bite (and I can eat more that way!). I like to grill these over the coals, with some smoke added. That way the brininess of the oyster has a delicate, smoky overlay.

Remove the oysters from the grill. Holding an oyster in one of your hands that is protected by either a thick glove or a folded towel, and using an oyster knife, cut the muscle inside the top shell of the oyster to free it, and discard the shell. Then free the oyster from the bottom shell, where it is snuggled, by severing the muscle that holds it. This isn't necessary, but it makes life easier for the oyster eater!

Drizzle each oyster with an equal amount of melted butter, then drizzle with an equal amount of Pommeau and serve immediately, while the oysters are still hot.

GRILLED BREAD WITH SMASHED TOMATOES

PAIN GRILLÉ AUX TOMATES ÉCRASÉES

Serves 4 to 6

Grilled bread. The first time I made this for French friends, they couldn't believe it. How could something so simple and basic be *so good?* The French have such a bread culture, yet bread has its place, and that place is sliced, in a basket, as a support for cheese, a pusher for salad, a sopper for sauce. Grilled? It really takes the Italians for that, and here I've crossed the border and introduced it to France! And just in case you wondered, everyone I know is making it now! Because this is quick, you can make it while the grill is heating and have it ready for guests when they arrive so they don't notice that dinner isn't quite ready!

SPECIAL EQUIPMENT: *Long tongs, pastry brush*

PREPARATION AND GRILLING TIME: *About 4 minutes*

DIFFICULTY LEVEL: *Simple*

---

4 slices sourdough or your favorite bread (½-inch; 1.25-cm thick)

2 tablespoons olive oil, or to taste

1 to 2 fat cloves garlic, peeled

4 ripe tomatoes, cut in half

Fleur de sel

ASTUCES: I brush the bread with oil—not too much—before grilling, then I brush it again once it's off the grill. This avoids flare-ups that might add a not-so-good flavor to the toasted bread. It also keeps the fat level down. I get a wonderful organic bread from the food co-op in Louviers. The loaf looks as though it was made for a giant—it's long and fat, studded with grains, and made with a great blend of spelt and wheat flours. Try to find something similar for this recipe.

BUILD A MEDIUM-SIZE FIRE IN THE BARBECUE.
When the coals are red and dusted with ash, spread them in a tight, single layer; they need to emit concentrated heat. Set the grill over the coals.

Brush the slices of bread on each side lightly but thoroughly with olive oil. Set the slices on the grill and toast until they are golden, 2 to 3 minutes. Turn the slices and repeat until the bread is crisp and toasty and even very dark on the outer edges (if you like really toasted bread the way I do).

Transfer the slices to a cutting board and brush them on one side with oil. Quickly and thoroughly rub them with the garlic cloves on one side. Cut them into serving-size pieces, then arrange them on a platter. Serve immediately with the tomatoes, with instructions to your guests to smash and rub the cut side of the tomato firmly over the surface of the hot grilled bread. Season with fleur de sel and enjoy!

SMOKY GUACAMOLE

GUACAMOLE FUMÉ

Serves 4 to 6

Guacamole, as it's translated by French chefs and cooks, is mild, consisting of avocados, garlic, and perhaps a shallot, maybe some cilantro but not usually, and maybe but not always lemon juice. It's actually more of an avocado puree than a highly seasoned, Latin dip. This version is subtle as well, yet heady with the smoky flavor that is imparted when the avocado is grilled over the coals. I add garlic, lemon or lime juice, salt, perhaps some roasted red bell pepper, and, depending on whom I'm serving, a pinch of spicy pepper. I suggest you leave it simple, like this, so the smoky flavor comes through.

SPECIAL EQUIPMENT: *Tongs, long metal spatula, mortar and pestle or food processor (you can also crush the avocados in a bowl using a fork)*

PREPARATION AND GRILLING TIME: *15 minutes*

DIFFICULTY LEVEL: *Simple*

---

4 medium avocados (4½ ounces; 135 g each), just ripe, cut in half, pitted, and removed from their peels

1 tablespoon olive oil

1 tablespoon freshly squeezed lemon or lime juice, or to taste

Generous pinch fine sea salt

1 large clove garlic

¼ roasted pepper (see Grilled Red Bell Peppers, page 177), diced

Piment d'Espelette or cayenne pepper, to taste

BUILD A FIRE AND WHEN THE COALS ARE red and dusted with ash, pour them into the barbecue. Spread them in a tight, single layer; they need to emit concentrated heat. Place the grill over the coals until it is hot.

While the fire is heating, place the avocados, cut side up, on a large plate and drizzle them with the olive oil. Gently rub it into them on both sides—this is a bit tricky as you don't want to break them, so be gentle. Drizzle the avocados with half of the lemon juice and season them with salt. Move them around a bit on the plate so they are evenly covered with the olive oil and the lemon juice.

When the grill is ready, place the avocados on it, cut side down. Grill, uncovered, until the avocados have grill marks on them, a bit more than 2 minutes. Turn the avocados carefully using tongs and a long metal spatula, and continue grilling them, carefully moving them off to the side if they are getting too dark, until they are nicely golden, which will take 5 to 6 minutes. You'll need to turn and shift them so they grill evenly; do so very carefully. Transfer them to the plate with the oil and lemon, and let cool to room temperature.

continued

ASTUCES: A sure-fire method for removing avocados from their peels (once the seed is removed) is to use a soup spoon. Simply scoop around the meat of the avocado and transfer it, unblemished, to a plate or other receptacle. It's very important, when grilling avocados, to stay close by. Overgrilling gives them an unpleasant texture. Finally, don't puree the avocados too much. You want this guacamole to have texture.

While the avocados are grilling, place the garlic and a generous pinch of salt in a mortar or the work bowl of a food processor, and puree it. When the avocados are cool, add them to the garlic and process them into a chunky puree. Add the remaining lemon or lime juice, the red bell pepper, and the spicy pepper. Serve with chips or fresh vegetables or . . .

GRILLED SHIITAKES

SHIITAKES GRILLÉES

Serves 4 to 6

The shiitake's claim to fame is as a little vitamin bomb (it's full of protein, B vitamins, calcium, magnesium, phosphorous), which may not make it sound appetizing, but just you wait! That something so good for you can be so exquisitely delicious may come as a big surprise. The shiitake's texture is like a cèpe (porcini); its flavor flirts with that of the truffle, and its texture is the stuff of dreams, tender and muscular at once. When grilled, it becomes crispy on the edges and mouth-melting in the center. Convinced?!

SPECIAL EQUIPMENT: *Long tongs, pastry brush, three long skewers*

PREPARATION AND GRILLING TIME: *7 to 10 minutes*

DIFFICULTY LEVEL: *Simple*

---

8 ounces (250 g) medium fresh shiitakes, trimmed if necessary

2 tablespoons untoasted sesame oil

Fleur de sel and freshly ground black pepper

ASTUCES: If your shiitakes are very fresh, you won't need to remove the stems because they'll be tender and great to eat. If your shiitakes are of very different sizes, I suggest cutting them so they are all roughly the same size.

PLACE THE SHIITAKES IN A LARGE BOWL.
Drizzle with the sesame oil and mix quickly so the oil touches all of the shiitakes. Reserve.

Build a medium-size fire in the barbecue. When the coals are red and dusted with ash, spread them in a tight, single layer; they need to emit concentrated heat.

Thread the shiitakes onto the long skewers, pushing them together very gently.

Set the grill over the coals. When it is hot, lay the skewers atop the grill and grill the shiitakes until they are golden, which will take 2 to 3 minutes. Continue grilling the shiitakes, turning the skewers every 1 to 2 minutes until the shiitakes are tender and golden on the outside, for a total grilling time of about 7 minutes. Remove them from the grill, then remove the shiitakes from the skewers and place them onto a serving plate, season lightly with fleur de sel and liberally with pepper, and serve immediately.

CUTE LITTLE MUSHROOMS ON THE GRILL

PETITS CHAMPIGNONS MIGNONS SUR LE GRILL

Serves 4 to 6

Once you've made these, you'll never grill mushrooms any other way. Not only is this appetizer simple to make, it results in mushrooms that are almost like a confit. Use the freshest button or crimini mushrooms you can, and don't weep over the discarded stems. If you find it impossible to throw them away, then use them to make a soup stock, or slice them in half, grill them on a plancha, and add them to an omelet.

SPECIAL EQUIPMENT: *Baking dish or platter, grill pan, long tongs*

PREPARATION AND GRILLING TIME: *12 to 15 minutes*

DIFFICULTY LEVEL: *Simple*

1 pound (500 g) medium button mushrooms (about 24 mushrooms), stems removed, brushed clean

2 tablespoons olive oil

Fine sea salt and freshly ground black pepper

1 bunch chives

ASTUCES: When you clean mushrooms, hold them stem side down so the grit doesn't fall into the mushroom cap. The mushrooms will become slightly crisp at the edges as they grill, which is what you're after.

SET THE MUSHROOMS IN A BAKING DISH OR on a platter, cap side down. Pour ¼ teaspoon of the oil into the stem end of each mushroom, strew them with salt, then grind fresh pepper over them.

Build a medium-size fire in a grill. When the coals are red and dusted with ash, spread them in a tight, single layer; they need to emit concentrated heat. Set the grill over them, and set a grill pan on the grill.

When the grill is hot, set the mushrooms on it, cap side down, cover, and cook until the mushrooms are golden and tender but not too soft, and the oil is bubbling inside of them, 5 to 6 minutes.

While the mushrooms are grilling, mince the chives.

When the mushrooms are cooked, transfer them to a serving platter. Sprinkle them with a generous amount of chives and serve immediately.

CHAPTER 2

FIRST COURSES

"A good meal should begin with hunger."

—FRENCH PROVERB

The first course, or the entrée, opens up the meal after the amuse-bouches. I always think of the first course as a work of art, something lively and gorgeous, something that's taken a bit of time to cook and then arrange on the plate or platter. It's delicious and complete, and it gets your palate ready for what is next to come. The first courses in this chapter are like that—they're little universes of goodness that introduce whatever you choose to serve next!

AIOLI WITH AUTUMN VEGETABLES FROM THE GRILL

AIOLI AUX LÉGUMES D'AUTOMNE GRILLÉES

Serves 6

Aioli is the kind of dish that creates a fête, even if it's just being served to the family. It's happy and cheerful, and creates a dish that can be eaten with the fingers, depending on how formal you are. Speaking of formal, this dish dresses up easily and well, so it's very versatile.

Use the recipe as a guide, and find the best seasonal vegetables you can. I recommend serving this with a lovely Côtes du Rhône or, if the weather is propitious, a rosé.

~~~~~~

SPECIAL EQUIPMENT: *Steamer, grill pan*

PREPARATION AND GRILLING TIME:
If making the aioli, about 45 minutes; if just grilling the vegetables, about 30 minutes

DIFFICULTY LEVEL: *Simple to moderate (because of timing)*

---

2 small heads broccoli, cut into large, bite-size florets, stems separated

1 small head cauliflower, cut into large bite-size florets

1 pound (500 g) Basic Potatoes on the Grill (page 196)

8 ounces (250 g) Sweet Carrots (page 172)

6 to 8 Whole Grilled Zucchini (page 205)

1 head lettuce, such as green leaf, red or green oakleaf, or romaine, trimmed, washed, and patted dry

Aioli (page 266)

BUILD A GOOD-SIZE FIRE IN THE BARBECUE, or light up the gas grill using all three burners.

Bring 3 cups water to a boil in the bottom of a steamer. When the water is boiling, add the broccoli stems, cover, and steam until they are just beginning to turn tender, about 4 minutes. Add the broccoli and the cauliflower florets, cover, and steam until the broccoli and cauliflower are tender-crisp, which will take 5 to 7 minutes.

When the coals are red and dusted with ash, spread them in a tight, single layer, leaving a perimeter of grill with no coals under it; they need to emit concentrated heat. Set the grill over the coals. Proceed to grill all of the vegetables, except the lettuce, to your liking.

To serve, arrange the lettuce leaves on a platter, then arrange the vegetables atop the lettuce leaves in an attractive fashion and serve with the aioli alongside.

ASTUCES: Different vegetables require different cooking times on the grill. However, they can all be done on the grill simultaneously. You'll want to use a grill pan for some of them, and you'll need to juggle and focus so that you remove each type of vegetable when it's perfectly grilled. This dish is served at room temperature, so there is no hurry to get everything to the table while it is hot. Note that there is some two-step cooking here.

TOMATOES PROVENÇALES

TOMATES PROVENÇALES

Serves 6 to 8

Oh my, these are good. Tomates Provençales are a French summer tradition, usually baked in the oven. Here, I grill them, using perfectly ripe tomatoes that sing with flavor. Something about the heady seasoning makes you feel like you're on vacation even if you're not—it evokes those hills, vineyards, and winding roads of Provence.

You can serve these glorious tomatoes hot (you do have to let them sit for a few minutes or they'll blister the mouth), warm, or at room temperature. I like to serve these as a first course—they're a terrific introduction to Steak with Smoky Olives (page 128).

SPECIAL EQUIPMENT: *Metal cooling rack, tea towel or plate, grill pan, metal spatula, tongs*

PREPARATION AND GRILLING TIME: *About 50 minutes, including draining time*

DIFFICULTY LEVEL: *Simple*

6 large tomatoes (6 ounces; 180 g each), cored, cut in half horizontally, seeds removed

2 generous teaspoons fine sea salt

2 large cloves garlic, minced

1½ cups (15 g) fresh basil leaves

2 tablespoons fresh thyme leaves

¼ cup (60 ml) olive oil

⅔ cup (about 50 g) fresh bread crumbs

Freshly ground black pepper

SPRINKLE THE TOMATOES EVENLY WITH THE salt (you may or may not use all of the salt, but give them a nice, even sprinkling). Place them, cut side down, on a wire rack over a baking pan or nonreactive surface, and let the tomatoes drain for 30 minutes.

Mince together the garlic, basil, and thyme. Place the mixture in a small bowl and whisk in the oil, then the bread crumbs, to make a thick paste.

Preheat all three burners of a gas grill, or build a medium-size fire in the barbecue. When the coals are red and dusted with ash, spread them in a tight, single layer, leaving a perimeter of grill with no coals under it; they need to emit concentrated heat. Set the grill over the coals and set the grill pan on top.

Turn the tomatoes cut side up. Spread each tomato with the herb mixture, letting some fall into the cavities left by the seeds and spreading it evenly over the cut side. You'll have plenty; use it all.

When the grill is hot, set the tomatoes on it, cover the grill, and cook until the tomatoes are bubbling on top and the bread crumb mixture is golden, 10 minutes. Transfer the tomatoes to a platter, season with pepper, then let sit for at least 10 minutes before serving.

ASTUCES: When you core the tomatoes, remove just the very core without making a huge hole in the tomato. Salting the tomatoes firms them up and seasons them through. These cook surprisingly quickly, and the tomatoes get quite soft, which is what you want. Transfer them carefully from grill to plate or platter, using tongs and a metal spatula. Don't be concerned if the skin is quite dark; as you eat the tomato you'll find the fleshy part separating from the skin, which will stay on your plate.

UPSIDE~DOWN ARTICHOKES

ARTICHAUTS À L'ENVERS

Serves 6

Artichoke season never comes too soon for me. I *love* this vegetable. It evokes so many happy memories of sitting at the family table, carefully peeling off the leaves, running them through my teeth to get the gorgeous meat at the ends, then finally landing on the soft, tender heart. We ate artichokes often growing up (long before anyone else we knew ate them), thanks to my mother's uncle, who grew them in his Portland, Oregon, garden. They were always a favorite of my mother's, and her early experiences inspired ours. In France, Brittany is home to the artichoke. There, in fields bathed by sea air, they grow to huge proportions, each head weighing a pound or more. They're nutty, meaty, simply delicious. And here, on the grill, well, you just have to try them!

SPECIAL EQUIPMENT: *Scissors (for trimming the leaves), stainless steel spoon*

PREPARATION AND GRILLING TIME: *35 minutes*

DIFFICULTY LEVEL: *Simple*

6 cups water

3 large artichokes (1 pound; 500 g total), leaves trimmed, cut in half, choke removed

1 large clove garlic

¾ cup (7.5 g) flat-leaf parsley leaves

2 tablespoons olive oil

Fine sea salt and freshly ground black pepper

BRING 6 CUPS (1½ LITERS) WATER TO A BOIL in the bottom of a steamer. When the water is producing steam, put the artichokes in the steamer. Don't be concerned if you need to layer them; they'll cook perfectly well that way. Cover the artichokes, using aluminum foil if a lid doesn't fit, and cook the artichokes until the hearts are tender but not mushy, 20 to 25 minutes. Remove the artichokes from the steamer.

Build a medium-size fire in the barbecue. When the coals are red and dusted with ash, spread them in a tight, single layer, leaving a perimeter of grill with no coals under it; they need to emit concentrated heat. Set the grill over the coals.

Mince together the garlic and the parsley leaves. Mix in 1 generous tablespoon of the oil.

When the artichokes are steamed, brush them all over with the remaining oil. If any oil remains, add it to the parsley mixture. Season them all over with salt and pepper.

continued

ASTUCES: This is a two-step recipe. Despite my efforts, I found it impossible to entirely grill an artichoke, thus the pre-steam. You can steam many at a time, piling them atop each other—they cook evenly and quickly. When shopping for artichokes, look for those with an even, dusty green color without dry, brown spots or streaks. The stem should be green at the cut end, as this indicates freshness. Not all artichoke varieties have sharp hooks at the end of their leaves, but if they do, cut them off; they hurt! Always use stainless steel with artichokes, because they'll turn any other metal black. Your hands will be black once you've worked with them, too, so keep half a lemon on hand to bleach them when you're finished. There's no point in rubbing these with lemon to keep them from discoloring; they'll turn dark on the grill. Incidentally, the blackening of artichokes comes from the oxidation of polyphenols they contain, resulting in nothing more serious than a color that stains.

When the grill is hot, set the artichokes on it, cut side down, cover the grill, and grill until they are golden, which will take 4 to 5 minutes. Turn the artichokes, and spoon equal amounts of the parsley and garlic mixture into each one, spreading it slightly to cover the inside of the heart where the choke was. Cover and grill until the artichokes are hot through and golden, an additional 4 to 5 minutes.

To serve, place an artichoke, cut side up, on each plate. As diners remove the leaves, they can brush them through the garlic and parsley mixture in the center of each artichoke. The real prize is the garlicky, parsley-flavored heart! Serve immediately, as these are best hot from the grill.

GAZPACHO, SMOKY FRENCH~STYLE

LE GAZPACHO FUMÉ À LA FRANÇAISE

Serves 6 to 8

Here, the simple purity of summer tomatoes and red bell peppers grilled gently over the coals, teamed with farm-fresh cucumbers, garlic, and onions, makes this the most refreshing gazpacho you're likely to taste. It speaks of the finest and freshest ingredients, softly spiked with smoke, hot pepper, and freshly squeezed lemon juice. Simple to prepare, I predict that once you've tried it, your summer meals will rarely be without it!

~~~~~~

SPECIAL EQUIPMENT: *Grapevine or other wood cuttings or chips, long tongs, metal spatula, food processor*

PREPARATION AND GRILLING TIME: *2 hours 25 minutes, including 2 hours chilling time (minimum)*

DIFFICULTY LEVEL: *Simple*

About 2 pounds (1 kg) medium tomatoes, firm yet ripe, sliced in half horizontally, seeded

1 medium red bell pepper (8 ounces; 250 g), cut in quarters, seeds and pith removed

2 tablespoons olive oil

Pinch fine sea salt

1 small onion (3 ounces; 90 g), preferably sweet, peeled and quartered

1 large cucumber (10 ounces; 300 g), peeled and cut into 1-inch (2.5-cm) pieces

1 clove new garlic

1 tablespoon freshly squeezed lemon juice

Piment d'Espelette or an equal mix of sweet and hot paprika, to your taste

Basil leaves, for garnish

BRUSH THE TOMATOES AND THE PEPPER
with oil.

Light a medium-size fire in the barbecue. When the coals are red and dusted with ash, spread them in a tight, single layer; they need to emit concentrated heat.

Place a handful of grapevine cuttings or wood chips over the coals and let them burn for a minute or two, then set the grill over the coals and put the barbecue cover in place, vents open.

When the grill is hot, place the tomatoes and the pepper directly over the coals, cut side down. Grill until the tomatoes and pepper are marked with grill marks, 2 to 3 minutes, then turn them, sprinkle with salt, cover the grill, and cook until the tomatoes are tender, about 4 minutes. Transfer the tomatoes from the grill to a shallow soup bowl or platter that will catch the juices. Cover the grill and continue grilling the pepper until its skin is blackened and the pepper is tender, an additional 5 minutes. Transfer the pepper to a paper bag to sweat.

Remove the skin from the tomatoes and pepper, and discard. Save all the juices from both the tomatoes and the pepper.

Place the tomatoes with their juices, all but one quarter of the pepper with its juices, the onion, the cucumber, and the garlic in the work bowl of a food processor fit with a steel blade, and

continued

ASTUCES: To remove the seeds from the tomatoes, simply shake the tomato, cut side down, over a bowl or compost bin. You may need to scoop out a few seeds, but generally this method works well. There isn't any need to peel the tomatoes before grilling as, once they are grilled, the skin peels off easily. Note that I suggest making and freezing this gazpacho in summer, when everything is fresh from the farm. Note, too, that when cooked on a gas grill this gazpacho doesn't seem to acquire the desired smoky flavor, so get out your barbecues! Finally, this soup is gorgeous when served chilled, but if served ice cold the flavors disappear. I recommend removing it from the refrigerator about 10 minutes before you plan to serve it.

process until you have a thick puree. Add the lemon juice and the piment d'Espelette, pulse, and adjust the seasoning. Place the gazpacho in the refrigerator, covered, to chill. This will take at least 2 hours.

About 10 minutes before serving the soup, remove it from the refrigerator. Dice the remaining quarter of grilled pepper. Adjust the seasoning of the soup and divide it among six to eight bowls. Drizzle each bowl with a bit of the remaining olive oil, garnish with some of the diced pepper and a basil leaf or two, and serve.

FOIE GRAS WITH GREEN BEANS

FOIE GRAS AUX HARICOTS VERTS

Serves 6

Fresh foie gras is great any way it is prepared, in my opinion. Here, I put grapevine cuttings on the hot coals to send up smoke, and then set a cast-iron skillet over the coals. When the skillet is blistering hot (this happens fast), put the frozen slices of fresh foie gras on it. They sizzle and brown to perfection within a minute and are gorgeous on these green beans!

SPECIAL EQUIPMENT: *Steamer, whisk, cast-iron or other heavy, fireproof skillet, grapevine or other wood cuttings, long tongs*

PREPARATION AND GRILLING TIME: *20 minutes*

DIFFICULTY LEVEL: *Simple*

---

1 pound (500 g) green beans, trimmed and cut into 3-inch (7.5-cm) lengths, on the bias

1 large clove garlic, minced

2 tablespoons walnut oil

Fine sea salt and freshly ground black pepper

6 ounces (180 g) fresh foie gras, cut into 6 equally thick slices and frozen

PLACE THE BEANS IN A STEAMER ABOVE boiling water, cover, and cook until they are tender through, which can take up to 14 minutes (if you like beans that are sweet and delicious and not crisp; if you want your beans crisp, time them accordingly).

While the beans are cooking, place the garlic and the walnut oil in a medium bowl. Whisk together with a bit of salt and pepper and reserve.

Light a medium-size fire in the barbecue, or light up the gas grill using two burners.

When the beans are cooked to your liking, add them to the walnut oil and garlic and toss well until they are thoroughly coated with the mixture. Reserve, keeping the beans warm. (You can do this by setting them on the side of the grill, away from the coals.)

When the coals are red and dusted with ash, spread them in a tight, single layer, leaving a perimeter of grill with no coals under it; they need to emit concentrated heat. Add the grapevine cuttings to the coals, then set the grill over the coals and set a cast-iron skillet on the grill.

Right before you cook the foie gras, plate the beans, dividing them among six plates. They should still be warm.

ASTUCES: If you don't have walnut oil (J. Leblanc brand), ideally from Burgundy, you may use a top-quality olive oil. Once the foie gras is sliced, place it on a piece of aluminum foil lined with parchment paper and put it in the freezer before cooking. Make sure to keep the beans warm, and once the foie gras is cooked, serve it immediately. If you don't find fresh foie gras in your local specialty grocery, you can order it online from retailers like D'Artagnan (www.dartagnan.com).

When the skillet is blistering hot, use long tongs to transfer all of the pieces of foie gras to the skillet. They will start to melt immediately. Season them with salt and pepper and cook until they are golden, a matter of seconds. Turn them, season, and cook until golden—the whole operation will take no longer than 2 minutes.

Transfer one piece of foie gras to each of the plates, placing it atop the beans. Give each one more sprinkle of salt and pepper and serve *immediately!*

BACON-WRAPPED GOAT CHEESE SALAD

FROMAGE DE CHÈVRE AU LARD FUMÉ EN SALADE

Serves 4 if each person wants 2 pieces of cheese; otherwise, serves 8

Bacon-wrapped goat cheese is a quintessential entrée in the French household. You can even purchase the goat cheese already wrapped in bacon at the épicerie (grocery store). Typically, the cheeses are heated in the oven until they begin to melt and the bacon softens. I've adapted this idea, putting the cheeses on the grill after tucking grilled pepper underneath the bacon for some extra lusciousness. The bacon entirely covers the cheese, and as the bacon crisps on the grill, the cheese softens so that when you cut into it, *oh my*. It's molten and delicious.

SPECIAL EQUIPMENT: *Trussing skewers, long tongs, long metal spatula*

PREPARATION AND GRILLING TIME: *7 to 8 minutes if not roasting the pepper; 27 minutes if roasting them*

DIFFICULTY LEVEL: *Simple*

---

4 round goat cheeses (about 2½ ounces; 75 g each), firm but young, cut horizontally in half

Piment d'Espelette or an equal blend of hot and regular paprika

Fine sea salt and freshly ground black pepper

½ roasted red bell pepper (Grilled Red Bell Peppers, page 177), cut into 8 equal pieces (about 2-by-2 inches; 5-by-5 cm)

8 slices slab bacon, rind removed, about 1 ounce (30 g) each

Classic Vinaigrette (page 252)

8 cups (210 g) lettuce leaves, rinsed, washed, and torn into bite-size pieces

Fleur de sel (optional)

SET THE PIECES OF CHEESE ON A WORK

surface, cut side up. Season each piece with piment d'Espelette and a bit of salt and some pepper. Lay a piece of red bell pepper atop each cheese, flattening it out gently so it covers the surface of the cheese. If it hangs over a bit, that's fine. Wrap each piece of cheese with a piece of bacon so the bacon almost entirely encases the cheese, and keep it held closed with a trussing skewer.

Build a medium-size fire in the barbecue, or light up the gas grill using all three burners. When the coals are red and dusted with ash, set the grill over them. When the grill is very hot, place the cheeses on it right over the coals and grill until the bacon is golden, about 30 seconds. Turn and repeat. Cover the grill and continue cooking until the cheese begins to melt, an additional minute or so. Transfer the cheeses from the grill to a plate or platter, using a long metal spatula.

Place the vinaigrette in a large bowl. Add the lettuce and toss well until it is coated with the vinaigrette. Divide the salad among four plates, setting it in the center of the plate. Transfer the hot cheeses to the salads, serving two pieces per person. Garnish with fleur de sel, if desired, and serve immediately.

ASTUCES: You can assemble the cheeses the morning of the day you plan to make this salad.

IMPRESSIONIST VEGETABLES FROM THE GRILL

LES LÉGUMES IMPRESSIONNISTES GRILLÉES

Serves 4

This is a beautiful first course inspired by chef and owner Bruno Verjus at Table restaurant in Paris. Chef Verjus is an aesthete who believes, as I do, that grilling is the most elemental style of cooking—the most "true" style. He wants everything on every plate he serves at his restaurant to be visually stunning, but more than that he wants it to taste better than anything you've ever eaten. I share this lofty goal.

This dish is pretty, happy, and more important than anything, delicious. I've served it many times, and every time I do it's as though I invited the vegetables and guests to a party, because it looks so celebratory on the plate. Because some of the vegetables are small, like the radishes, I use a perforated grill pan with holes in it so they don't fall into the fire. If you don't have a perforated grill pan, don't worry. Just pay careful attention and do your best. If you lose a radish, weep for it and then let it go.

SPECIAL EQUIPMENT: *Tongs, grill pan, metal spatula, cheesecloth, sieve*

PREPARATION AND GRILLING TIME: *25 minutes*

DIFFICULTY LEVEL: *Moderate*

¾ cup (185 ml) full-fat yogurt

2 tablespoons olive oil

Fleur de sel or coarse sea salt

12 radishes, with greens, rinsed, roots removed

12 small spring onions, trimmed, with 2 inches (5 cm) stem (or scallions)

8 stalks asparagus, trimmed, peeled halfway up from the root end

12 leaves spinach, or ramps or other tender green

PLACE THE YOGURT IN A SIEVE LINED WITH cheesecloth one hour before you plan to serve this dish. Set the sieve over a bowl and reserve, at room temperature.

Build a medium-size fire in the grill. While the coals are heating, pour the olive oil into a large, flat dish. Add a generous amount of salt, mix it with your fingers, then place all the vegetables except the greens in the oil and turn them until they are lightly covered with oil and salt.

When the coals are red and dusted with ash, divide them in the barbecue, putting half the coals on either side. Set the grill over the coals. If you've got a grill pan, place it on top of the grill, with half of it over the coals and the other half over the part of the barbecue without coals.

When the grill is hot, place the radishes, spring onions, and asparagus over the coals and leave them there just long enough until they are golden all over, turning them once. Depending on the heat of your grill and the vegetables, this can take from

½ teaspoon smoked paprika, or more if needed

Cilantro Oil (page 271)

Fleur de sel

ASTUCES: You may use any vegetable you like here, in any quantity you like. But small spring vegetables are best, and radishes, which keep their cheery color, are essential. Sometimes I use baby turnips; if I can't find spring onions, I use shallots; and occasionally I double the amount of asparagus. If cilantro is hard to find, simply use the finest extra virgin olive oil all by itself. You'll miss the vivid green color and the subtle flavor of the cilantro, but the dish will be delicious. Have fun!

2 to 4 minutes. When they're golden on both sides, move them to the side of the grill away from the coals, cover the grill, and cook them until they are tender, which will take from 2 to 4 minutes.

While the vegetables are grilling, place the spinach leaves in the remaining oil and salt and rub them so they are lightly covered with oil.

Remove the vegetables from the grill and place the spinach leaves on the grill above the coals. They will brown quickly, so turn them until they wilt and are golden to almost black, which will take just seconds. Remove them from the grill.

To serve, place a dollop of yogurt in the center of each of four plates. Sprinkle it liberally with smoked paprika. Arrange the vegetables around it. Drizzle some cilantro oil around the vegetables. Season with fleur de sel and serve immediately.

A VERY SPECIAL SEASONING

My favorite variety of black pepper is voatsiperifery (*Piper borbonense*). It is a wild pepper picked when immature, by hand, in the wilds of the humid south of Madagascar, then sun-dried. The tiny berries are reddish with little tails that, when dried, turn a rich, dark brown that is almost black. This pepper emerged on the French culinary scene about five years ago, but it is still not widely known or used. Its wonderful name comes from the words *voa* (the Malagasy term for "fruit") and *tsiperifery* (the local name of the plant). This is a pepper that I use for

very special dishes: Its earthy citrus and floral aromas are intense, and it makes everything it touches better. But it's not, in my opinion, an everyday pepper because it's so remarkable. With melon particularly, its light, fragrant spiciness shines as it picks up the flavor of the fruit and takes it to a higher level. If you don't have this pepper on hand or can't find it, any black pepper will be wonderful. Another great choice is Tellicherry, which is perhaps easier to find, though voatsiperifery is available online from retailers like Spice Ace (www.spiceace.com).

MELON DE CAVAILLON WITH AIR~CURED HAM

MELON DE CAVAILLON AU JAMBON SÉCHÉ

Serves 6

This dish is a play on a very French first course—slices of sweet, flowery, juicy melon de Cavaillon (Tuscan melon, or cantaloupe)—combined with air-cured ham. Normally, each slice is simply wrapped with a slice of ham. Here, I've spiced it up by grilling the ham so it is just this side of crisp (if it gets crisp it takes on a burnt flavor), and seasoning the melon with freshly squeezed lime juice and flavorful black pepper.

SPECIAL EQUIPMENT: *Pastry brush*

PREPARATION AND GRILLING TIME:
10 minutes

DIFFICULTY LEVEL: *Simple*

---

4 ounces (120 g) air-cured ham, such as prosciutto, very thinly sliced

1 tablespoon olive oil

2 medium (about 2 pounds; 1 kg) or 1 large (4 pounds; 2 kg) Cavaillon or Tuscan cantaloupe, skinned, seeded, and cut into thin slices

2 tablespoons freshly squeezed lime juice

Freshly ground black pepper

BRUSH THE SLICES OF HAM ON EACH SIDE with oil.

Light the gas grill using all three burners or build a good-size fire in the barbecue.

When the coals are red and dusted with ash, spread them in a tight, single layer, leaving a perimeter of grill with no coals under it; they need to emit concentrated heat. Set the grill over the coals.

When the grill is hot, place the ham on it and *don't leave!* The ham will begin to curl almost immediately—grill it, turning regularly, until it is curled but not darkened or crisp, for about 2 minutes total. Consider this like sautéing on the grill!

Transfer the ham to a plate and let it cool.

Just before serving, arrange the melon on a serving platter. Drizzle it with the lime juice and season liberally with pepper. Thinly slice the ham crosswise into strips that are about ¼-inch (0.60 cm) wide. Strew the ham strips over the melon and serve immediately.

ASTUCES: Nearly every French region has its own version of air-cured ham. I vary between using Norman ham, which is smokier and generally more thickly cut than Italian ham, and ham from Aosta in Italy. For a dish like this, Italian air-cured ham is best. That's what the French would use, too. This is a great recipe for the gas grill, as you don't need any smoky flavor added to it.

SPICED MELON SALAD

SALADE DE MELON ÉPICÉE

Serves 4 to 6

Summer brings us the best melons on earth, first from southern France and finally from gardens in our own backyard. This way the season extends from the end of June to the end of September, and we eat them for breakfast, lunch, and dinner, as a sweet and as a savory.

This is one of my favorite preparations because it features that gorgeous sweetness of melon with the zing of pepper and a touch of basil. It wakes you up with its surprising flavors and brightens any meal it accompanies. I particularly like it alongside Curry Beef and Zucchini Brochettes (page 140), but you can serve it with Rotisserie Chicken (page 99) or even Chicken Wings with Herbes de Provence (page 88). Or you can make it and eat it all by itself for lunch.

SPECIAL EQUIPMENT: *Whisk*

PREPARATION TIME: *10 minutes*

DIFFICULTY LEVEL: *Simple*

---

1 small cantaloupe-type melon (1 pound 6 ounces; 680 g), peeled, seeded, and cut into ½-inch (1.25-cm) cubes

1 large shallot, minced

Zest from 1 large lime, preferably organic, minced

2 tablespoons freshly squeezed lime juice, or to taste

Fine sea salt, to taste

½ teaspoon piment d'Espelette or hot paprika, or to taste

2 tablespoons olive oil

½ cup (5 g) fresh basil leaves

PLACE THE MELON CUBES IN A MEDIUM bowl with the shallot and the lime zest, and gently toss them together.

In a small bowl whisk together the lime juice, a good pinch of salt, and the piment d'Espelette. Whisk in the olive oil and adjust the seasoning.

Pour the sauce over the melon and toss it gently. Let the melon sit at room temperature for at least 30 minutes and up to 1 hour.

Just before serving, mince the basil, add it to the melon, toss well, and adjust the seasoning. Transfer the melon to a serving bowl and serve.

ASTUCES: There are a million suggestions for finding the perfect melon. My two sure-fire tips: aroma and cracks around the stem end, as though it is separating from the melon. Another tip is weight for its size. A heavy melon is one that's mature, but you've got to have the wonderful melon aroma to be sure that flavor follows. Note that this recipe isn't grilled, but it is a perfect accompaniment to so many grilled foods.

SWEET POTATOES WITH QUAIL EGGS

PATATE DOUCE AUX OEUFS DE CAILLE

Serves 8 for a first course or 4 for a main course

I love sweet potatoes, and like every French person I know, I love eggs. Here the two combine to make an amusing and simple dish that can be an easy weeknight supper. It's a gorgeous blend, with the sweetness of the potato enveloping the little savory eggs. I like to garnish this with tarragon, because tarragon and eggs are a match made in heaven.

After using every size of egg and having various messes on my hands (but always great flavor), my daughter, Fiona, suggested I use quail eggs. It was a perfect idea, and they're so easy to get here in France from the supermarket or the cheese truck at the market. In the United States, quail eggs are available from certain supermarkets such as Whole Foods or other specialty food shops. This dish is delicious, and your guests will love its flavor and the way the two bright little eggs sitting in their orange bed of sweet potato make them smile! As for the little balls of sweet potato that are removed to make room for the eggs, they are for the chef. Or, better yet, you can set them alongside each potato. Try a white Burgundy (un-oaked Chardonnay) here—you'll love it!

SPECIAL EQUIPMENT: *Pastry brush*

PREPARATION AND GRILLING TIME: *32 to 38 minutes*

DIFFICULTY LEVEL: *Moderate*

ASTUCES: If you cannot find small sweet potatoes, you may cut larger ones in half, crosswise, and then halve those lengthwise. Note that the cooking times for both potatoes and eggs will vary depending on the type of heat you use; it's all very simple, just check on the potatoes from time to time. Note that the quail egg shells break easily, but the inner membrane can be tough—you can pierce it with the tip of a sharp knife, then open up the shell and release the egg. Finally, you may substitute flat-leaf parsley or basil leaves if you can't find fresh tarragon.

BUILD A MEDIUM-SIZE FIRE IN THE BARBECUE, or light all three burners on the gas grill. When the coals are red and dusted with ash, spread them in a tight, single layer, leaving a perimeter of grill with no coals under it; they need to emit concentrated heat. When the grill has reached 450°F (235°C), it's more than ready. Turn off the middle burner.

Brush each potato with olive oil on both sides and season generously with salt and pepper.

Place the potatoes on the grill, cut side down, and brown for 2 minutes, until they have stripes on them. Turn the potatoes and brush the cut side with more oil. Cover the grill and cook the potatoes until they are tender through, which will take from 25 to 30 minutes, depending on the potato. Check them every 10 minutes, and if they are browning too quickly, turn them over again. To test for doneness, pierce the potatoes with a trussing skewer—it should slide easily through the potato.

continued

4 small sweet potatoes (5 ounces; 150 g each), preferably organic, rinsed, unpeeled, cut in half lengthwise (or 2 large 10-ounce; 300-g potatoes, cut in half crosswise, then cut in half lengthwise)

1 scant tablespoon olive oil

Sea salt and freshly ground black pepper

8 quail eggs

Piment d'Espelette, or a mix of hot and mild paprika, to taste

1 generous tablespoon butter, chilled, thinly sliced into 8 small slices (optional, but delicious)

2 tablespoons fresh tarragon leaves (don't use dried; see Astuces)

Remove the potatoes from the barbecue, and when they are cool enough to handle, scoop out two rounds with a ⅛-inch (standard) melon baller, making sure to go fairly deep into the potato without piercing the skin. Break an egg into each. Season the eggs with salt and pepper, place the potatoes on the grill again, cover, and cook until the eggs are to your liking. At 2 minutes, the yolks and whites will be slightly runny but set; 3 minutes, the yolks will be runny; 4 minutes, the yolks will be cooked through, what might be called "hard" yet still tender.

Remove the potatoes from the grill. Sprinkle each egg with a bit of piment d'Espelette. Place a slice of butter atop each potato, if desired, and drizzle with a bit of the olive oil that remains. Season with salt and pepper, and garnish with the tarragon leaves, leaving them whole. Serve immediately.

POTATOES WITH ONIONS AND MAPLE SYRUP

POMMES DE TERRE AUX OIGNONS ET SIROP D'ÉRABLE

Serves 8 as a first course or 4 as a main dish

The French are artists with the potato, and here the wonderful tuber is taken to new heights. Brushed with oil and maple syrup, infused with garlic, onion, and bay leaf, it is one of the best possible side dishes I can think of. If you're not in the mood for meat or poultry, one or two of these potatoes make a fine main course. They are simple to prepare, out of the ordinary, and will appeal to everyone.

SPECIAL EQUIPMENT: *Tongs, aluminum foil, 1 cup wood chips*

PREPARATION AND GRILLING TIME: *About 55 minutes*

DIFFICULTY LEVEL: *Moderate*

4 medium potatoes (about 5 ounces; 150 g each)

2 tablespoons olive oil

1 tablespoon maple syrup

Fine sea salt and freshly ground black pepper

2 cloves garlic, minced

2 medium onions (about 4 ounces; 120 g each), cut into 12 thick slices

12 fresh or dried (from Turkey) bay leaves

WASH THE POTATOES AND MAKE THREE partial cuts in each, crosswise. Be careful not to cut through the potatoes.

Using a pastry brush, paint the exterior of the potato and inside of the cuts with olive oil, then with the maple syrup. Season with salt and pepper, making sure some of the seasoning gets inside the cuts. Rub the minced garlic over the potatoes, pushing some of it into the cuts in the potatoes.

Light a medium-size fire in the grill.

Brush the slices of onion on either side with remaining oil and maple syrup, season them on each side, then slip one slice into each cut in the potato, pushing them down as far as you can. Slip a bay leaf into each slit of the potato alongside the onion slices. Season the potatoes all over with salt and pepper.

Place the wood chips in a bowl and cover with water.

Cut four large pieces of aluminum foil and set a potato in the center of each. Pour 2 teaspoons of water around each potato, then seal the packets. When the coals are red and dusted with ash, divide them in the barbecue, putting half the coals on either side. Place the grill over the coals. When the grill is hot, place the potato packets in the center of the grill and close the top. The temperature should rise to about 400°F (200°C). Cook the

ASTUCES: The cooking time will vary depending on the size and freshness of the potato. Also, I *adore* bay leaves. If you love them but don't adore them, you may use fewer. Should you have any leftover potatoes, dice them up, add some bacon, and serve them for . . . an American breakfast or a French first course!

potatoes for 20 minutes, then check them for doneness. The potatoes should be nearly tender. Open the packets, and then drain the wood chips and place them under the grill onto the hot coals. Close the grill and continue cooking the potatoes until they are tender through, 10 to 15 additional minutes. Remove the potatoes from the grill and transfer them from the foil to a serving platter or four warmed plates. Remind guests to remove the bay leaves from the potatoes before eating.

ROMESCO: SUMMER'S PERFECT SAUCE

SAUCE ROMESCO: LA SAUCE D'ÉTÉ PARFAITE

Makes 2 very generous cups (500 ml)

Be prepared to see your most selfish instincts emerge when this sauce is nearby. Heady with the grilled flavor of charred peppers, tomatoes, garlic, and almonds, then made doubly smoky from paprika, you'll want to eat it by the spoonful. A recipe brought to me by my dear friend and noted gourmand, Nelleke Geel, from her beloved Catalonia region in northeastern Spain, this is often served with Grilled Spring Onions (page 178) or Basic Grilled Leeks (page 175), a tradition I've copied. I don't just use Romesco with leeks, though. Serve it with Grilled Bread with Smashed Tomatoes (page 41), with Garlic Polenta with Olives (page 194), with grilled fish, roast chicken, steak frites—you get the idea; it's good with everything! Serve a Catalan wine here, such as a Côtes Catalanes.

SPECIAL EQUIPMENT: *Food processor, long tongs*

PREPARATION AND GRILLING TIME: *About 45 minutes*

DIFFICULTY LEVEL: *Simple*

---

1 pound (500 g) red bell peppers

1 pound (500 g) ripe red tomatoes

3 cloves garlic, peeled and cut in half lengthwise

Generous ⅓ cup (55 g) raw almonds

¾ cup (50 g) fresh bread crumbs

1 tablespoon sherry vinegar

2 tablespoons olive oil

Fine sea salt and freshly ground black pepper

¼ teaspoon smoked paprika, such as pimentón de la Vera, or to taste*

PREHEAT THE GAS GRILL USING TWO burners (350°F; 180°C). Grill the peppers and tomatoes until they are soft and darkened, turning them every 5 minutes so they grill evenly. The tomatoes will take about 15 minutes to grill; the peppers will take 20 to 25 minutes. Remove the vegetables from the grill as they're cooked, putting the tomatoes into a shallow bowl and the peppers into a paper bag to steam.

Place a medium cast-iron skillet on the grill and let it heat. When it is hot, place the garlic and almonds in it and grill until the garlic is golden and the almonds are toasted, stirring and shaking the pan often so they don't burn. It should take about 10 minutes. Transfer the garlic and almonds from the grill to a bowl. Add the bread crumbs to the pan and toast them until they are golden, stirring almost constantly; they will take 5 to 7 minutes to toast.

Peel and seed the peppers and the tomatoes. For the tomatoes, because they are ripe and turn to a delicious softness, just pluck out the seeds that stay in a gelatinous mass. Use a scraper to scrape the tomato flesh from the skin.

ASTUCES: If serving with leeks, which I do, particularly during midsummer to early fall when they are slim, simply wash and trim them, removing just the very outer leaves but keeping some of the tough leaves. They will char as the leeks grill, and your guests can pull them off to reveal the tender, juicy interior of the leeks. This makes for a mess, but it's such a delicious one that no one will mind. Just be prepared with lots of napkins and a bowl for the discarded leaves. Traditionally, this sauce is made in a mortar with a pestle, so do this if you like. I opt for the food processor.

*If you like spicy, use the hot version of pimentón de la Vera.

Place the peppers, tomatoes, garlic, almonds, and bread crumbs in the work bowl of a food processor and process until they are reduced to a puree—it will not be a smooth puree and should be quite thick. Add the vinegar, oil, and salt and pepper and process, then add the smoked paprika. Adjust by adding more of any seasoning that you like.

To serve, transfer to a bowl and issue a spoon to all the guests . . . !

GRILLED VEGETABLE SALAD

SALADE DE LÉGUMES GRILLÉES

Serves 6 to 8

Oh my, what a salad! It's Mediterranean and purely French at the same time because of the vegetable varieties, the mushrooms, and the lovely vinaigrette, which brings everything together and turns this into a meal in itself. The vegetables are cooked the French way, which means all the way through, so that they give up all their sweetness and flavor. This salad can be served as a main course with air-cured ham, as a first course before Smoky Pork Shoulder à la Française (page 166), or all on its own with some wonderful crusty bread. Try a gutsy Languedoc-Roussillon alongside.

SPECIAL EQUIPMENT: *Long tongs, pastry brush, perforated grill, gloves, platter*

PREPARATION AND GRILLING TIME: *25 to 30 minutes*

DIFFICULTY LEVEL: *Simple*

FOR THE SALAD:

2 medium zucchini (about 5 ounces; 150 g each), cut in half lengthwise

2 medium eggplants (7 ounces; 210 g each), rinsed, dried, cut in half lengthwise

2 medium bell peppers (about 5 ounces; 150 g each), seeds and pith removed, cut in quarters

4 spring onions (about 0.75 ounce; 22 g each), trimmed

8 ounces (250 g) medium crimini or regular mushrooms, stems removed, wiped clean

1 cup cherry tomatoes (8 ounces; about 250 g), preferably red and yellow, cut in half lengthwise

1 to 2 tablespoons olive oil

BRUSH ALL OF THE VEGETABLES BUT THE mushrooms and the cherry tomatoes on both sides with olive oil. Brush the mushrooms first with lemon juice, then with olive oil. Set all of the vegetables on a large platter near the grill, so they are all at hand. Season them lightly with salt.

Build a good-size fire in the grill.

Make the vinaigrette: In a medium bowl, whisk together the mustard, honey, and vinegar. Whisk in a large pinch of salt and some freshly ground pepper along with the garlic and the piment d'Espelette, then slowly whisk in the olive oil. Taste for seasoning and set aside.

When the coals are red and dusted with ash, spread them in a tight, single layer, leaving a perimeter of grill with no coals under it; they need to emit concentrated heat. Set the grill and a perforated grill pan over the coals.

When the grill pan is hot, place all of the vegetables atop it, except for the mushrooms and cherry tomatoes, and brown them for 2 minutes. Turn them, brush them with oil, and brown for 2 minutes. Close the grill and cook the vegetables until they are tender through, which will take 10 to 12 minutes for the zucchini, peppers, and white eggplant if using, 12 to 14 minutes for the purple eggplant and the onions. Check the vegetables on the grill at least once during cooking; if they are browning too

1 tablespoon freshly squeezed lemon juice

Fine sea salt

FOR THE VINAIGRETTE:

1 teaspoon Dijon mustard

1 teaspoon honey

2 tablespoons balsamic vinegar

Fine sea salt and freshly ground black pepper

1 clove garlic, minced

¼ teaspoon piment d'Espelette or a blend of mild and hot paprika

¼ cup (60 ml) olive oil

½ cup (about 4 g) lightly packed fresh tarragon or basil

FOR THE GARNISH:

Herb sprigs

Fleur de sel

ASTUCES: I leave the stem end on the eggplant, because it looks so pretty even when the eggplant is grilled. Just give your guests a heads-up that it's not really edible. I also love to use a mix of white and purple eggplants that are so common now at the French market. Note that the cooking times differ, however, with the white eggplant cooking more quickly than the purple variety.

quickly, move them to the edge of the grill, where they will continue to cook but won't brown so quickly.

Transfer the vegetables to the platter and place the mushrooms on the grill pan. Brown on each side for about 2 minutes, cover the grill, and cook until the mushrooms are tender, about 5 minutes. Transfer the mushrooms to the platter.

To serve the salad, cut the vegetables into large, bite-size pieces in an attractive manner (zucchini on the bias, eggplant lengthwise, etc.), and arrange them back on the platter. Strew the cherry tomatoes over all.

Mince the tarragon and whisk it into the vinaigrette.

Drizzle the vegetables with the vinaigrette, season with fleur de sel, garnish with herb sprigs, and serve either warm or at room temperature.

CHAPTER 3

POULTRY, FISH, RABBIT, AND SOME TOFU

"The weariness of life disappears among friends, at table."
—MICHEL ONFRAY, FRENCH PHILOSOPHER

Poultry and fish may well be the stars of the grill. Always versatile, they are even more so on the grill. For instance, poultry can be roasted whole, cut down the back and flattened, spiced, herbed, and turned into a meal for a few or many. As for fish, well, it is wonderful on the grill with a caveat—it needs protection from ultra-hot temperatures, as the recipes here recognize. Fish becomes more moist and tender when treated gently, and no matter the temperature, it always cooks more quickly than you think it will, which is *fast*.

You'll find a recipe for rabbit here, and that's because in France rabbit is always classified with poultry. Why? Because it was traditionally raised in the *basse cour*, or farmyard, by the farmwife. She either raised rabbits and poultry to sell so she could buy what she needed, or she raised them for her family. Either way, rabbit is "poultry" to the French! As for tofu, it seems to fit here as well, though it's neither fish nor fowl.

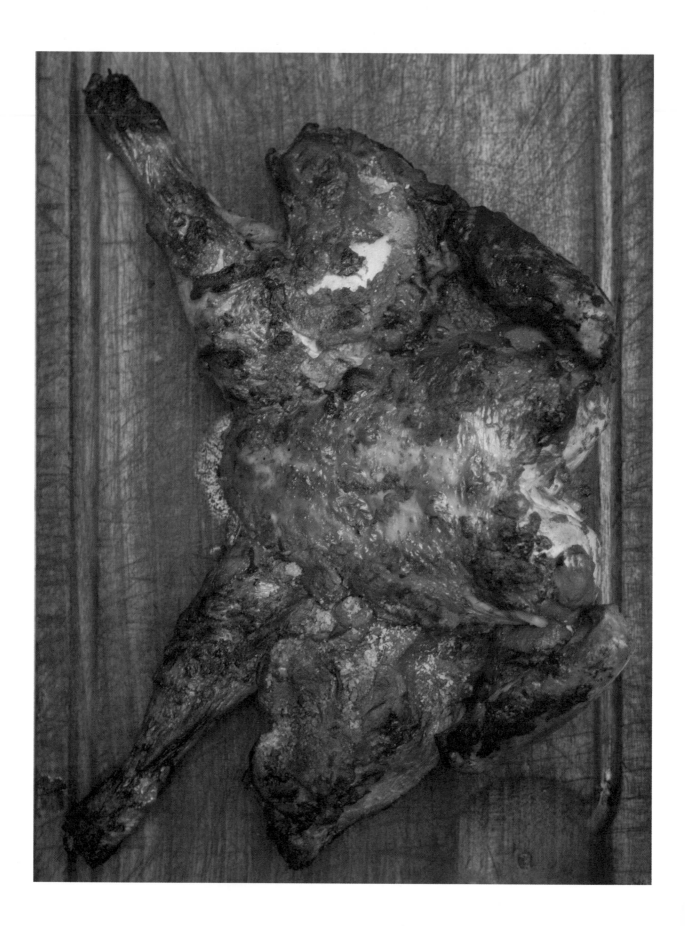

THE DEVIL'S HOT TOAD CHICKEN

LE POULET DE DIABLE EN CRAPAUD

Serves 6

A crapaud is a toad, which is what this chicken looks like when its backbone is removed and it's flattened—it resembles a toad that's about to hop! But don't worry, it will sit still as you rub butter under its skin, then slather it with a gorgeously piquant mixture of mustard and peppers, à *la diable.* Why go to the effort of removing the backbone? Well, it's no effort, first of all (see instructions below). Once you get the hang of cutting out the backbone, you'll be able to do it with your eyes closed in seconds. Second of all, by flattening out the chicken, it cooks evenly over the coals and ends up looking intriguingly delicious. Serve this with a microbrew, one that's not too dark.

SPECIAL EQUIPMENT: *Poultry shears or heavy chef's knife, pastry brush (for brushing butter and mustard mixture on chicken), tongs, gloves*

PREPARATION AND GRILLING TIME: *About 1½ hours*

DIFFICULTY LEVEL: *Moderate*

1 chicken (about 3½ to 4 pounds, 1.75 to 2 kg), at room temperature

2 tablespoons (30 g) unsalted butter, melted

Fine sea salt

½ teaspoon piment d'Espelette, or to taste

½ teaspoon sweet paprika, or to taste

¼ teaspoon spicy smoked paprika, or to taste

⅓ cup (75 ml) Dijon-style mustard

2 tablespoons fresh bread crumbs, lightly toasted

Flat-leaf parsley or other herb sprigs, for garnish

TURN THE CHICKEN ON ITS BREAST.

Using poultry shears, cut from the tail toward the neck on the right side of the backbone; you'll need to feel your way through this, but it's easy to do. Repeat on the other side of the backbone; remove the backbone piece and reserve it (it's great on the grill). Flip the chicken and remove the giblets, which you can grill or use for something else. If your chicken isn't completely flat, you can make a short vertical cut at the top of the sternum/base of the neck (this is advisable for true free-run chickens with actual tensile strength; not necessary for flabbier varieties). This will allow the chicken to lie flat.

Carefully loosen the skin from the meat of the chicken, making an effort not to tear or poke a hole in it, by gently inserting a finger between skin and meat. Brush the meat with half the butter as evenly as you can, then pull the skin back over the meat.

Salt the chicken all over.

Build a fire in the grill, and when the coals are red and dusted with ash, divide them in the barbecue, putting half the coals on either side. Place a drip pan in the center. Set the grill over the coals.

continued

ASTUCES: Remember to cut the bones at either side of the base of the neck. Doing so allows you to flatten the chicken easily. And if you want this chicken to be truly "devilish," then you'll likely want to increase the amount of spicy smoked paprika and piment d'Espelette.

While the grill is heating, whisk together the piment d'Espelette, paprikas, and mustard in a small bowl.

Place the chicken, skin side down, in the center of the hot grill. Cover and cook until the skin begins to turn golden, about 15 minutes (the temperature of the grill should be about 325°F; 165°C). If the skin isn't golden at this point, remove the cover of the grill and move the chicken over the coals, watching it until the skin browns nicely, which will take just a few minutes.

Flip the chicken onto the meat side and rub the skin with two-thirds of the mustard mixture. Cover the grill and cook the chicken for 10 minutes, then flip the chicken back to the skin side. Rub the remaining mustard mixture on the meat of the chicken and sprinkle it with half the bread crumbs, pressing them into the mustard. Shake a few drops of butter over the bread crumbs. Cover the barbecue and grill the chicken until it is nearly cooked through, about 15 minutes. The bread crumbs will be crisp and lightly golden. Turn the chicken onto the meat side, sprinkle the skin with the remaining bread crumbs and press them onto the chicken. Drizzle with the remaining butter. Cover and continue to cook until the bread crumbs are golden and the meat is cooked through, an additional 10 minutes.

Remove the chicken from the grill and place it, meat side down, on a warmed platter. You can serve it either immediately, when it's lukewarm, or at room temperature. Garnish with herb sprigs before serving.

RABBIT WITH MUSTARD AND CRISPY BACON

LAPIN À LA MOUTARDE ET LARD CROUSTILLANT

Serves 4 to 6

Rabbit is a frequent visitor to the French table, primarily in the cooler seasons of fall, winter, and spring. There isn't any reason for this seasonality aside from tradition, as rabbit's light, tender, and lean meat is ideal for summer, too.

On the advice of my butcher (and in the interest of dramatic presentation!), I roast whole rabbit after macerating it in mustard and wrapping it with bacon. Rabbit and bacon are like a horse and carriage—they simply go together. There is a reason for this: As the carriage needs a horse, so the rabbit needs the bacon, or some source of fat and moisture, because rabbit is very lean. They are such a duo that when the butcher sells rabbit, he always asks the customer if he needs bacon, too. The added gift the bacon gives to the rabbit is flavor and crisp texture—try this, you'll see. Serve a lovely, lean Saumur here for a real treat.

SPECIAL EQUIPMENT: *Trussing string, rotisserie (really a great tool), long tongs, long gloves, cutting board, trussing skewers for recalcitrant pieces of dangling bacon*

PREPARATION AND GRILLING TIME: *2 hours to marinate, about 1 hour to grill, 10 minutes sitting time*

DIFFICULTY: *Moderate*

FOR THE MUSTARD SAUCE:

1 shallot, diced

2 cloves garlic, minced

2 tablespoons olive oil

¼ cup (60 ml) Dijon mustard

Pinch sea salt

Freshly ground black pepper

BLEND ALL OF THE INGREDIENTS FOR THE mustard sauce in a small bowl. In a nonreactive baking dish, place the rabbit and rub it all over with the sauce. Cover and let sit at room temperature for at least 2 hours. You may also do this the night before you plan to cook the rabbit and refrigerate it, covered. Remove it from the refrigerator at least 2 hours before you plan to grill it.

Build a medium-size fire in the barbecue or light the gas grill using the two outside burners. When the coals are red and dusted with ash, divide them in the barbecue, putting half the coals on either side. Set a grill pan in the center of the barbecue to catch any drippings.

continued

1 whole rabbit (about 3 pounds; 1.5 kg)

Fine sea salt and freshly ground black pepper

10 to 12 slices slab bacon, rind removed (about 1 ounce; 30 g each)

FOR THE GARNISH:

Fresh bay leaf, or sprigs of other fresh garden herbs

ASTUCES: In the United States rabbits don't grow on trees. They don't in France, either, but they're easily obtainable. When you want to cook rabbit, I suggest you contact a local chef. Likely, she or he can order a rabbit for you. Otherwise, check the frozen foods section at a relatively upscale grocery. You're likely to find rabbit there. Before you marinate the rabbit, slice through the meat at the four leg joints so that you can bend them back and turn the rabbit into a long roast. I like to add bay leaves to the coals right before I put the rabbit on (you can add them to your gas grill, too). They add some sweet, smoky flavor to the rabbit. If you don't have the rotisserie attachment, you'll need to turn the rabbit three or four times during the roasting process.

Season the marinated rabbit all over with salt and pepper, then wrap it with the bacon strips and tie them into place. This is a bit of an athletic endeavor, be calm and go slowly. (I lay the bacon strips on the cutting board, slightly overlapping at the ends. I place the rabbit atop them, then slide the string under the bacon and bring it up—and the bacon with it—and around the rabbit, tying firmly to hold the bacon in place. Another option is to fit the rabbit on the rotisserie bar, then tie the bacon around it.) Use as many pieces of string as you need. If some of the bacon refuses to get caught in the string, simply skewer it into the rabbit using trussing skewers.

If using the rotisserie, fit the rabbit firmly on the rotisserie bar.

When the fire is hot, put the rotisserie bar in place; if not using, set the grill over the coals, and when the grill is hot, place the rabbit directly on the grill over the drip pan. You don't really need to check the rabbit if you're using the rotisserie; if you're grilling the rabbit, you need to turn it every 15 minutes, or as often as necessary to keep it golden without it getting too dark, until it is cooked through. Either way you cook, it will take 1 hour. Halfway through the cooking time, brush the rabbit with any of the leftover mustard sauce.

When the rabbit is cooked, transfer it to a cutting board and let it rest for 10 minutes before cutting off the string. Cut the rabbit into serving pieces and cut the bacon into large bite-size pieces.

If you have the rabbit liver, rub it all over with oil and place it on the grill until it is golden on all sides and slightly rosy inside, 6 to 7 minutes. Remove from the grill and season with salt and pepper.

To serve, place the rabbit pieces and the bacon on a platter. Cut the liver into several pieces and arrange it on the platter with the rabbit. Garnish with the bay leaf or herb sprigs and serve immediately.

GRILLED CHICKEN WITH SWEET, SPICED RHUBARB

POULET À LA RHUBARBE DOUCE ET PIQUANTE

Serves 6

In France we often use rhubarb in savory dishes. It adds so much, with its tang and color. This particular rhubarb sauce is simple to make. I've used it to accompany everything from mackerel to lamb, and it's delicious every time. I think it's best with chicken, and I've no doubt you'll love it here—the play of sweet, spicy, and crisp is gorgeous. The sauce keeps in the refrigerator, and it gets even better after a day or two.

~~~~~~~~~~~~~~~~~~

SPECIAL EQUIPMENT: *Large rubber spatula, tongs*

PREPARATION AND GRILLING TIME: *2 hours macerating time; about 45 minutes*

DIFFICULTY LEVEL: *Moderate*

FOR THE RHUBARB SAUCE:

¾ cup (185 ml) filtered water

½ cup (100 g) Vanilla Sugar (page 281)

3 bird's eye peppers (or other spicy pepper)

½-inch (1.25-cm) piece peeled ginger, cut in very thin coins

4 stalks rhubarb (about 11 ounces; 330 g total), cut into ¼-inch (0.6-cm) thick rounds

FOR THE SAUCE: WHISK TOGETHER THE

water and vanilla sugar in a large saucepan. Place it over medium-high heat. Add the bird's eye peppers and coins of ginger and bring to a boil, stirring occasionally. When the sugar is dissolved, fold in the rhubarb with a large heat resistant spatula and cook, folding gently so the rhubarb and syrup are combined, until the rhubarb softens but doesn't turn mushy. This will take 2 to 4 minutes. After 2 minutes, watch the rhubarb carefully, as you don't want it to overcook. When it is tender (it can be tender-crisp), remove it from the heat. It will hold very well at this stage.

In a small bowl, mix together the coconut, powdered ginger, and salt. Stir in the olive oil to make a thick paste. Pull back the skin on the chicken thighs and rub equal amounts of the paste over the meat, then pull the skin back over the meat. Let the chicken sit for at least 2 hours at room temperature or overnight in the refrigerator.

Light a good-size fire in a grill or heat the gas grill using all three burners.

When the coals are red and dusted with ash, divide them in two, placing half on each side of the barbecue. Set a drip pan in the center. Set the grill over the coals, and when the grill is hot, lay the chicken on the center of the grill, skin side down. Cover and

FOR THE CHICKEN:

3 tablespoons unsweetened coconut

3 teaspoons powdered ginger

Large pinch sea salt

2 tablespoons olive oil

6 large chicken thighs (about 9 ounces; 270 g each), with skin

Geranium blossoms or flat-leaf parsley leaves, for garnish

ASTUCES: If for some reason your rhubarb turns to instant mush—this can happen in a very wet year—remove the bird's eye peppers and puree the remaining sauce ingredients. Then add the peppers back to the puree so they continue to add flavor as it sits, but remove them again just before serving. It won't be as pretty, but the flavor will be the same. If you are unable to find bird's eye peppers, you can use any little hot pepper. Just remember to remove them before serving the dish.

cook until the skin is pale golden, for 10 minutes. Turn it and repeat. Finally, place the chicken over the coals, cover, and grill until the skin is golden and the chicken is cooked through—the meat should be at 160°F (71°C), which will take an additional 5 minutes.

To serve the chicken, transfer each piece from the grill to a warmed dinner plate. Remove the bird's eye peppers from the sauce and evenly divide the sauce among the plates, drizzling some of it (including the coins of ginger, which are delicious) over the chicken. Garnish with the geranium flowers and serve immediately.

CHICKEN WINGS WITH HERBES DE PROVENCE

LES AILES DE POULET AUX HERBES DE PROVENCE

Serves 2 to 4

The best butcher in my town is right next door to my house. Not only does he opt for locally raised meat and poultry, but he's ready to help out with any project that comes my way. When I was filming a day-in-the-life documentary of Louis XIV, he not only made a special Louis XIV pâté for the shoot, but he offered to do most of the meat and poultry roasting for it. Incredibly, he had everything fresh and ready to go just minutes before we needed it.

The other service he provides, aside from great meats and poultry, is preparing chicken wings. This is my favorite part of the bird, but it is not esteemed by the French. When he cuts apart a chicken, most people don't want the wings, so he puts them aside and waves to me from behind the counter when I walk by. "I've got wings. Do you want them?" he asks. Sometimes there are pounds of wings, sometimes just enough to serve four as an appetizer or two as a main course. No matter, I always take what he offers.

This recipe is a reflection of his kindness and the emergence of summer herbs in the garden. I put it together quickly, and all of my guests enjoyed it immensely. I do recommend making a double or triple batch and serving the wings with Grilled New Potato Salad (page 199).

~~~~~~~~~~~~~~~~~~~~~~~~~~~~~~~~~~~~~~~

SPECIAL EQUIPMENT: *Nonreactive dish, long tongs*

PREPARATION AND GRILLING TIME: *1 to 2 hours to marinate; 30 minutes to grill*

DIFFICULTY LEVEL: *Simple*

Eight chicken wings (about 1½ pounds; 750 g)

2 tablespoons olive oil

2 teaspoons freshly squeezed lemon juice

½ cup (5 g) fresh Herbes de Provence (page 261) or 1½ teaspoons dried

Fine sea salt and freshly ground black pepper

PLACE THE CHICKEN WINGS IN A NON-
reactive dish in one layer. In a small bowl whisk together the oil and the lemon juice.

Mince the herbes de Provence and whisk them into the oil and lemon juice. Pour this mixture over the chicken wings and turn each one so it is covered with the mixture. Strew the chicken wings with salt and pepper, cover, and let sit at room temperature for 30 minutes and up to 2 hours.

Light a good-size fire in the barbecue. When the coals are red and dusted with ash, divide them in the barbecue, putting half the coals on either side. Set a grill over the coals.

When the grill is hot, place the chicken wings in the center, cover the barbecue, and cook the wings until they are golden

ASTUCES: Make sure the wing tip is tucked under the little drumstick part of the wing so that the wings grill evenly. Chicken wings in France are heftier than those in the US, which is why this is a recipe for four and not for two. This recipe is easily doubled or tripled.

on both sides and cooked through, which will take about 30 minutes total. Turn the chicken wings at least twice, and if they aren't getting golden enough for your taste, place them directly over the coals for 5 minutes on each side toward the end of the cooking time, that is, after 20 minutes.

Transfer the chicken wings to a warmed platter and serve immediately, or let them come to room temperature before serving.

DUCK BREAST À LA VOÛTE

MAGRET À LA VOÛTE

Serves 4 to 6

I had this lovely preparation at La Voûte restaurant in Gap, a bustling city in the Hautes-Alpes, where the snow stays in the mountains all the way through summer. Duck breast has such intensely rich and special flavorings that most preparations are simple. I'm the first to stand aside and let the meat speak for itself, but here the seasoning elevates the flavor of the duck breast. That said, it's important not to overseason duck breast. I like to serve these with Honeyed Turnips (page 201) and a gorgeous, robust Côtes du Rhône.

SPECIAL EQUIPMENT: *Tongs*

PREPARATION AND GRILLING TIME: *2 hours to marinate; 20 minutes to grill*

DIFFICULTY LEVEL: *Simple*

THE DUCK:

2 medium magrets (about 12 ounces; 360 g each), at room temperature

FOR THE MARINADE:

Zest from 1 lime

¼ cup (60 ml) tamari

1 fat coin fresh ginger (½-inch; 1.25-cm thick), peeled, minced (about 2 tablespoons minced ginger)

1 medium clove garlic, minced

1 teaspoon sugar

¾ cup (7 g) cilantro leaves

Fleur de sel (optional)

SCORE THE FAT ON EACH DUCK BREAST

right to, but not into, the meat. Place the duck breasts in a nonreactive dish.

Mince two-thirds of the lime zest. Reserve the remaining zest in a covered ramekin.

Place the minced zest in a medium bowl. Whisk in all of the ingredients for the marinade except for the reserved zest, cilantro leaves, and fleur de sel.

Mince ½ cup of the cilantro leaves and whisk them into the marinade. Reserve the remaining ¼ cup.

Pour the marinade, which is quite thick, over the duck breasts. Rub it into them on both sides, and marinate for at least 1 hour and up to 2 hours at room temperature, turning the duck breasts two or three times so they marinate evenly.

Build a charcoal fire in the barbecue. When the coals are red and dusted with ash, divide them in the barbecue, putting half the coals on either side. Place a drip pan in the center.

continued

ASTUCES: Magret, or fattened duck breast, comes from a duck that has been raised to provide foie gras. The breast is tender, delicate, yet very meaty and infused with very special flavor. Ideally, the breast meat is served very rare. Here, it is medium-rare, which is the best way to cook it on the grill. You'll note that the seasoning is delicate. In the US, magret de canard is now available at most high-end supermarkets or online from retailers like D'Artagnan (www.dartagnan.com).

Set the grill atop the coals, and when the grill is hot, place the duck breasts in the center of the grill, skin side down, above the drip pan. Close the grill and cook until the skin is golden, about 12 minutes. Remove the cover and turn the duck breasts onto their meat side. Leaving the grill open, grill the breasts until the meat has changed color from red to "cooked" looking, which should take 2 to 4 minutes. Turn the duck breasts back onto their skin and continue grilling, uncovered, until the skin is deep golden and crisp and the meat is done to your liking. Medium rare, ideal for duck breast, will take 4 to 6 additional minutes.

Transfer the duck breasts to a cutting board, meat side down, and let them rest for about 5 minutes and up to 10 minutes. While the meat is resting, mince together the remaining ¼ cup cilantro leaves and the remaining lime zest.

To serve, slice the duck breasts into thin, diagonal slices and arrange them in the center of four to six warmed plates. They will give off quite a bit of juice; make sure you corral it to pour over the slices once they are on the plates. Sprinkle equal amounts of the minced lime zest and cilantro over the slices, season with fleur de sel if desired, and serve immediately.

DUCK BREAST À L'ORANGE

MAGRET À L'ORANGE

Serves 6

This favorite recipe for fattened duck breast (magret) is a riff on the classic duck à l'orange, though the resemblance stops with the name. There is no caramel here, just pure orange juice with a touch of fresh ginger, reduced to a syrup, then drizzled over duck breast that has grilled enough to crisp the skin and give a smoky tone. Duck breast is poultry, but it's also like red meat, one of the best there is. I suggest serving this with Grilled Asparagus (page 174). You'll want a rich red wine here, such as a Gaillac Vieilles Vignes from Peyres Roses.

SPECIAL EQUIPMENT: *Long tongs, small saucepan*

PREPARATION AND GRILLING TIME: *27 minutes, not including at least 1 hour macerating time*

DIFFICULTY LEVEL: *Simple*

FOR THE DUCK:

2 large magrets (15 ounces; 450 g each), at room temperature

1 teaspoon smoked paprika

1 teaspoon hot smoked paprika

Fine sea salt

FOR THE ORANGE SAUCE:

1 cup (250 ml) freshly squeezed orange juice

2 thin coins peeled ginger

FOR THE GARNISH:

Fleur de sel (optional)

Flat-leaf parsley or other herb leaves, for garnish

SCORE THE SKIN SIDE OF THE DUCK

through the skin to the meat, but not into the meat. This will allow the duck breast to cook evenly.

Mix the paprikas in a small bowl, then pat them into the duck breasts on both sides and the ends. You can do this up to several hours before you grill the duck breasts, leaving them at room temperature, covered, to macerate.

To make the orange sauce, place the orange juice and the ginger in a small, heavy saucepan over medium-high heat and bring it to a boil. Reduce the heat so it is simmering, and reduce the orange juice by about three-fourths, to ¼ cup (60 ml). Remove from the heat.

Build a good-size fire in the barbecue. When the coals are red and dusted with ash, divide them in the barbecue, putting half the coals on either side and placing a drip pan in the center. Set the grill over the coals.

continued

For this you'll want to use magret de canard, which is the breast from a fattened duck. In the US, it is now available at most high-end supermarkets or online from retailers like D'Artagnan (www.dartagnan.com). The layer of fat on the magret will astonish you. Don't trim it off, because duck fat is a good fat (being low in saturated fat), and it's filled with flavor that enhances the meat.

Lightly salt the duck breasts on all sides, and when the grill is hot, after about 5 minutes, place the duck breasts in the center of the grill, skin side down, above the drip pan. Close the grill and cook until the skin is golden, about 12 minutes. Remove the cover and turn the duck breasts onto their meat side. Leaving the grill open, grill the breasts until the meat has changed color from red to "cooked" looking, which should take 2 to 4 minutes. Turn the duck breasts back onto their skin and continue grilling, uncovered, until the skin is deep golden and crisp, and the meat is done to your liking. Medium rare, ideal for duck breast, will take 4 to 6 additional minutes.

Transfer the duck breasts from the grill to a cutting board and let them rest for at least 5 and up to 10 minutes, meat side down. Reheat the orange sauce over medium heat until it simmers, then reduce it a bit more, so that it is quite thick. Remove from the heat and remove and discard the ginger coins.

To serve, slice the duck breasts into thin, diagonal slices and arrange them in the center of four to six warmed plates. Drizzle equal amounts of sauce over and around them, season with fleur de sel if desired, garnish with herb leaves, and serve immediately.

GRILLED, STUFFED TURKEY NOT LIKE THANKSGIVING

DINDE FARCIE—PAS COMME LE JOUR DONNANT

Serves 4

This is a quintessentially French recipe, where humble turkey (which the French love) is turned into something rather elegant. Escalopes of turkey, which are cut from the breast and don't have the tenderloin attached, are stuffed with a sweet mixture of onions and peppers, set on a bed of grilled pepper sauce, and then garnished with herb oil. Despite the number of steps, this recipe is easy to make. What's more, you can do many things simultaneously, so it really doesn't take long: You grill the peppers while you make the stuffing; make the oil while the packets grill; and so on. I predict this dish will become a favorite. I suggest serving a red Sancerre alongside—its mineral tones are perfect here.

SPECIAL EQUIPMENT: *Tongs, trussing skewers (at least 8, maybe more), food processor*

PREPARATION AND GRILLING TIME: *45 minutes*

DIFFICULTY LEVEL: *Moderate*

FOR THE TURKEY:

18 ounces (550 g) turkey breast, cut into four slices (about ¼-inch; 0.6-cm thick, and measuring about 4-by-8 inches; 10-by-20 cm)

2 to 3 tablespoons olive oil

Piment d'Espelette or hot paprika

Fine sea salt and freshly ground black pepper

IF YOU NEED TO, *GENTLY* POUND THE SLICES of turkey to get the correct dimensions. Pour half the oil in a nonreactive dish, set the turkey slices atop the oil, and push them around so one side is covered with oil. Drizzle with the remaining oil and spread it completely over the turkey. Sprinkle the turkey on one side with a generous amount of piment d'Espelette or the amount of hot paprika that suits your heat palate. Cover and let sit at room temperature for at least 2 hours and up to 4 hours (if the room is hot, refrigerate the turkey, remembering to remove it from the refrigerator an hour before you plan to cook it so that it can come to room temperature).

Build a medium-size fire in the barbecue.

To make the stuffing, place the oil with the onion in a large skillet over medium-high heat. When the onion begins to sizzle, season it with salt and pepper, reduce the heat to medium, and cook, stirring occasionally, until the onion is nearly translucent, about 5 minutes. Add the garlic and the red bell pepper and cook, stirring, until the red bell pepper is mostly tender, for about 5 minutes. Stir in the turmeric. Adjust the seasoning.

FOR THE FILLING:

1½ tablespoons olive oil

2 medium onions (8 ounces;
250 g each), minced

Sea salt and freshly ground black
pepper

2 large cloves garlic, minced

1 large red bell pepper (8 ounces;
250 g), pith and seeds removed,
minced

¾ teaspoon turmeric

¾ cup (8 g) gently packed flat-leaf
parsley leaves

FOR THE SAUCE:

2 large red bell peppers

1 tablespoon olive oil

Fine sea salt

Piment d'Espelette

FOR THE GARNISH:

Flat-leaf parsley leaves

Parsley Oil (page 272)

ASTUCES: Put the breast in the freezer for about 10 minutes before slicing. This makes the meat firmer so that it is easier to slice. If the piece of tenderloin is left on the turkey, remove it before slicing the breast thin. You'll be tempted to add more oil to both stuffing and turkey, but don't. This dish ends up being light and almost refreshing. More oil would make it heavy. Note that this is a two-step recipe, with the stuffing cooked on the stovetop.

Mince the parsley and stir into the filling. Adjust the seasoning. Remove from the heat.

When the coals are red and dusted with ash, divide them, putting half of the coals on each side of the barbecue. Set the grill atop them, and when it is hot, place the two whole red bell peppers on the grill over the coals. Grill the peppers until they are black all over, which requires turning regularly but not often; this doesn't require close supervision and should take about 10 minutes. When they are blackened, transfer them to a paper bag, close it, and let them steam.

To make the turkey packets, lay out the slices on a work surface and season generously with salt and lightly with pepper. Cut them in half crosswise, so that you have eight pieces of roughly equal size. Put a generous tablespoon of filling on the bottom third of each slice, and fold the top of the slice over that to make a packet. Secure the slices closed with a trussing skewer.

Place the packets in the center of the grill. Cover the grill and cook the packets until they have golden grill marks on one side and the meat begins to turn translucent, about 5 minutes. Turn them, cover, and cook until they are golden, an additional 5 minutes. Turn them twice more until they are evenly golden and cooked through, for a total grilling time of 20 minutes.

While the packets are cooking, remove the skin, the pith, and the seeds from the peppers and puree them with 1 tablespoon of oil. Season to taste with salt and piment d'Espelette. If there is leftover filling, stir it into the red pepper sauce.

To serve, place a thick round of sauce in the center of four warmed dinner plates. Set two packets atop the sauce, and drizzle a bit more sauce over the top. Garnish with parsley leaves, dot the plate with parsley oil for decor, and serve immediately.

ROTISSERIE CHICKEN

POULET RÔTI SUR LES BRAISES

Serves 6

I believe the rotisserie chicken was invented in France, most likely by the Gauls, though the first bird on a spit probably wasn't a chicken, and electricity was far in the future. Most likely, the bird in the *Gaulois* diet was a goose, a duck, or a pigeon, or maybe all three. All of these birds were domesticated early on, and all of them were grilled over the coals.

Here, though, I present the humble French chicken. They seem to be roasting everywhere in France, on sidewalks in front of the butcher shop, inside the butcher shop, and at market stands. When I walk by one of the vertical grills at my weekly farmers' market, I often wonder why I bother to cook—they smell so good and look so succulent. Sometimes I buy one. They are sumptuous—fresh farm chicken, roasted to perfection, slipped into a special bag along with its juices, to be opened with great fanfare at home. And there you have it, a Saturday market picnic at the dining room table.

Even better than this, though, is roast chicken from the grill at home. There is nothing quite like the slightly smoky, juicy, and tender bird that results when you take this off the rotisserie. You get a hint of smoke and a crisp skin that crackles when you cut into the chicken. Using the great technique of indirect heat, the juice from the bird drips into a pan. Those drippings, in turn, become a luscious sauce. Enjoy this with a lightly chilled Brouilly.

SPECIAL EQUIPMENT: *Rotisserie, long tongs, trussing string*

PREPARATION AND GRILLING TIME: *1 hour 10 minutes*

DIFFICULTY LEVEL: *Simple*

LIGHT A GOOD-SIZE FIRE IN THE BARBECUE.

Mince the zest and the garlic together and place in a small bowl. Pour over the oil, stir, then season the mixture with salt and pepper. Loosen the skin on the chicken, detaching it carefully from the meat, including the legs. Rub the oil and zest mixture onto the meat of the chicken.

Place a bay leaf and a lemon, cut in half, inside the chicken, and season the cavity with salt and pepper. Truss the chicken well and carefully so it will roast evenly.

When the coals are red and dusted with ash, divide them in the barbecue, putting half the coals on either side. Set a drip pan in the center.

continued

3 strips of zest each from an orange, a lemon, and a lime

1 large clove garlic

2 tablespoons olive oil

Fine sea salt and freshly ground black pepper

1 roasting chicken (4 to 5 pounds; 2 to 2½ kg), with giblets if possible, at room temperature

1 bay leaf

1 lemon

½ cup (125 ml) water

2 to 3 tablespoons freshly squeezed lemon juice

ASTUCES: You can vary the seasonings you put under the skin of the chicken, depending on your mood. If you don't have an electric rotisserie, you will still roast the chicken using the indirect method. Simply set the grill over the coals, which are banked toward the sides. When the grill is hot, set the chicken in the center of the grill so it isn't over the coals. Cover the grill and roast the chicken, turning it every 20 minutes, until it is golden and the interior temperature is 165°F (74°C).

Place the chicken on the rotisserie bar, making sure it is firmly in place. Set it over the coals; start the rotisserie and make sure the chicken is turning. Cover and cook until the chicken is golden brown and about 165°F (74°C) on the interior, which will take about 1 hour 15 minutes. You don't have to check the chicken until after at least an hour, but I always peek a couple of times to be sure all is well.

When the chicken is roasted, transfer it to a cutting board, breast side down, and let it rest for at least 20 minutes and up to 40 minutes. Take the drippings in the roasting pan, add the water, place it over medium heat, and bring the liquid to a boil, scraping up any browned bits from the bottom of the drip pan. Add the lemon juice to taste, then adjust the seasoning with salt and pepper if necessary.

Carve the chicken and serve with the sauce alongside.

SALMON WITH TARRAGON BUTTER, GRILLED ON THE SKIN

SAUMON À L'UNILATÉRALE AU BEURRE D'ESTRAGON

Serves 4

Cooking fish on the skin side, which protects the meat from direct heat, leaves it so moist and tender that I can't quite imagine any other way to cook it. In the case of salmon, you are also left with strips of golden skin that are shatteringly crisp and delectable. To finish here, add a bit of melted butter, a squeeze of lemon juice, a shower of freshly minced tarragon, and *voila!* This makes for quite a lunch or supper, particularly when you serve it with Basic Grilled Leeks (page 175) and a chilled Saumur-Champigny.

SPECIAL EQUIPMENT: *Long metal spatula, plancha*

PREPARATION AND GRILLING TIME: *10 to 12 minutes*

DIFFICULTY LEVEL: *Simple*

---

2 salmon fillets (8 to 10 ounces; 300 g each), bones removed, rinsed quickly and patted dry

2 to 3 teaspoons olive oil

4 tablespoons (60 g) unsalted butter

Fine sea salt and freshly ground black pepper

1 cup (10 g) gently packed tarragon leaves, minced

4 teaspoons freshly squeezed lemon juice, or to taste

LIGHT ALL THREE BURNERS OF A GAS GRILL. Place a plancha on the grill; let it heat to blistering and the grill to about 425–450°F (220–230°C).

Rub each salmon fillet all over with a light coating of oil. Put the butter in a medium heatproof pan and place it on the grill to melt.

When the plancha is hot, place the salmon fillets on it, skin side down. The butter is most likely melted at this point, so remove it and keep it warm. Close the grill and cook the salmon fillets until they are opaque through, about 8 minutes; if they are almost but not quite opaque, remember they will continue to cook once off the grill. Slip a sturdy metal spatula between the meat and the skin of each fillet, and transfer the meat to a cutting board with a trough around it to catch the juices or a large plate or platter. Carefully remove the skin from the plancha—it will be golden and crisp—and reserve. Season the salmon with salt and pepper and let it sit for a few minutes so that the fillets give up their juices.

continued

ASTUCES: Always let fish sit for a few minutes after cooking, as it will give up juices that have little flavor. Pour away this juice; it dilutes any sauce that you serve and will make the plate unattractive. Also note that each serving here is 5 ounces (150 g), half of the salmon fillet per perosn. If you want a heartier serving, simply increase the weight of the salmon fillets. The cooking time should remain the same. This recipe is ideal for a gas grill; if you don't have a plancha, use a cast-iron skillet set on your grill.

Stir the tarragon into the melted butter, then stir in the lemon juice to taste.

To serve, cut each piece of salmon fillet in half crosswise, and use a slotted spatula (so their juices don't come with them) to transfer one piece each to the center of a warmed plate. Drizzle the butter mixture over each piece. Cut each piece of salmon skin in two, and balance each piece at an angle on a piece of salmon. Serve immediately.

DRUNKEN LOBSTER

HOMARD IVRE

Serves 4

This recipe comes directly from Baptiste, a grower at my Saturday market and a natural-born gourmand. He described how his father, a professional chef, made this one evening over the grill at their home. His description was so mouthwatering that I decided to try it. I also decided to invite Baptiste and his parents for the evening, figuring that they could guide me along the flaming way. They did—it was fabulous. And I've made it many times since! Grilled lobster all by itself is an exceptional treat. The heat of the fire and the protection of the shell allow the meat to cook into mouth-melting tenderness, retaining all of its flavor with a slight hint of smoke. With a touch of alcohol the lobster becomes ethereal, because the alcohol just kisses the lobster meat with flavor, enhancing its natural and briny sweetness.

SPECIAL EQUIPMENT: *Small, heatproof saucepan, long tongs, gloves, and crackers and picks for eating the lobster*

PREPARATION AND GRILLING TIME: *10 minutes*

DIFFICULTY LEVEL: *Moderate*

3 tablespoons unsalted butter

2 medium live lobsters (about 1¾ pounds; 800 g each), cut in half lengthwise

⅓ cup (80 ml) whiskey, Pernod, grappa, or your liqueur of choice (use half this amount if grilling over gas)

BUILD A GOOD-SIZE FIRE IN A BARBECUE,
or heat up the gas grill using all three burners.

When the coals are red and dusted with ash, spread them in a tight, single layer, leaving a perimeter of grill with no coals under it; they need to emit concentrated heat. Set the grill over the coals.

Place the butter in a small, completely heatproof saucepan.

When the grill is hot, lay the lobster on it, shell side down. Cover and cook until the lobster tail meat turns almost completely translucent, the tomalley inside the lobster turns opaque, and the outer shell turns red, then golden, 7 to 9 minutes. If grilling over the coals, quickly throw half the whiskey over each lobster so some hits the coals and *stand back!* Flames will engulf the lobster, then almost immediately die down.

continued

ASTUCES: Place the lobster in the freezer for about 15 minutes before you plan to cut it in half. The lobster will sleep, making the job of dispatching it easier. Also, if you're grilling over gas, don't throw alcohol on the gas burners. Use about half the amount of alcohol, flame it in a pan, and then drizzle it over the lobster tails. Before you flame anything, tie back your hair, put on your gloves, and stand back. If you love the tomalley, or fatty part of the lobster (it's delicious), then drizzle it with alcohol, too.

Place the pan of butter on the grill next to the lobster, cover for 1 minute, then remove the lobsters from the grill, transferring them to a serving platter. Leave the pan with the butter on the grill until it is melted, then drizzle the butter over the lobster tails.

If you are grilling over gas, place half the alcohol in a shallow, completely heatproof saucepan and place it over the heat. Once it is hot, touch a live flame to it and *stand back*! Flames will ignite, then die down. Divide the alcohol among the lobster tails.

Serve the lobster immediately.

SARDINES, OH! SARDINES

LES SARDINES, O! LES SARDINES

Serves 4 to 6

They swim into our lives in the summer, these little blue-striped fish. Part of the herring family, sardines are small and simple (anatomically), but they nonetheless pack a wollop of flavor. They're a natural for the grill. The purist way to cook them is over a hot fire for just a few minutes, head, insides, and all. They emerge from the grill crisp on the outside, their fillets molten and tender.

I prepared these recently for the sardine expert in my midst, Nathalie Souchet, my neighbor and a native of Brittany, where some of France's best sardines come from. She grew up eating everything from the sea, and she remembers when her mother grilled sardines in the family fireplace. "No sardines will ever taste as good as my mother's," she said the other day, sitting in my kitchen and about to eat these off the grill.

She took her first bite. "Ahhh, I adore sardines," she said, her eyes closed. "Simple, the way my mother cooked them . . . these are delicious!" I took that as an imprimatur for publishing this recipe! These are delicious with a lovely Bandol—the Mourvèdre grape, particularly, loves sardines!

SPECIAL EQUIPMENT: *Long tongs, platter*

PREPARATION AND GRILLING TIME:
About 7 minutes

DIFFICULTY LEVEL: *Simple*

1½ pounds (750 g) sardines fresh from the water, rinsed and refrigerated

1 tablespoon olive oil

Fine sea salt and freshly ground black pepper

Fresh sage leaves or other herb, for garnish

BUILD A MEDIUM-SIZE FIRE IN THE BARBECUE
or turn on the gas grill, using all three burners.

Rub the sardines with oil and refrigerate them until you're ready to put them on the grill.

When the coals are red and dusted with ash, spread them in a tight, single layer; they need to emit concentrated heat. Set the grill over the coals.

When the grill is hot, place the sardines on it right over the coals and cook until they are golden, about 2½ minutes, turn, and cook until they are golden on the other side and cooked through, another 2½ minutes.

Transfer the sardines to a serving platter, strew them generously with salt and pepper, garnish with sage leaves, and serve immediately.

ASTUCES: Sardines swim in the Pacific, the Atlantic, and the Mediterranean. In the US, they're most available on the West Coast. But don't give up if you live elsewhere, as chances are you can find them, even if you have to beg your favorite chef to order them through her or his private channels. It will be worth it, because freshly grilled sardines are one of the wonders of the culinary world. And when you grill them, I hope you'll follow my advice and keep things simple. There are countless additions you can make to this recipe, but eating these fish right off the grill, crisp and tender at the same time, is the very best.

There isn't any need to clean a sardine, because the heat from the grill does that for you. That said, if you decide you want to clean them, simply make a cut through the backbone behind the head and pull—out will come everything you don't want to eat. Give them a quick rinse, and keep them cold until you put them on the grill.

COD WITH CHERMOULA, FROM THE MAGHREB

CABILLAUD AU CHERMOULA DU MAGHREB

Serves 4 to 6

This is a simple, exotic presentation based on the principles of North African, or Maghreb, flavors, which are so prevalent now in French cooking. As we say, "France went out to colonize the world; the world has come back to colonize its cuisine." Lucky for our palates. There are so many variations on chermoula; it reflects the cook who makes it. That said, it always includes cilantro and flat-leaf parsley, a touch of olive oil, lemon juice, garlic, and paprika. From there, it can vary. Here, instead of adding turmeric and cumin to the chermoula as some cooks do, I sprinkle them directly on the cod. *Miam* (which is Frenchly onomatopoeic for "yum")!

Serve this with couscous, Bulgur (page 179), or rice. And when you've made this sauce for fish, you can then move along to try it on chicken or pork! As an accompaniment, I like to serve a deeply flavored rosé or a fruity red wine such as a Sancerre.

SPECIAL EQUIPMENT: *Whisk, plancha, pastry brush*

PREPARATION AND GRILLING TIME: *about 15 minutes*

DIFFICULTY LEVEL: *Moderate*

FOR THE COD:

1½ pounds (750 g) cod loin, bones removed

1 teaspoon olive oil, or more if necessary

1 teaspoon ground turmeric

1 teaspoon ground cumin

1 teaspoon piment d'Espelette or medium-hot paprika

¼ teaspoon fine sea salt

½ teaspoon freshly ground black peppercorns

PLACE THE PLANCHA ON THE GAS GRILL, then heat the grill to 400°F (200°C), using two burners.

Rinse the cod and pat it dry. Remove any bones. Rub the cod all over with half the olive oil.

Whisk together the turmeric, cumin, piment d'Espelette, and salt and pepper in a small bowl, then sprinkle it evenly over the cod. You are likely to have a bit leftover; save it in an airtight container for another dish.

Make the chermoula: Place the cilantro, parsley, and garlic in a small bowl, and pour over the 2 tablespoons olive oil. Mix to make a paste. Stir in the lemon juice, then the paprika. Reserve.

Brush the plancha evenly and generously with the remaining oil. Place the fish on it, cover the grill, and cook until the cod is cooked through, 5 to 6 minutes—you won't turn it, because it's too fragile and will fall apart.

FOR THE CHERMOULA:

½ cup (5 g) cilantro leaves, minced

½ cup (5 g) flat-leaf parsley leaves, minced

3 medium cloves garlic, minced

2 tablespoons olive oil

3 tablespoons freshly squeezed lemon juice

1 teaspoon sweet paprika

FOR THE PLANCHA:

1 teaspoon olive oil

FOR THE GARNISH:

Cilantro leaves

ASTUCES: Cod is the fish of choice here. Given that, there are many members of the cod family to try, and a few cousins as well. Flounder works here, as does lingcod, halibut, even tilapia. While I recommend serving other starches with this dish, it is essential to offer bread, because if there is a bone that gets caught in the throat, a bite of bread will push it down and remove the danger.

Transfer the cod to a platter and let it rest while it gives up some of its liquid, just a minute or two.

Transfer the cod to four warmed dinner plates. Evenly divide the chermoula among the four pieces of cod, garnish with cilantro leaves, and serve immediately.

———

My son, Joseph, was home for the Christmas holidays, and I was firing up the grill to cook the huge number of cod loins my friend Bruno-the-fishmonger had given me. As usual, I'd invited a lot of people in to celebrate. The kitchen was crowded and bustling, and everyone was happy and drinking little hot toddies. I was threading my way in and out of the kitchen to supervise the fire in the courtyard, but I was starting to panic because the fire was doing miserably.

Joe caught a whiff of my panic and said, "Mom, let me take care of it," which I happily did, melting into the group to make merry and play hostess.

Joe had cooked on the grill at Pok Pok NY restaurant in Brooklyn for more than a year, and he knows his way around fire. He took control, brought the chimney starter filled with charcoal into the kitchen, set it over one of the huge gas burners on my stove, and turned it to maximum heat. I was only half paying attention as I mingled, until I smelled smoke. The kitchen began to fill with it. Joe, oblivious, was deftly assembling tools and not realizing that guests were starting to cough. Bits of newspaper and charcoal from the chimney were floating into the air and falling onto the little crescent rolls rising nearby, and everything else.

"Joe!" I cried, running to the stove. He beat me there, grabbed the chimney (with his gloves on, good grill chef), and ran out the door to the barbecue in the courtyard, where he tipped the by-now red-hot coals into it.

I turned on the fan inside, blew a few errant ashes from the rolls, and followed him.

"Well, that's the way we did it at the restaurant," he shrugged, shifting around the burning coals. My panic gone, I burst into laughter, the fire burst into flame, and pretty soon we all sat down to some amazing grilled cod.

BACON AND ROSEMARY GRILLED COD

CABILLAUD AU LARD FUMÉ ET ROMARIN

Serves 4

Cod is one of the wonders of the seafood world. It spawned exploration and discovery, fortunes won and lost, tragedy and prosperity. Today, in France, it is still almost always *sur l'étalage,* or "on the fish counter." The stocks are well managed, for now, so I enjoy its tender, white meat with abandon. The most coveted cut is the *dos,* or "loin," which is perfect for grilling. Because cod is so lean, it has to be protected from the direct heat, which is the main reason for using the bacon in this dish. Of course, everything is better with bacon, something the French have known for centuries; they put bacon in everything but dessert (and I'm sure that is coming).

Many herbs are good with cod, though rosemary is exceptional. However, try pineapple sage, regular sage, basil, thyme, tarragon. For woody herbs, you'll need to remove them from the fish right after you take it from the grill. For leafy herbs, just leave them with the fish as they almost melt while the fish is cooking over the grill. I recommend serving this with either Grilled Asparagus (page 174) or Basic Grilled Leeks (page 175) and a spicy white wine such as a Cassis.

SPECIAL EQUIPMENT: *Trussing skewers, plancha or large cast-iron skillet, sturdy metal spatula, tongs, platter*

PREPARATION AND GRILLING TIME: *20 to 25 minutes*

DIFFICULTY LEVEL: *Moderate*

RINSE THE COD AND PAT IT DRY. RUB IT ALL over with the olive oil, then season it evenly with salt and pepper on all sides.

Lay out two slices of bacon on a work surface, slightly overlapping, and set a piece of cod atop the bacon so that the slices will wrap it lengthwise. Set a branch of rosemary atop the cod, then bring the bacon slices up and around the cod so it is completely enclosed. Secure the bacon slices with two trussing skewers. The cod should be nearly completely wrapped by the bacon. Repeat with the remaining cod, bacon, and rosemary sprigs.

Heat a gas grill with a plancha set on it to high heat, about 500°C. When the plancha is hot, set the bacon-wrapped cod pieces on it. Cover and cook for 4 minutes. Turn the cod, cover

continued

1½ pounds (750 g) cod loin or other thick (1½ inches; 3.75 cm) white fish loin or fillet from lingcod, halibut, or flounder, bones removed, refrigerated

1 to 2 teaspoons olive oil

Fine sea salt and freshly ground black pepper

8 ounces (250 g) thinly sliced slab bacon, rind removed if necessary

4 freshly picked sprigs rosemary (5 to 6 inches; 12.5 to 15 cm), or other herb leaves

Extra rosemary, for garnish

ASTUCES: Fish always seeps after it is cooked, so let it sit for 5 minutes on a platter. Place it somewhere it will stay warm so it can give up its juice. Remove the skewers immediately after taking the cod from the grill, and remove the rosemary (or other herb) sprigs. Then, once the fish has given up its juices, transfer each piece to a warmed dinner plate.

the grill, and cook until the bacon is golden, about 3 minutes. Balance the cod pieces against each other so they stand on their sides, for about 30 seconds per side, so the bacon turns uniformly golden.

Transfer the cod to a plate or platter and let it sit so its juices seep out. Meanwhile, usher everyone to the table and make sure the wine is poured. If you've used rosemary to flavor the cod, remove the sprigs by gently pulling them out from under the bacon. Transfer each piece of cod to the center of a warmed plate, garnish with a rosemary sprig or leaf, and serve the vegetable of your choice alongside.

BAY~GRILLED MONKFISH

LOTTE GRILLÉ AU LAURIER

Serves 6

This recipe is inspired by Chef Bruno Verjus, who prepares it at his chic little restaurant, Table, in Paris. The preparation involves fire and smoke, yet it's done on your stove and will not make your smoke detector whine (at least it didn't mine). Although this is an indoor grilling recipe, your guests will be convinced that you somehow hung from the balcony with a grill and produced this amazing fish. I include it here precisely for those of you who have neither garden nor balcony but love the smoky grilled taste of foods. Try this, and your "grill envy" will disappear. Serve a lightly chilled white Burgundy here.

SPECIAL EQUIPMENT: *Heavy, nonstick skillet, tongs, perforated spatula for lifting fish from one plate to another, one plate or platter to receive the fish from the pan, which you won't use for serving the fish*

PREPARATION AND GRILLING TIME: *About 20 minutes*

DIFFICULTY LEVEL: *Moderate*

1½ pounds (750 g) monkfish fillets, without the central bone, inner skin trimmed away

1 tablespoon olive oil

1 to 2 tablespoons neutral oil, such as grape seed or sunflower

1 small branch fresh bay leaves with about 6 leaves on it, or 6 dried bay leaves

Fleur de sel

Freshly ground black pepper

Additional fresh bay leaves or herbs (flat-leaf parsley leaves, tarragon leaves), for garnish

TRIM THE MEMBRANE FROM THE MONKFISH if necessary. Rinse and pat the fillets dry and refrigerate.

Place 1 tablespoon of each of the oils in a skillet over medium-high heat. Place one bay leaf in the pan, and when it begins to sizzle, add the branch or remaining bay leaves to the pan and cook them until they begin to blacken and smoke, which will take 3 to 4 minutes. Using the tongs, place the monkfish in the pan, gently nudging the bay leaves to the side. Shake the pan so that the bay leaves catch fire. Continue to shake the pan gently, and turn the fish, as the bay leaves go out and relight, for about 2 minutes, then place a lid on the pan and remove it from the heat. Let it sit without looking at it for 8 minutes. If the monkfish isn't cooked after 8 minutes, let it cook for an additional 2 minutes, then transfer it to a plate, season it with fleur de sel and pepper, and let it sit for 5 minutes. The monkfish will be golden on one side.

To serve, use a perforated spatula or tongs to transfer each piece of monkfish, golden side up, to the center of a warmed plate. Garnish with the additional bay leaves.

ASTUCES: Monkfish has an outer and an inner skin. Usually the fishmonger trims away the gray outer skin, but not always the inner skin, which is very fine, almost more of a membrane. If this inner skin is still on the fish, simply trim it away using a very sharp knife, preferably one that is flexible bladed, like a fish fillet knife. Otherwise the membrane will shrink during cooking and your fish will be pulled every which way. When searing the bay leaves, take care that there is nothing flammable near your stove, that your hair is tied back, and that you stand a good length away from the pan, tending to things in it with a pair of tongs, preferably a pair that is extra-long. If you have a fan above the stove, you may also want to switch it on. Once the fish is cooked, remember to let it sit for at least 5 minutes once you've taken it from the pan to allow its juices to emerge. When you serve it, simply lift it from the plate with a perforated spatula to leave the juices behind.

———————

Many years ago I tasted the most amazing dish near Bordeaux—local mussels cooked in a nest of pine needles set over hot coals. Called éclade, the origins of the dish sit with the mussel fishermen there who landed their boats, arranged mussels on a wood plank, then buried them in a deep layer of pine needles that they set afire. By the time the needles were burnt, the mussels were open, their cream to orange colored meats scented with pine smoke.

I've never forgotten the dish, and lo and behold, when I climbed up from the beach at Trébeurden in Brittany not long ago, I noticed a thick layer of pine needles alongside the path on both sides. Of course there would be pine needles—craggy maritime pines (*Pinus pinaster*), their arthritic branches shaped by the coastal winds, lined both shoreline and roads. In short order I had a big bagful of needles. It was no effort at all to find gorgeous Locquémeau mussels from nearby Lannion, and I was on my way.

According to tradition I should have pounded four nails in a wooden plank and used them to wedge a first whorl of mussels balanced on their edges. This would have anchored the rest of the blue-shelled molluscs until the plank was covered with them. But I didn't have a plank let alone nails, so instead I built a fire. Then, when it was ready, I laid down a very thick layer—4 to 6 inches (10 to 15 cm)—of pine needles, strew the mussels on it, covered the whole affair with another thick layer of needles, and waited for the coals to light the needles, which happened almost immediately. They burst into flame and, as the mussels heated and let loose their liquid, curls of white smoke and then an entire mushroom cloud emerged from the grill. I covered it, but the smoke found its way out from under the edge and out of the holes of the grill.

After about 10 minutes, I lifted the cover of the grill and swept back the needles, half of which were charred and half of which were heavy with steam from the mussels. Those that were dry lit right back on fire, so I worked gingerly, extracting the open mussels one by one, blowing off the ashes and charred pine needles as best I could before putting them in a bowl. Surrounded, buried almost, by the heady-smelling smoke, I didn't even notice the small crowd that had formed to watch. We were a group of about 20 on a spectacular terrace in Trébeurden overlooking the bay; most everyone was standing around the grill to see what on earth I was doing. Those among the group who know me well weren't surprised—they had shared such experiences with me before. Those who didn't know me well probably thought I was crazy.

Until they tasted the mussels. Smoky, tender, juicy, salty, and marvelous. It was a messy business (just the kind I love), and I became something of a star, if a slightly smoky one. I didn't care about smoke or stardom though. To be able to make éclade was a dream come true, and the result as delectable as I remembered.

I will say, however, that despite the supply of pine needles I brought home with me in the car, I'm not sure I'll do this again anytime soon. Éclade is the kind of thing that you have to just make happen in the right environment, with the right ingredients, surrounded by the right kind of people, those who don't mind a few charred pine needles in their food. As in so much traditional cooking over fire, it is nearly impossible to reduce something like this to times and method. Once those flames get going and that smoke starts roiling, it's *sauve qui peut*—"everyone for themselves." Nonetheless, the few guidelines that follow should help if you ever decide you want to make your own éclade!

ÉCLADE

Serves 20 as a very satisfying appetizer

A nonrecipe for the intrepid and the fortunate to serve with Muscadet.

~~~~~~

SPECIAL EQUIPMENT: *Lots of dry pine needles, long tongs, long gloves*

PREPARATION AND GRILLING TIME:
35 minutes, including debearding the mussels; if you have a grill without a cover, the mussels will take about 25 minutes to cook; if you have a covered grill, they should be cooked in about 15 minutes

DIFFICULTY LEVEL: *Challenging*

---

6 pounds mussels

ASTUCES: Debeard mussels right before you cook them, never in advance, because the mussels spoil quickly once debearded.

RIGHT BEFORE YOU PLAN TO COOK THEM, debeard the mussels.

Build a good-size fire in a barbecue, and when the coals are red and dusted with ash, place a very thick layer—about 4 inches (10 cm)—of dry pine needles atop it, and pour the mussels on top of it in a single layer. Top with another thick layer of pine needles, cover the grill, leaving all vents open, and wait for the spectacle. After about 10 minutes, remove the cover and push back the top layer of pine needles, some of which will be burnt, some of which will be damp, to uncover the mussels using long tongs. Remove any that are open, and push the needles back over those that are still closed. Leave the cover off until the steam and smoke start going again, then replace the cover and cook for another 5 minutes. Repeat the process until all the mussels are open.

There is little left to do but serve the mussels with a wonderful, crisp Muscadet.

LEMONY TOFU SKEWERS

LES BROCHETTES DE TOFU CITRONNÉ

Serves 4

This is a bright and lively preparation for the vegetarians and vegans in your life, or for anyone who wants a meatless meal. It goes together quickly and tastes like a bit of sunshine on the plate. Here I call for spring onions, which are mature versions of a scallion that have been left in the ground long enough to form a bulb. Hot and sweet and fabulous, they are available for about two months a year, from late March to late May. If you can't find them, use small dry white onions. I recommend serving this with Lemon and Ginger Rice (page 263) and a lovely bottle of Sancerre blanc.

SPECIAL EQUIPMENT: *Zester, 4 long skewers, long tongs, gloves, pastry brush, plancha (optional, but easy)*

PREPARATION AND GRILLING TIME: *20 minutes, not including 2 hours marinating time*

DIFFICULTY LEVEL: *Moderate*

13 ounces (400 g) firm tofu, cut into 8 blocks (about 1-inch, 5-cm thick; 2¼-inches, 2.5-cm long; and 2½-inches, 3.25-cm wide)

¼ cup (60 ml) olive oil

Zest from 2 lemons

1 large clove garlic

Fine sea salt and freshly ground black pepper

8 spring onions, roots trimmed, stems trimmed down to about 2 inches (5 cm), cut in half

GENEROUSLY BRUSH THE TOFU PIECES ALL over with 1 tablespoon of the olive oil.

Mince the lemon zest with the garlic, and press half of this mixture all over the pieces of tofu. Season the tofu with salt and pepper on all sides and let sit, covered, for at least 2 hours at room temperature, or in the refrigerator overnight. Let it come to room temperature before cooking.

Mix the remaining lemon zest mixture with the remaining oil in a small bowl.

Build a medium-size fire in the barbecue.

Thread the tofu pieces and the vegetables on the four skewers, alternating so there are two pieces of tofu per skewer and so the tofu pieces are separated by a vegetable or two. Brush the skewers evenly, but not so they are dripping, on all sides with the lemon zest and oil mixture, then season the skewers lightly with salt and pepper. There should be some lemon zest and oil mixture left over.

When the coals are red and dusted with ash, spread them in a tight, single layer, leaving a perimeter of grill with no coals under it; they need to emit concentrated heat. Set the grill over the coals and set a plancha (if using) on the grill to heat.

1 small (125 g) red bell pepper, seeded, pith removed, cut into 1½-inch (3.75-cm) squares

8 fat asparagus stalks, rinsed, ends trimmed, stalks peeled halfway up toward the head, cut on the bias into 2-inch (6.25-cm) lengths

1 tablespoon freshly squeezed lemon juice

1 batch Lemon and Ginger Rice (page 263)

ASTUCES: Tofu prepared and served this way comes into its own as a center-of-the-plate offering. It's important to let it macerate and absorb the flavors of the lemon and garlic, which combine perfectly with the quick, hot cooking and the subtle smoke from the fire. Using a plancha for the tofu makes the whole recipe come together easily, but if you don't have one, you can cook these directly on the grill.

When the plancha is hot, set the skewers atop it and cook, covered, for 3 to 4 minutes. Turn the skewers and cook them for an additional 3 minutes, and continue turning the skewers regularly until they have cooked a total of 12 minutes and the tofu and vegetables are golden. If you don't have a plancha, divide the coals in half, placing each half to the side of the barbecue, and set the grill over it to heat up. When the grill is hot, place the skewers in the middle of the grill to cook. The timing will be the same. If the tofu and vegetables aren't golden at the end of the cooking time, place them directly over the coals for a minute or two on each side.

While the brochettes are cooking, stir the lemon juice into the remaining lemon zest and oil mixture.

To serve, place the rice on a platter, lay the brochettes on top, and drizzle them with the lemon zest and oil mixture, or serve on individual plates.

GINGER TOFU STEAKS WITH MELTED SPINACH

STEAK DE TOFU ET ÉPINARDS FONDUS

Serves 4

My daughter, Fiona, has joined an increasing number of French eaters and become a vegan. This means I have lots of fun trying out vegan recipes on the grill. I like to keep them simple, fresh, and fanciful, yet full of everything she needs. This dish fits the bill—it's delicious, balanced, and colorful. Its Asian overtones reflect the Asian influences in French cuisine so present because of the multitude of culinary exchanges among chefs from Japan and France.

I buy firm organic tofu at our local organic cooperative, and then slice it into steaks. If I'm preparing a weeknight meal, I marinate it for about 2 hours. If I've got more time, I might marinate it overnight. Either way, it's filled with texture and flavor.

The spinach here is a simple miracle. By cooking it this way you preserve everything: flavor, color, and texture, yet you have something that quite nearly melts in your mouth.

SPECIAL EQUIPMENT: *Grill pan, long tongs, grilling gloves, long metal skewers, large saucepan*

PREPARATION AND GRILLING TIME: *2 hours minimum to marinate; about 15 minutes to grill*

DIFFICULTY LEVEL: *Simple*

WHISK TOGETHER ALL THE INGREDIENTS for the marinade in a small bowl until combined. Place the tofu in a single layer in a nonreactive dish, pour the marinade over it, turn the tofu, and let it marinate for at least 2 hours, turning it occasionally, or overnight. Remove it from the refrigerator at least 1 hour before you plan to grill it.

About 25 minutes before you plan to cook the tofu, build a fire in the barbecue, or light up the gas grill with all three burners. When the coals are red and dusted with ash, spread them in a tight, single layer, leaving a perimeter of grill with no coals under it; they need to emit concentrated heat. Set the grill over the coals and, if using a grill pan, set the pan on the grill.

Thread each tofu steak lengthwise on a long metal skewer; you can put two pieces of tofu on each skewer, with about ¼ inch between them. Place the steaks on the grill pan and grill until

2 teaspoons Dijon mustard

2 tablespoons freshly squeezed orange juice

1 tablespoon freshly squeezed lemon juice

⅓ cup (75 ml) tamari

2 tablespoons sesame oil

Freshly ground black pepper

2 cloves garlic, minced

2-inch (5-cm) length fresh ginger, skinned, minced (or finely grated)

FOR THE TOFU:

12 ounces (430 g) firm tofu, cut into 4 (¾-by-4½-inch; 2-by-11.25-cm) pieces

1 batch Melted Spinach (page 206)

FOR THE GARNISH:

2 generous teaspoons freshly squeezed lemon juice

Chive tips or other herb

they turn golden, which, depending on the heat of the fire, will take 3 to 4 minutes. Turn and continue to cook until the tofu is golden, 2 to 3 minutes. Transfer the tofu to a platter.

Place the remaining marinade in a small, heavy saucepan over medium heat and reduce it by one-third.

While the marinade is reducing, transfer the spinach to a cutting board and coarsely chop it. Return it to the saucepan to keep warm.

To serve, evenly divide the spinach among four warmed plates. Drizzle with equal amounts of lemon juice, and season with salt if you like. Place a tofu steak atop each one. Drizzle with the reduced marinade and garnish with a chive tip. Enjoy!

ASTUCES: Baby spinach will cook much more quickly than the larger leaves, so do take this into account. Add the lemon juice to the spinach right before you serve it, as it turns the spinach an unappetizing color if you add it sooner than that.

CHAPTER 4

LAMB, BEEF, VEAL

"One becomes a cook; one is born a grill chef."

—JEAN ANTHELME BRILLAT-SAVARIN,
JUDGE, POLITICIAN, WRITER ON GASTRONOMY

The French are experts at grilling meat, from a shoulder of lamb to fat pork chops. The French grill chef has an inherent understanding of how to get the best from meat (there is that Gallic DNA again), so that it's perfectly seared on the outside and perfectly juicy on the inside. They know to let meat come to room temperature, to give it enough time on the grill so that it is gentled into perfection, and to serve it after it has sat just long enough for it to relax. If I had to choose my favorite meat from the French grill I'd say lamb, though beef and veal are jewels from the grill, too. Enjoy the dishes from the recipes here!

GRILLED BEEF CHOP

CÔTE DE BOEUF SUR LE BARBECUE

Serves 6 to 8

Côte de boeuf is an iconic French summer offering from the grill. When someone plans a summer get-together to impress, côte de boeuf is on the menu; when someone invites the in-laws, the same. It's understandable—côte de boeuf is not only succulent but impressive, a huge, bone-in hunk of meat that is cooked just so that it is well-browned on the outside and perfectly red and juicy inside. There is no seasoning except a shower of coarse salt and pepper once off the grill. I love a hearty Crozes-Hermitage with this. Yum.

SPECIAL EQUIPMENT: *Long, sturdy tongs, grapevine or other "sweet wood" sticks (like apple or hickory)*

PREPARATION AND GRILLING TIME: *15 minutes*

DIFFICULTY LEVEL: *Simple*

---

1 côte de boeuf (T-bone), about 3 pounds (1.5 kg), at room temperature

Coarse sea salt

Freshly ground black pepper

Herb leaves, for garnish

ASTUCES: In the United States, the closest cut we have to the French côte de boeuf is a T-bone steak. Get one that is thick cut so that you can cook it as described here. Regarding smoke—you want the côte de boeuf smoky but not overly smoky. To achieve what I think is a perfect result, I throw grapevine cuttings on the fire about 3 or 4 minutes before I put the côte de boeuf on the grill. The cuttings flare up, then die down, filling the covered grill with smoke to bathe the côte de boeuf.

BUILD A GOOD-SIZE FIRE IN THE BARBECUE. When the coals are red and dusted with ash, spread them in a tight, single layer, leaving a perimeter of grill with no coals under it; they need to emit concentrated heat. Set the grill over the coals.

When the grill is very hot, and before putting on the côte de boeuf, add a large handful of grapevine or other "sweet wood" (like apple or hickory) sticks, if desired, on the coals, putting them off to one side where they will flare.

Put the côte de boeuf on the grill away from the flames; cover the grill and cook until the côte de boeuf is browned on the grill side, 5 minutes. Turn the meat and cook for 5 minutes, uncovered; turn it again and cook for 5 minutes, uncovered, and turn it again. Cook uncovered for 3 minutes, then for the last 2 minutes cooking time, cover the barbecue. At this point, the côte de boeuf is perfectly rosy and rare, the way it should be, and nice and almost crisp on the outside, with a gorgeous smoky flavor. If you like your meat cooked more, then leave it on the grill longer, but not more than 5 extra minutes.

Transfer the côte de boeuf to a cutting board. Shower it with salt and pepper, turn it, repeat, then let it sit for about 15 minutes before you cut it into slices that are just less than ¼-inch (0.6-cm) thick. Arrange the slices on a platter, garnish with the herb leaves, and serve with salt and pepper alongside.

STEAK WITH SMOKY OLIVES

STEAK AUX OLIVES FUMÉ

Serves 4 generously

This dish has turned me into an enthusiastic steak eater, which I'd never been. Oh, I have enjoyed a perfectly grilled steak with a big mound of crisp, golden frites from my favorite bistro from time to time, but otherwise beef was never on my list of favorite foods. This recipe, though, makes my mouth water just thinking about it. Perhaps it's the sirloin I get from a local butcher who specializes in aged beef from the Norman cow. Perhaps it's the smoky olives that accompany it. Whatever it is, I highly recommend you make this, because you will love it. And though it is simple to make, it works for a formal occasion. So, you can serve it and act as though you've labored over a hot stove all day!

SPECIAL EQUIPMENT: *Cherry or olive pitter, wooden cutting board, long tongs, gloves, grill pan, bowl, 2 cups wood chips or two handfuls grapevine cuttings or other fruit wood cuttings*

PREPARATION AND GRILLING TIME: *25 to 30 minutes (pitting olives takes time)*

DIFFICULTY LEVEL: *Simple*

FOR THE STEAK:

1 pound (500 g) top-quality sirloin (about 2-inches thick, 7- to 8-inches long; 5-cm thick, 17.5-to 20-cm long)

½ teaspoon olive oil

Fine sea salt

LIGHT A MEDIUM-SIZE FIRE IN THE

barbecue. When the coals are red and dusted with ash, spread them in a tight, single layer, leaving a perimeter of grill with no coals under it; they need to emit concentrated heat. Set the grill over the coals. Set a grill pan on the grill.

Rub the steak all over with the ½ teaspoon olive oil, massaging it into the meat.

Right before placing the steak on the grill, place the wood chips or the grapevine cuttings on the coals. Let them flame up, then when they've died down and are smoking, place the steak on the grill over the coals, season with salt, cover, and cook until the steak is golden, about 3 minutes. Turn the steak, season it with salt, cover, and cook until it is golden, about 3 minutes. If you like your steak rare, it is cooked; if you prefer it medium, keep the grill covered for another 3 to 4 minutes.

While the steak is grilling, coarsely chop the olives and the parsley together—they don't need to be minced, but the mixture shouldn't be too coarse either. Place it in a bowl and pour the ¼ cup olive oil over it. Season with salt and pepper and reserve.

1 cup Smoky Olives (page 36)

½ cup (5 g) flat-leaf parsley leaves

¼ cup (60 ml) top-quality olive oil

Fine sea salt and freshly ground black pepper

Fleur de sel, for garnish (optional)

ASTUCES: Make sure the steak is at room temperature before you put it on the grill. Note that I call for olives with pits, then ask you to pit them. I find that pre-pitted olives are of low quality, so it's worth the extra effort. Use a cherry or an olive pitter to remove the pits. Also, make sure your olive oil here is of the very best quality—I use a special AOP oil from Aix-en-Provence. It isn't the same oil I use for cooking. The distinction is subtle. Quality cooking oil is delicious, but the oil here is reserved for using as a condiment so that all of its richness in flavor can be appreciated. Note that the amount of meat in this recipe allows for 4 ounces (120 g) of beef per person. If you want to serve a more ample amount, simply adjust the recipe accordingly. You may want to increase the amount of olives.

Transfer the steak to a cutting board, season it with salt and several grinds of black pepper. Let it rest for at least 5 minutes before cutting into it.

To serve, slice the steak on an angle into pieces that are about ¼-inch (0.6-cm) thick. Arrange them in the center of four dinner plates. Spoon over the parsley and olive mixture, using it all, drizzling the steak with any olive oil that remains in the bowl. Garnish with fleur de sel and serve.

GOLDEN VEAL CHOP WITH VANILLA LIME BUTTER

CÔTES DE VEAU DORÉ AU BEURRE DE LA VANILLE ET CITRON VERT

Serves 6

Once you've made this dish, you'll become a loyal convert to using vanilla in a savory dish! And don't be prejudiced against veal, the meat from a young cow. Avoid industrially produced veal in favor of that which is humanely raised and you'll find it a toothsome, flavorful meat. It's a French favorite from the farm, where calves are allowed to gambol in the pasture so their meat is red and has some texture. Vanilla is a very French flavoring, too—coming from the former French colony of Madagascar. Though France is no longer officially involved in the island's government, it is its biggest customer. And one of the things that Madagascar sends to France is plump, moist, and flavorful vanilla beans. So the combination of vanilla and veal seems almost inevitable. As for the lime, it's magic here! Serve this with a not-too-chilled white Burgundy or a dry Muscat from Barroubio.

SPECIAL EQUIPMENT: *Zester, long tongs, gloves*

PREPARATION AND GRILLING TIME: *20 minutes*

DIFFICULTY LEVEL: *Simple*

---

3 tablespoons unsalted butter, softened

Seeds from 1 vanilla bean

Zest from 1 lime, minced

Six veal chops (6 to 8 ounces; 180 to 250 g each), at room temperature

2 teaspoons olive oil

Fine sea salt and freshly ground black pepper

1 lime, cut in wedges

BUILD A GOOD-SIZE FIRE IN THE BARBECUE.
When the coals are red and dusted with ash, divide them in the barbecue, putting half the coals on either side. Place a drip pan between them. Set the grill over the coals.

Place the butter in a small bowl and mix the vanilla seeds and lime zest into it. Divide the butter into six even pieces, and place them in the refrigerator.

Rub the veal chops all over with the oil.

When the grill is hot, place the veal chops on it in the center, close the grill, and cook until the chops are golden, about 4 minutes. Turn the chops, strew them with salt and pepper, cover, and cook until they are golden on the other side, an additional 4 minutes. If the chops aren't golden enough for your liking, place them directly over the coals for a minute or so to get the golden allure. If you like veal rare, it is cooked. If you prefer your veal more cooked, add an additional minute or two to the cooking time.

ASTUCES: You can make the composed butter with the vanilla and lime the night before you plan to serve this dish. You may want to keep the lime and vanilla butter on hand (it freezes very well) so that you can use it for this dish or any grilled fish or poultry. Freeze the composed butter in individual portions so that you can use it as you need it! You may want to get fancy and pipe the butter into fanciful shapes before chilling!

Transfer each chop to a dinner plate. Season generously with salt and pepper. Place a nugget of butter on top of each chop and lime wedges on the side. Serve immediately.

HANGER STEAK WITH HORSERADISH SAUCE

ONGLET À LA SAUCE AU RAIFORT

Serves 4 to 6

Onglet, or hanger steak, is a very special cut of beef. It is highly regarded in France because of its flavor and its tender, slightly elastic texture. It is considered an organ meat because it hangs from the diaphragm of the cow, and because it needs to be treated carefully and cooked quickly. It is perfect on the grill because it emerges with the exterior deep golden and almost crisp, and the interior juicy and red. The horseradish is a spicy counterpoint. I recommend a rich yet smooth Bordeaux Supérieur, such as a Château Panchille.

SPECIAL EQUIPMENT: *Kitchen twine, tongs, cutting board*

PREPARATION AND GRILLING TIME:
25–30 minutes if preparing the Turkish Kebab Sauce and depending on how rare you like your steak; 10 minutes maximum if the Turkish Kebab Sauce is already prepared

DIFFICULTY LEVEL: *Moderate*

---

1 generous pound (525 g) hanger steak, at room temperature

⅔ cup Turkish Kebab Sauce (page 275)

3 generous tablespoons (55 ml) horse-radish

Fine sea salt and freshly ground black pepper

⅔ cup (6 generous g) flat-leaf parsley leaves, minced

1 tablespoon olive oil

Flat-leaf parsley leaves, for garnish

Freshly ground black pepper, for garnish

Fleur de sel, for garnish

CUT THE HANGER STEAK IN HALF CROSSWISE.
Cut along the length of each piece but not all the way through, and open each piece like a book.

In a medium bowl, whisk together the kebab sauce and the horseradish. Taste for seasoning and adjust with salt and pepper if necessary.

Spread 1 generous tablespoon of the sauce on one side of the partially cut surfaces of the hanger steak. Sprinkle each steak with the minced parsley. "Close" the steak and tie the pieces together in four or five places. Rub the steaks all over with the olive oil, and season them with salt and pepper.

Heat all three burners of the gas grill, or build a medium-size fire in the barbecue. When the coals are red and dusted with ash, spread them in a tight, single layer, leaving a perimeter of grill with no coals under it; they need to emit concentrated heat. Set the grill over the coals.

When the grill is very hot, set the steaks on it right over the coals. Close the grill and cook until the steak is brown on one side, about 3 minutes. Turn it to the other side and, keeping the grill open, grill it until the steaks are golden on the other side, another 2 to 3 minutes. At this point, the steaks are quite rare and just the way most people in France eat it. If you prefer your

ASTUCES: Hanger steak is best served rare because it stays tender that way. But, as always, this depends on your taste. Also, the weight called for is with the hanger steak trimmed of any nerve tissue (most likely this is the way you will purchase it). I cut the hanger steak in half crosswise, because I find two pieces much easier to handle than one long, narrow steak. After this, each piece of hanger steak is cut along its length, but not all the way through, per the instructions. Finally, don't let the instructions for tying the hanger steak intimidate you—just cut pieces of string, slip them under the steak, and tie a bow or a quick little knot. Simple.

steak more cooked—say, medium—then turn it again and cook it for 2 minutes, then turn it again and cook for 2 additional minutes, for a total of 9 minutes. Remove from the grill and let the steaks sit for about 10 minutes.

Transfer the steaks from the grill to a cutting board and let them rest for 10 to 20 minutes. They will stay hot, don't worry.

Remove the strings from the steaks and cut the steaks into thick slices. Place about 2 tablespoons of the horseradish sauce in the center of four to six warmed dinner plates (four servings are generous; six are slight), and spread it into a small, thick round. Lay the slices atop the sauce and garnish with parsley sprigs. Grind a little mound of black pepper alongside each serving, and then place a little mound of fleur de sel alongside each serving. Serve immediately.

CAMEMBERT BURGER: THE BEST CHEESEBURGER YOU'VE EVER HAD

HAMBURGER AU CAMEMBERT—
LE MEILLEUR CHEESEBURGER QUE VOUS N'AYEZ JAMAIS DÉGUSTÉ

Serves 8

Every time I see the word *hamburger* I can't help but think of Steve Martin in *The Pink Panther*. During his English lesson he twists his tongue and his face around the word *hamburger* in such delicious ways that it is impossible for me to keep a straight face, even years later. All I can say is a good laugh is a wonderful thing, and so is this burger. It's Norman, no doubt about it, with its slices of perfectly melted Camembert, which gives the burger a nutty, rich dimension, and the traditional garnish of apples and onions. This is fantastic with hard apple cider or a microbrew.

SPECIAL EQUIPMENT: *Metal spatula, long tongs, plancha or cast-iron skillet*

PREPARATION AND GRILLING TIME: *About 35 minutes if you've already made the buns, 3 hours 10 minutes if you haven't*

DIFFICULTY LEVEL: *Simple*

FOR THE BURGERS:

2 pounds (1 kg) medium-fat ground beef

Fine sea salt and freshly ground black pepper

½ teaspoon ground allspice

½ cup firmly packed, flat-leaf parsley leaves, minced

1 Camembert (about 8 ounces; 250 g), skin left on, cut into ¼-inch (0.62-cm) strips, which you cut in half crosswise

PLACE THE GROUND MEAT IN A MEDIUM bowl and add the seasonings and parsley.

Mix all the ingredients together, preferably with your hands, so they are thoroughly combined. Take a small piece of the meat and cook and taste it so that you can adjust the seasoning to your liking. Form the meat into eight individual burgers, flattening them.

Build a medium-size fire in the grill. When the coals are red and dusted with ash, divide them in the barbecue, putting half the coals on either side. Set the grill over the coals. If you've got one, light up the gas grill, too, using all three burners.

First, prepare the onions and the apples. You can do this either on a plancha or in a cast-iron skillet right on the gas grill or the barbecue over a very hot fire. Melt the butter and the oil together and add the onions. Stir, season lightly with salt, cover

continued

2 tablespoons unsalted butter, more if needed

1 tablespoon olive oil, more if needed

12 ounces (360 g) onions, trimmed and thinly sliced

Fine sea salt

4 medium (about 6 ounces; 180 g) flavorful apples, such as Pink Lady or Cox's Orange Pippin, cored, peeled, and cut into ⅓-inch (0.62-cm) sections

FOR THE FINISHED SANDWICH:

8 Hamburger Buns (page 258)

About ¼ cup (60 ml) Mayonnaise (page 264, optional but delicious)

ASTUCES: Make sure that the ground beef you get is medium-fatty, not too lean. Also note that I use both a charcoal and a gas grill for this recipe because I'm lucky enough to have both options. The onions and the apples cook better over gas because the heat is a bit more even. But I love the burgers over the coals, because they pick up a slight smoke flavor. You may, though, decide to make life simple by cooking everything over the coals or over gas. Finally, you are likely to have Camembert left over. Don't despair—it's amazing at room temperature with bread or atop a salad.

the grill, and cook until the onions soften and turn golden, 5 to 8 minutes, checking them often and stirring to be sure they don't burn. If they turn dark golden at the edges, don't be concerned; this enhances their flavor. Remove the onions from the pan and add the apples, stirring into the remaining oil in the pan. (If there isn't enough, add 2 teaspoons oil and a scant tablespoon of butter.) Cook the apples until they are golden, 3 minutes, stir, and continue to cook until they are tender and golden through, an additional 5 minutes. Remove from the pan. Taste both the onions and the apples for seasoning, and reserve.

When the grill is hot, place the burgers right over the coals and cook until they are golden and beginning to cook through, about 4 minutes. Turn, cook each burger until it is golden, about 2 minutes, then top each burger with two slices (or more, to your taste) of Camembert, cover the grill, and cook until the burgers are the doneness you like and the cheese is softened but not entirely melted, an additional 2 minutes for medium-rare. If you like your burger closer to medium, leave it on the grill for an additional 2 to 3 minutes (not too much longer or the meat will be dry).

Transfer the burgers from the grill to a plate or platter and let them rest. Place the buns, cut side down, right over the coals until they are toasted, about 2 minutes. Remove them from the grill.

To assemble the burgers, slather the cut sides of the buns with mayonnaise (if desired). Divide the apples among the bottom half of the buns. Top with the burgers, cheese side up. Garnish with the onions, and top with the other half of the bun. Press down firmly on the burger, which helps to keep the whole thing together. Serve immediately.

MEDITERRANEAN BURGERS

BURGERS À LA MÉDITERRANÉE

Serves 6

When I think of a burger, my mind instantly goes to lamb, because I grew up in a lamb-loving household, and then moved to a lamb-loving country. The French use lamb in so many different dishes, often influenced by the Mediterranean culture to the south and the east, where the flavors evoke the spice markets, or souks, of northern Africa or the Middle East.

This is a great dish to prepare for a crowd. It's simple and unexpected, the meat is flavorful, the two sauces keep it all moist, and the cucumber adds a crisp touch. The burgers are best rare, but of course you can grill them to your taste—just know that as with any ground meat dish, the more you cook it, the drier it will become.

As for the spices, many Americans are surprised at how delicately spiced much Mediterranean food is. If your palate needs more, increase the amount of spices you use here. Try a Minervois here, from Domaine de Barroubio.

SPECIAL EQUIPMENT: *Long tongs, spatula, lemon zester*

PREPARATION AND GRILLING TIME: *20 to 25 minutes if you've made the Red Pepper Sauce, the Turkish Kebab Sauce, and the Hamburger Buns; 3 hours 55 minutes if you haven't yet*

DIFFICULTY LEVEL: *Simple*

Zest from 1½ lemons (if you love lemon, use all the zest from the second lemon)

2 cloves garlic

1 cup (10 g) gently packed, flat-leaf parsley leaves

½ cup (5 g) mint leaves

1½ pounds (750 g) ground lamb, a mix of lean and medium-fat

MINCE TOGETHER THE LEMON ZEST, GARLIC, parsley, and mint. Place these in a medium bowl with the ground lamb, cinnamon, ½ teaspoon salt, and several grinds of pepper, and mix everything together using your hands until the ingredients are thoroughly combined. Take a thimble full of the meat and cook it in a small skillet over medium-high heat, then let it cool for a moment before you taste it. You can then adjust the seasoning.

Form six flattish burgers, and if the meat isn't at room temperature, let it sit until it is.

Build a medium-size fire in the barbecue, or light up all three burners on the gas grill. When the coals are red and dusted with ash, spread them out in a tight, single layer, leaving a perimeter of grill with no coals under it; they need to emit concentrated heat. Set the grill over the coals.

When the grill is hot, place the burgers on it. Grill them until they are golden, 4 to 5 minutes, then flip and grill them until they are the doneness you prefer—another 3 to 4 minutes

½ to 1 teaspoon ground cinnamon

½ teaspoon fine sea salt, and more to taste

Freshly ground black pepper

6 Hamburger Buns (page 258), cut in half horizontally

6 tablespoons Red Pepper Sauce (page 255), more if needed

1 medium cucumber, peeled, cut in half crosswise, then cut into thin slices lengthwise (at least 2 slices per burger)

Freshly squeezed lemon juice (optional, but recommended)

Turkish Kebab Sauce (page 275)

ASTUCES: A lemon zester is best to use here rather than a rasp, as you want bits of lemon zest that explode with flavor when you bite into them.

and they will be medium-rare; 5 to 6 minutes and they will be well-done. Two minutes before the burgers are cooked, place the buns, cut side down, on the grill to toast.

Transfer the burgers to a plate and let them sit while you prepare the buns.

Slather each cut side of each bun with 1 tablespoon (or more) of the red pepper sauce. Lay two to three strips of cucumber on the bottom half of each bun. Season with salt and pepper, top with a burger, season with salt and pepper and a squeeze of lemon juice if desired, drizzle with kebab sauce, top with the other half of the bun, and *voila!* Dinner is prepared.

CURRY BEEF AND ZUCCHINI BROCHETTES

BROCHETTES DE BOEUF ET COURGETTES AU CURRY

Serves 6

The other day, I went next door to my butcher, Mr. Coutard, and asked him for beef to make brochettes. He turned to his small cooler and pulled out two different pieces, *le filet et le rumsteak* (the tenderloin and the rump steak). "Either will do, but this is best for you," he said, choosing the tenderloin. He then asked me if I wanted him to cut them into pieces for the skewer. Of course I wanted him to do this—I love to watch him work, and I wanted to see what size pieces he thought were right. They were surprisingly small. I also knew he'd tell me exactly how long to cook the brochettes and over what size fire. He did. The results are here for you in this easy dish that is as perfect for a weeknight supper as it is for a weekend party. You must serve this with Spiced Melon Salad (page 68) and a glorious Saint-Émilion.

SPECIAL EQUIPMENT: *Long metal skewers, gloves, tongs, platter for serving*

PREPARATION AND GRILLING TIME: *Up to 2 hours to marinate; 12 minutes to grill*

DIFFICULTY LEVEL: *Simple*

---

1 pound (500 g) beef tenderloin, cut in small (0.75-by-1.5-by-1-inch; 2-by-3.25-by-2.5-cm) cubes

1 medium yellow or green zucchini (4 ounces; 120 g), trimmed, cut in half lengthwise, then cut into ½-inch (1.25-cm) half-moons

1 bunch small spring onions (about 1 pound; 500 g—about 1½ ounces; 45 g each), stems and root ends trimmed

7 tablespoons (100 ml) olive oil

5 to 6 scant teaspoons Curry Powder (page 257) or Madras

Fine sea salt and freshly ground black pepper

PLACE THE BEEF, ZUCCHINI, AND ONIONS IN a large, nonreactive bowl. In a small bowl, mix together 5 tablespoons of the oil and the curry powder, and pour it over the meat and vegetables. Toss the meat and vegetables with the oil mixture so they are thoroughly combined, and let sit at room temperature for at least 30 minutes and up to 2 hours, covered. You may also marinate the ingredients in the refrigerator, covered, overnight.

Build a medium-size fire in the grill. When the coals are red and dusted with ash, spread them in a tight, single layer; they need to emit concentrated heat.

Thread the beef and the zucchini onto the same skewers, alternating several pieces of zucchini with the beef, beginning and ending with beef. Thread all of the onions onto one or two skewers, as they will cook longer than the other ingredients.

continued

ASTUCES: Note that the onions are cooked separately, because they take longer than the zucchini and the beef. You might say "Why include them, then?" The answer is because they go so well with the beef and zucchini. Note, too, that yellow zucchini makes this recipe sit up and sing. Milder than their green cousins but equally delicious, they add a festive note to the brochettes. I like to remove the ingredients from the skewers before serving so there isn't fumbling with skewers at the table. If you want this dish to have a more intense curry flavor, simply use the larger amount of curry powder, or add it to your liking.

Place the grill over the coals. When it is hot, add the onion skewers and cook until the onions are golden on one side, about 2 minutes. Turn and cook until the onions are golden on the other side, about 2 minutes. Season with salt and pepper, cover the grill, and cook until the onions are tender, 8 to 10 minutes.

About 5 minutes into grilling the onions, add the beef and zucchini skewers to the grill. Brush them with the reserved oil and season them with salt and pepper. Cover and cook until the meat and vegetables are golden, about 3 minutes, then turn the brochettes and repeat. The meat will be quite rare at this point, which is ideal. If you like your meat cooked more, leave it on the grill another 2 to 3 minutes.

Remove the brochettes from the grill and let them set for a minute or two, then either serve them, or remove the ingredients from the skewers, transferring them to a serving platter, and serve immediately.

LEMONY, GARLICKY, ROSEMARY LAMB SHOULDER OVER THE COALS

ÉPAULE D'AGNEAU AU CITRON, AIL ET ROMARIN SUR LES BRAISES

Serves 6 to 8

The shoulder is my favorite cut of lamb. It's got lots of texture yet is tender and delicate. What's more, it has enough personality to stand up well to seasonings like those used here. The foreshank attached to the shoulder is a *lagniappe*, a little extra treasure that tastes so good and is so very buttery. I always make sure each guest gets a piece, it's so delicious. This is a simple recipe, but it will wow your family and guests. I recommend serving it with a Domaine de Barroubio or richly flavored Bordeaux from Château Penin.

~~~~~~~~~~~~~~~~~~~~~~~~

SPECIAL EQUIPMENT: *Drip pan, long tongs, fork, gloves, zester*

PREPARATION AND GRILLING TIME: *45 to 50 minutes grilling time, 20 minutes resting time*

DIFFICULTY LEVEL: *Moderate*

⅓ cup (3 g) fresh rosemary

2 cloves garlic

Zest from 1 lemon

1 lamb shoulder (3 to 3½ pounds; 1.5 to 1.75 kg), boned

1 tablespoon olive oil

About 2 teaspoons coarse sea salt

About 1 teaspoon coarsely ground green, white, and black peppercorns

MINCE TOGETHER THE ROSEMARY, GARLIC, and lemon zest and transfer to a small bowl.

Make six ½-inch (1.25-cm) deep slits in the lamb shoulder. Insert as much of the rosemary mixture as you can in each slit. Mix the remaining mixture with the olive oil and rub it over the lamb shoulder. Let the lamb sit at room temperature for 2 hours or up to overnight. If leaving the lamb overnight, wrap and refrigerate it, and remove it from the refrigerator at least 2 hours before grilling so it is at room temperature.

About 25 minutes before you plan to cook the lamb shoulder, build a good-size fire. When the coals are red and dusted with ash, divide them in the barbecue, putting half the coals on either side. Set a drip pan in the middle of the coals, then set the grill over the coals.

When the grill is hot, place the lamb shoulder in the center, over the drip pan, strew salt and a bit of freshly ground pepper over the shoulder, and close the grill, making sure the air holes are open in the top and the body of the barbecue. Grill for

continued

ASTUCES: I like to use a traditional zester here to get pieces of zest that burst with lemony flavor. Note that the cooking times I give result in lamb that is medium, which is the way I think lamb shoulder is best. If you want it rare, just cut back on the cooking time while the shoulder is in the center of the grill, before you brown it over the coals.

12 minutes, until the shoulder is pale golden on the grill side. Turn the shoulder, season with salt and pepper, and grill for another 12 minutes. Transfer the shoulder to the part of the grill that is over the coals, cover, and grill until the shoulder is deep golden, about 10 minutes. Turn and repeat. The interior temperature of the lamb should now be about 150°F (65.5°C), which means it is medium and, to my way of thinking, perfectly cooked; if you like it more rare, brown it on just one side; if you like it more well done, adjust the initial cooking time in the center of the grill accordingly.

Transfer the lamb from the grill to a cutting board that will catch the juices, and let it sit for at least 10 minutes and up to 20 minutes before slicing the lamb. Drain the juices into a small pitcher and serve it alongside.

LAMB CHOPS WITH GARLIC AND PARSLEY SAUCE

CÔTES D'AGNEAU AU PERSILLADE

Serves 6

This is the meal you make when you get home late from work. It's easy to light up the gas grill or build a fire in the barbecue, make the persillade, and fling those chops on the grill! I like to serve this with a green salad, nothing more, nothing less except for bread, which *always* has pride of place on the French table. Serve this with a Côtes du Rhône such as an AOP Ventoux from Domaine Aymard.

SPECIAL EQUIPMENT: *Long tongs*

PREPARATION AND GRILLING TIME: *15 minutes*

DIFFICULTY LEVEL: *Simple*

12 small (about 3-ounce; 90-g) or 6 large (about 5-ounce; 150-g) lamb chops, at room temperature

Fine sea salt

Freshly ground black pepper

⅓ cup Garlic and Parsley Sauce (page 273)

ASTUCES: Once you've minced together the parsley and garlic, put it in a bowl and pour over the oil immediately. The oil traps the flavor that would otherwise dissipate into the air.

BUILD A MEDIUM-SIZE FIRE IN THE BARBECUE, or light the gas grill using all three burners. When the coals are red and dusted with ash, spread them in a tight, single layer, leaving a perimeter of grill with no coals under it; they need to emit concentrated heat. Set the grill over the coals.

When the grill is hot, sprinkle the chops evenly with salt and place them on the grill. Cover and cook until they are dark golden, about 4 minutes. Flip the chops, season them with salt and pepper, and spread equal amounts of garlic and parsley sauce on each chop, pressing it firmly into the chop. Cook for an additional 4 minutes. This will result in chops that are medium-rare; if you prefer your chops cooked longer, then leave them on the grill for an additional 1 to 2 minutes. Right before the chops are cooked, flip them quickly onto the garlic and parsley sauce side, just so the sauce gets very hot, 30 seconds to 1 minute.

Transfer the chops to a platter, season them lightly with salt and pepper, and serve immediately.

GRILLED STEAK WITH FRITES

STEAK FRITES

Serves 4

This quintessential meal makes the world go 'round, particularly if you're French. It's the equivalent of the American hamburger, pizza, or subway sandwich. What's fantastic is that you can get an amazing steak frites at just about any brasserie or café in the country, though none are quite as good as this one! Here, the steak is grilled just enough to make it golden on the outside, heated through, but left very rare, just the way we like it here in France! If you like your steak more well done, just grill it longer! You can add all manner of spices and flavors to the steak, but the most pure, and most French way, is to let a nugget of gorgeous butter melt over it once it's off the grill, then season it with coarsely ground pepper and coarse sea salt. *Miam!* Steak frites usually includes a green salad, which I've done here. Though steak frites is simple, it merits something special like a delicious red from Château Croix Beauséjour from Saint-Émilion.

SPECIAL EQUIPMENT: *Deep fat fryer, long tongs, long metal spatula, gloves*

PREPARATION AND GRILLING TIME: *For the steak, about 5 minutes; for all the elements, about 30 minutes*

DIFFULTY LEVEL: *Simple*

1 pound (500 g) flank steak, or the cut of your choice

2 teaspoons olive oil

Coarse sea salt

Coarsely ground black pepper

Classic Vinaigrette (page 252)

1 medium head salad greens (about 5 cups; 130 g), rinsed and spun dry

2 tablespoons unsalted butter, cut in three pieces

1 batch French Fries (page 188)

Mustard (optional)

Mayonnaise (page 264, optional)

RUB THE STEAK ALL OVER WITH THE OLIVE

oil and let it sit, at room temperature, for at least 1 hour.

Build a good-size fire in the barbecue. When the coals are red and dusted with ash, spread them in a tight, single layer, leaving a perimeter of grill with no coals under it; they need to emit concentrated heat. Set the grill over the coals.

When the grill is blistery hot, set the steak on it, season it with salt and pepper, and grill until the steak is golden and can easily be removed from the grill (which shows it is seared enough on the exterior), about 1½ to 2 minutes. Turn the steak—it should be nicely browned. Salt and pepper the steak and continue to grill it until it is done to your liking. For rare (the French way), cook it an additional 1½ to 2 minutes. If you would like it more cooked, simply leave it on the grill for a minute or two longer than that.

continued

ASTUCES: Instead of grilling individual steaks, grill the flank steak as a whole piece and cut it into serving pieces once off the grill. It stays moister that way. The tricky part here is timing. Get the frites fried the first time, build the fire, get the grill hot, then start putting the frites into the oil for their second frying. When they're all fried, grill the steaks.

Pour the vinaigrette into a large bowl, whisk, add the lettuce leaves, and toss well until the lettuce is coated with the vinaigrette.

Transfer the steak to a cutting board. Set the butter atop it and move it around atop the steak with a fork or a knife so it melts evenly into the meat. Give the steak a quick seasoning with more pepper and salt if desired, then cut it into serving-size pieces. Place a piece of steak on each of four warmed plates. Garnish with a generous amount of salad, and pass the frites separately, with mustard or mayonnaise, if desired.

SYRIAN SPICED LAMB CHOPS

CÔTES D'AGNEAU À LA SYRIENNE

Serves 4

The lamb here, spiced with flavors from the Middle East, is both exciting and haunting, conjuring up images of craggy landscapes, lilting music, flowing robes, and song and dance. I recommend a shoulder chop here because it's more tender and moist than a loin chop. You'll need to cook it a few minutes longer than a loin chop, but it's worth the wait! Try a lush and spicy Côtes du Rhône from La Roche Buissière with this dish, and serve grilled onions and grilled zucchini alongside.

SPECIAL EQUIPMENT: *Long tongs*

PREPARATION AND GRILLING TIME: *About 10 minutes if the spice is made; 20 minutes if not*

DIFFICULTY LEVEL: *Simple*

1 generous tablespoon Syrian Spice Mix (page 276)

8 small shoulder chops (8 ounces; 250 g), or 4 larger chops (12 ounces; 360 g) that are about ¾-inch (1.8-cm) thick

Fine sea salt

Fleur de sel (optional)

ASTUCES: Remember to let the lamb come to room temperature before you grill it, as the result will be more tender if you do. The French much prefer rare lamb; if you prefer it more cooked, just increase the cooking time.

RUB A LIGHT LAYER OF SYRIAN SPICE MIX over each lamb chop and let sit at room temperature for at least 30 minutes and up to 2 hours. You may also do this the night before and refrigerate the lamb. Remember to bring it out of the refrigerator at least 2 hours before you plan to grill it.

Light a good-size fire in a barbecue or light the gas grill, using all three burners. When the coals are red and dusted with ash, spread them in a tight, single layer, leaving a perimeter of grill with no coals under it; they need to emit concentrated heat. Set the grill over the coals.

Sprinkle the chops evenly with salt and place them on the grill right over the heat. Cover and cook until they are dark golden, about 4 minutes. Flip the chops and repeat. This will result in chops that are medium rare; if you prefer your chops cooked longer, then leave them on the grill for an additional 1 to 2 minutes.

Remove the chops from the grill and transfer them either to a warmed serving platter or warmed plates. Sprinkle them lightly with more of the Syrian spice mix, a bit of fleur de sel if desired, then serve immediately.

CHAPTER 5

PORK

DE LA BARBE À LA QUEUE (FROM BEARD TO TAIL)

"Everything is beautiful. We must speak of a pig as a flower."

—JULES RENARD, WRITER AND PLAYWRIGHT

Pork keeps France on its feet. It is by far the most popular meat in the French culinary lexicon, and the French eat the pig from head to tail, which engendered the term *de la barbe à la queue* or barbecue. They say nothing is wasted in the pig but its cry, and if you go into a butcher shop or charcuterie you'll see that is true. But more than that, pork that's raised on small farms here in France has unparalleled flavor, is abundant, and is so easy to prepare. I use it liberally in many forms, from sausages to bacon to fat chops to tender shoulders. Look for local, farm-raised pork, and I predict you will, too.

SAUERKRAUT WITH TONS OF PORK

CHOUCROUTE AVEC DES TONNES DE PORC

Serves 6

French *choucroute,* which is redolent of herbs and tender apples and onions, bears little resemblance to the mouth-puckering sauerkraut of my youth, even though both are thinly sliced, fermented cabbage. In France, choucroute hails from Alsace, yet it's a national treasure sold from market stands, at every butcher shop, and in most charcuteries throughout the land. Its crowning glory is the pork that adorns it, from thick and smoky slab bacon, to fat and thin sausages, to small ham hocks or pork chops. Traditionally, pork destined to serve with choucroute is braised and boiled, but here it is grilled. I've chosen three cuts that are perfect cooked over the coals. You'll love this, and you may want to plan a party to do it justice! Serve, as they do in Alsace, with chilled Riesling.

SPECIAL EQUIPMENT: *Long tongs, fireproof baking dish with cover (Le Creuset recommended), long spatula*

PREPARATION AND GRILLING TIME: *About 1½ hours, which includes the cooking time for choucroute*

DIFFICULTY LEVEL: *Simple*

FOR THE SAUERKRAUT:

2 pounds (1 kg) sauerkraut (salted, fermented cabbage)

1 tablespoon goose or duck fat, or unsalted butter

2 medium onions (5 ounces; 150 g each), thinly sliced

3 medium sweet apples such as Pink Lady, cored, peeled, and thinly sliced

1¾ cups (435 ml) Riesling or other fruity white wine

¾ cup (185 ml) water

Freshly ground pepper to taste

LIGHT THE GAS GRILL, LIGHTING ALL THREE burners. Thoroughly rinse the sauerkraut in cold water and let it drain.

Melt the fat with the onion in a large, flameproof saucepan over one of the burners on the gas grill, stirring as the fat melts. Cover the saucepan, cover the grill, and cook, stirring the onions often until they are tender, which will take about 8 minutes.

Add the sauerkraut and the apples to the onions and gently fold the ingredients together with a wooden spoon. Pour the wine and water over all, stir a little bit so that all the ingredients are mixed, add a few grinds of pepper, the cloves, juniper berries, bay leaves, and garlic, and push them down into the sauerkraut. Cover the pan and close the grill. Check the sauerkraut after about 10 minutes; the liquid will be boiling furiously. Turn off two of the burners, making sure the sauerkraut is simmering merrily and not directly over the burner that remains lit. Close the grill and cook the sauerkraut for about 1½ hours, checking it and stirring from time to time and adding a bit of water if

continued

2 whole cloves

6 juniper berries

2 fresh bay leaves

2 cloves garlic, peeled, cut in half

FOR THE GRILL:

3 thick-cut pork chops
(about 12 ounces; 360 g each)

6 fat pork sausages (about 5 ounces;
150 g each)

1 to 2 teaspoons olive oil

1 pound (500 g) slab bacon or salt
pork, rind removed, cut into 2½-inch
(6.25-cm) chunks

1 pound (500 g) Basic Potatoes on the
Grill (page 196)

TO SERVE:

Grainy mustard

ASTUCES: I like to use both grills to make this—the gas grill is perfect for the choucroute, and the barbecue is perfect for the meat. I suggest getting sausages from Aidells (www.aidells.com). If you are using salt pork instead of slab bacon, place it in a saucepan and cover with cold water. Bring the water to a boil, remove from the heat, and drain the salt pork. Rinse, repeat once more, then proceed with the recipe. You'll want to get thick cut chops for the grill. Note that I call for three thick pork chops for six servings; one chop per person is a lot of meat with the sausage and bacon in this dish. However, do as your taste dictates.

necessary—you want it moist, not soupy. The grill should be at about 350°F (180°C) for the sauerkraut to cook properly, so check the temperature and adjust if necessary, either by turning on or off a burner, or by opening up the grill.

While the sauerkraut is simmering, build a good-size fire in the barbecue. When the coals are red and dusted with ash, spread them in a tight, single layer, leaving a perimeter of grill with no coals under it; they need to emit concentrated heat. Set the grill over the coals.

Rub the pork chops and the sausages lightly with oil, and place them on the perimeter of the grill. Close the grill and cook until the sausages and the pork chops are golden, about 10 minutes. Turn the chops and the sausages, and place the slab bacon on the center of the grill. Close the grill and cook until the bacon is golden on one side, about 5 minutes. Turn the bacon, cover the grill, and cook until it is golden, an additional 5 minutes. Turn the pork chops, the sausages, and the bacon, cover the grill, and cook until the pork chops are golden and cooked through and the sausages and the bacon are deep golden, an additional 5 minutes.

To serve, transfer the sauerkraut to a serving platter, removing the bay leaves, cloves, and juniper berries if you find them. Strew the potatoes over it, then top with the meats. Serve immediately with mustard on the side.

CHOUCROUTE

I grew up eating sauerkraut from a jar. It was my father's fault. He was raised in a German household in Chicago, and his palate had a predilection for all things German.

My father also loved kimchi, and it was a frequent visitor on the family table. From whence such tastes? My father was a career military man with a palate as adventuresome as his spirit; he quailed at nothing when it came to food. The weirder and the spicier, the better for him.

His preference for kimchi turns out to be coherent with his love for sauerkraut because they have the same origins. It all has to do with the construction of the Great Wall of China. There are legends to explain this, and the one I prefer involves wooden barrels filled with cabbages that were placed strategically along the wall's length. The cabbages were fermented because the Chinese believed fermentation filled them with medicinal virtues and properties essential to the strength of the workers.

The rest of the story is a wild one involving Mongols, Huns, Tartares, and the conquest of Europe, ending up ultimately in the territory now called Alsace. There, in 451, the very first cabbages destined for pickling were, apparently, cultivated. It wasn't until the fifteenth century, though, that written reference is made to a dish sometimes referred to as *chou compost,* or "compost cabbage," and other times referred to as *chou acide,* or "sauerkraut," that was prepared in monasteries of the region.

The beauty of that "sauerkraut," which was basically thinly sliced cabbage layered with salt and kept hermetically sealed for several weeks until it "cooked" to a tender crispness, was its high content of vitamin C. From the builders of the Great Wall to the roving bands of Mongols, Huns, and Tartares, to the monks, and to the mariners who ultimately made it an essential part of their foodstuffs for seagoing voyages, sauerkraut kept strength high and scurvy at bay.

Fast-forward to the nineteenth century, when sauerkraut was well established in Germany (and ultimately wound up jarred and on supermarket shelves in the United States) and *choucroute* was well established in Alsace, now garnished with its retinue of pork products. The fermented cabbage had given its name to a dish that has become a vaunted regional specialty, always accompanied by mustards and beer or, even better, Riesling.

DINNER IN TWENTY: SAUSAGES, VEGETABLES, AND GARDEN HERBS

LE DÎNER DANS VINGT—SAUCISSES, LÉGUMES, ET LES AROMATES DU JARDIN

Serves 4 to 6

Don't we all wish for recipes like this, something quick and gorgeous, a little wild and lively, that goes together in no time at all? I know I do, and this is why I turn to this recipe. It's so easy, so pretty, and so seasonally perfect because it takes best advantage of the lively vegetables of summer's end. I make sure to always have rosé chilling, as it goes perfectly with this dish.

SPECIAL EQUIPMENT: *Plancha or cast-iron skillet, long tongs, gloves, metal spatula*

PREPARATION AND GRILLING TIME: *15 to 20 minutes*

DIFFICULTY LEVEL: *Simple*

---

8 sausage links (a generous 3 ounces; 95 g each), at room temperature

1 generous tablespoon olive oil

1 pound (500 g) onions, cut in ½-inch (1.25-cm) pieces

2 medium red bell peppers (about 7 ounces; 210 g), seeds and pith removed, cut in ½-inch (1.25-cm) pieces

Fine sea salt and coarsely ground pepper

4 large cloves garlic, cut in thick matchsticks

15 stems fresh thyme

LIGHT A GOOD-SIZE FIRE IN THE BARBECUE. When the coals are red and dusted with ash, spread them in a tight, single layer, leaving a perimeter of grill with no coals under it; they need to emit concentrated heat. Set the grill over the coals. Set the plancha or a large cast-iron skillet on the grill.

Rub the sausages lightly with about 1 teaspoon of the oil.

When the plancha is hot, pour the remaining oil on it. When the oil is hot—it will be almost instantly—place the onions and the bell pepper on it, stir, season with salt and pepper, and cook until the onions are turning deep golden at the edges and the peppers are getting black spots on them, about 7 minutes.

Simultaneously, place the sausage links on the grill around the plancha and cook, turning once or twice, until they are golden all over, which will take about 7 minutes, too.

continued

1 teaspoon fennel seeds

1 pound multihued cherry tomatoes, trimmed and cut in half

½ cup basil leaves

Basil sprigs, for garnish

ASTUCES: If you don't have a plancha, you can cook the vegetables in a cast-iron skillet and the sausages right on the grill. I suggest using sausages from Aidells (www.aidells.com) or any artisanally made sausages that contain quality ingredients.

Add the garlic to the vegetables, stir, then cover the barbecue. After 3 minutes, stir the vegetables, turn the sausage, and peel the leaves off the thyme right over the vegetables. Add the fennel, too. Stir and continue cooking until the vegetables are nearly tender through, stirring them, about 4 minutes.

Add the cherry tomatoes to the vegetables, stir, and season with a bit of salt and more pepper. Tear the basil leaves over the mixture, cover the barbecue, and cook just until the cherry tomatoes are softened, which will take about 3 to 5 minutes.

Transfer the vegetables to a large platter. Arrange the sausages around the vegetables, garnish with basil sprigs, and serve immediately.

GRILLED BABY BACK RIBS, FRENCH STYLE

CÔTES DE PORC GRILLÉE

Serves 4 to 6

The French are artists with pork, and this recipe reflects the simplicity with which they approach it. A touch of toasted cumin, a sprinkle of smoked paprika from neighboring Spain, and that most traditional accompaniment to pork, minced garlic, and you've got a dish fit for a king. In fact, with its blend of spices it would have suited a king like Charles V, who reigned during part of the Middle Ages, when spices were a sign of wealth. They were used in abundance and often rubbed on meat to enhance its flavor (and not to hide its "off" flavor as is often claimed). As it stands, this thoroughly contemporary recipe pleases all, and it is sure to please you, too! I recommend serving this with a rich Madiran from Château Aydie.

SPECIAL EQUIPMENT: *Nonreactive dish, long tongs, fork*

PREPARATION AND GRILLING TIME: *Macerating, 1 to 3 hours; preparation and grilling, about 50 minutes*

DIFFICULTY LEVEL: *Simple to moderate*

---

2 large cloves garlic, minced

1 teaspoon toasted, ground cumin

½ teaspoon smoked paprika

½ teaspoon fine sea salt

Freshly ground black pepper

2 tablespoons olive oil

2 pounds (1 kg) baby back ribs in one long piece, at room temperature

IN A SMALL BOWL BLEND TOGETHER THE garlic, spices, and oil. Rub this all over the pork, place it in a nonreactive dish, cover, and let sit at room temperature for at least 1 hour and up to 3 hours. If you like, you may do this the night before you plan to grill the ribs. In that case, refrigerate them, covered, and bring them out of the refrigerator 2 hours before you plan to grill them.

Build a good-size fire in the barbecue or turn on all three burners of the gas grill. When the coals are red and dusted with ash, spread them in a tight, single layer, leaving a perimeter of grill with no coals under it; they need to emit concentrated heat. Set the grill over the coals. (If you have very fatty ribs, see the Astuces.)

When the grill is hot, place the ribs right over the coals on their fattiest side, cover, and let them grill until they are deep golden, about 15 minutes. Turn them on their side, standing up, and grill until they are golden, about 6 minutes. Turn them on the other side, cover, and grill until they are golden, 6 to 7 minutes. Finally, turn them on their leaner side and finish the grilling until they are golden, an additional 12 minutes. Transfer the ribs to a serving platter and let them sit for about 10 minutes before cutting and serving.

ASTUCES: Toasting cumin enhances its flavor. To do this, simply place the seeds in a small pan on the grill or over medium heat, stirring/shaking them in the pan until you can smell them browning. This should take 4 to 5 minutes. Remove them from the heat and pour them onto a plate or into a bowl so they stop toasting. When they are cool, grind them in a spice grinder. Ground cumin keeps well in an airtight container in a dark, cool spot. The baby back ribs in France are not overburdened with fat, so there is practically no dripping on the coals to create flames. If your ribs are very fatty, I suggest you separate the coals and use a drip pan to catch the fat. And don't be surprised at the short cooking time—it works and the results are delicious!

WOOD~FIRE GRILLED PORK CHOPS

CÔTES DE PORC GRILLÉS AU FEU DE BOIS

Serves 6

Pork is easily the most common meat on the French grill and table. It emerges from the grill juicy and tender, and if it's still a bit pink, there is nothing to worry about. Why not try these with the Grilled New Potato Salad (page 199)? I like a Côtes de Roussillon from Ferrer-Ribière here, too, for a real treat.

~~~~~~~~~~~~~~~~~~~~~~~~~

SPECIAL EQUIPMENT: *Nonreactive dish or pan, long tongs, long metal spatula, gloves, wood cuttings or chips, bowl*

PREPARATION AND GRILLING TIME: *About 30 minutes*

DIFFICULTY LEVEL: *Simple*

---

6 thick (about 1½ inches; 4 cm) pork loin chops (8 to 9 ounces; 250 to 280 g each)

2 tablespoons olive oil

Coarse sea salt

Freshly ground black pepper

½ cup (5 g) fresh Herbes de Provence (page 261) or use ½ teaspoon dried herbes de Provence per chop

ASTUCES: The key to tender pork chops on the grill is slow cooking. I use the indirect method and leave the chop in the center of the grill for 10 to 12 minutes per side. If you want a more caramelized chop, though, set it directly over the wood or charcoal for a couple of minutes on one side, and serve browned side up! I prefer the (sir)loin chop over the loin end chop, because it is less dry and offers more texture when slow-cooked on the grill.

RUB THE PORK CHOPS ALL OVER WITH THE olive oil. Sprinkle them on both sides with salt and pepper and set them in a nonreactive dish or pan.

Mince the herbes de Provence and rub them on both sides of each chop. Let sit at room temperature for about 30 minutes, or up to 2 hours in the refrigerator. Remove from the refrigerator at least 30 minutes before grilling.

Build a medium-size fire in the grill. When the coals are red and dusted with ash, divide them, putting half on either side of the grill. Set the grill over the coals and when it is hot, lift up the side of the grill and insert the wood cuttings or chips, putting half on either side of the grill, right on the hot coals. They'll flare, but then the flame will die back.

Place the chops in the center of the grill.

Cover and cook until the chops are grilled to a deep golden on one side, about 10 minutes. Turn the chops and cook them on the other side until they are deep golden and cooked through, which, depending on the thickness of the chops, will take an additional 10 to 12 minutes. Transfer the chops from the grill to a serving platter, strew some salt and grind some pepper over them, and let them sit for about 10 minutes before serving so they have a chance to reabsorb some of their juices and relax.

HONEY GRILLED PORK CHOPS

CÔTES DE PORC GRILLÉES AU MIEL

Serves 6

Simple and elegant, this is a dish you can grill for a quick family weeknight dinner as easily as you can for a more dressed up Saturday night meal with friends. Pork is often served with something sweet, like apples or pears. Here, I put the sweetness right on the pork; it lifts its flavor with deep caramelization. I suggest serving it with Grilled Asparagus (page 174) or Whole Grilled Zucchini (page 205), a mound of toasty Bulgur (page 179), and a light red wine such as Saumur-Champigny.

SPECIAL EQUIPMENT: *Whisk, bowl, rubber spatula, long tongs, long metal spatula*

PREPARATION AND GRILLING TIME: *At least 2 hours to marinate; 30 minutes including resting time*

DIFFICULTY LEVEL: *Simple*

FOR THE MARINADE:

3 tablespoons freshly squeezed lemon juice

2 tablespoons olive oil

3 tablespoons mild honey, such as wildflower

3 large cloves garlic

3 teaspoons piment d'Espelette or 1½ teaspoons each hot and mild paprika

Generous pinch of salt

Several grinds of black pepper

THE CHOPS:

6 thick (about 1½ inches; 4 cm) pork loin chops (8 to 9 ounces; 250 to 280 g each)

WHISK TOGETHER THE MARINADE INGREDI- ents in a small bowl and pour into a nonreactive dish.

Place the pork chops in the marinade and turn them. Using a rubber spatula, rub the marinade evenly into the pork chops. Turn them again and repeat so they are completely covered in marinade. Cover the chops and marinate them at room temperature for at least 2 hours and up to several hours at room temperature, or overnight in the refrigerator, covered. Remove the meat from the refrigerator at least 2 hours before grilling them.

Build a medium-size fire in the grill. When the coals are red and dusted with ash, place half of the coals on either side of the grill. Place the grill over the coals, and when it is hot, place the chops in the center of the grill. Cover and cook until the chops are grilled to deep golden on one side, about 10 minutes. Turn the chops and cook them on the other side until they are deep golden and cooked through which, depending on the thickness of the chops, will take an additional 5 to 8 minutes.

Transfer the chops from the grill to a serving platter, strew some salt and grind pepper over them, and let them sit for about 10 minutes before serving so they have a chance to reabsorb some of their juices and relax.

ASTUCES: Before you put the pork chops in the marinade, slit the fat around the edges so the chop won't curl as it grills.

SMOKY PORK SHOULDER À LA FRANÇAISE

ÉPAULE DE PORC FUMÉ À LA FRANÇAISE

Serves 8, generously

No flavors are more French than the combination of grainy mustard, herbes de Provence, garlic, and beer. There are several regional influences at play here, I must admit. Beer and mustard are used in the north of France, where breweries abound; herbes de Provence and garlic are from the south. In today's France, blending regional culinary cultures is allowed when the result is as flavorful as this. Try this with a delicate Arbois from the Jura area, which is perfect with full-flavored pork dishes.

SPECIAL EQUIPMENT: *Rotisserie attachment (advised), kitchen twine, long gloves, nonreactive baking dish, wood chips or grapevine cuttings*

PREPARATION AND GRILLING TIME: *1½ hours*

DIFFICULTY LEVEL: *Medium (because of the rotisserie)*

FOR THE MARINADE:

3 tablespoons grainy mustard

2 cloves garlic, minced

1 tablespoon dried Herbes de Provence (page 261); if using commercial herbes de Provence, try 2 teaspoons

1 teaspoon mild honey

2 tablespoons (30 ml) mild-flavored beer

FOR THE PORK:

1 boneless pork shoulder (about 3 pounds; 1.5 kg)

½ cup (125 ml) mild-flavored beer

Fresh herb sprigs (parsley, sage, rosemary, thyme), for garnish

IN A MEDIUM BOWL, WHISK TOGETHER THE mustard, garlic, herbes de Provence, honey, and 2 tablespoons of the beer.

Place the pork in a nonreactive baking dish and pour the marinade over it. Turn the pork and rub the marinade into it. The marinade is quite liquidy, so be sure to turn the pork several times while it is marinating, which should be for at least 2 hours and up to 4 hours at room temperature, or overnight.

Build a good-size fire in the barbecue. When the coals are red and covered with ash, divide them in half, placing half the coals on either side of the barbecue. Place a drip pan in the center of the barbecue. Place the rotisserie motor on the barbecue.

Tie the pork shoulder to make a narrow roast; this is a bit messy, but persevere because your roast will cook more evenly once it is tied.

Thread the roast onto the rotisserie bar and secure it at each end. (If you don't have a rotisserie, you can roast this directly on the grill; you will need to turn it every 15 minutes to make sure it roasts evenly.)

Just before putting the roast on the rotisserie or the grill, place a handful of wood chips or grapevine cuttings on the coals. They will smoke and flame up a bit, but will very soon die down and just emit smoke.

ASTUCES: Pork shoulder is one of the best cuts because its gelatinous tissue turns mouth-meltingly tender when cooked. I highly recommend this cut, particularly when prepared as here. Remember to allow resting time for the shoulder and to recuperate any juices it gives up to add to the sauce. When you tie the roast, all you are concerned with is making a uniform packet. Just fold the edges toward the center and do the best you can. There is no particular technique involved. Note, too, that if you've made and dried your own Herbes de Provence (page 261), they will be less concentrated than what you purchase, in part because the herbs won't have been ground into small pieces. So, use a smaller amount of commercial herbes de Provence than your own fresh version.

Cover the barbecue and roast the pork shoulder for 1 hour. The rotisserie will make sure it's cooked evenly; if you don't have one, remember to turn it regularly.

When the roast is browned on the outside and cooked through (155–160°F; 68–71°C), remove it from the grill and let it rest on a cutting board for about 15 minutes.

While the pork is resting, place the remaining marinade and the ½ cup (125 ml) of beer into a small saucepan and bring to a boil over medium-high heat. Pour any juices that the pork shoulder gives up into the sauce. Reduce the mixture by half, taste for seasoning, then keep warm.

Remove the rotisserie clamps and the bar from the pork and slice the shoulder into the thickness you prefer. Arrange them either on warmed plates or on a warm platter. Pour the reduced juices over the pork, garnish with the herbs, and serve immediately.

CHAPTER 6

SIDE DISH VEGETABLES AND A FEW GRAINS

"The artichoke is a vegetable for solitude,
difficult to eat when you're sitting
across from someone, divine when you're alone.
It's a vegetable for the meditative,
the tinkerer, the gourmet."

—PAUL FOURNEL, WRITER

The vegetable is a relative newcomer to the French grill. But as in all things culinary, the French chef/cook has quickly tamed grilling techniques, combinations, and flavors for vegetables. You'll find many of these in this chapter. It's so important when cooking any ingredient to buy seasonal and local, but this is particularly the case for vegetables. Waiting for a vegetable to come into season is like waiting for a long-lost friend to show up at the front door—so exciting and satisfying. I have tried to avoid "two-step cooking methods," yet for some vegetables it's the only way to get their goodness from the grill.

GRILLED LEMON AND THYME BROCCOLI

BROCCOLI AU CITRON ET THYM SUR LE GRILL

Serves 4 to 6

Spring and early summer broccoli is tender and sweet, and when prepared this way it is almost impossible to resist. I like to serve this as a side dish to accompany just about anything. But here's a confession: sometimes this is our supper, with cheese and salad to follow!

SPECIAL EQUIPMENT: *Steamer, grill pan, long tongs, spatula*

PREPARATION AND GRILLING TIME: *25 minutes*

DIFFICULTY: *Simple*

1½ pounds (750 g) broccoli, cut into large, bite-size florets with stems

Zest from 1 lemon

3 tablespoons olive oil

1 large clove garlic

1 scant tablespoon fresh thyme leaves

Fine sea salt and freshly ground black pepper

ASTUCES: Cutting the broccoli florets into bite-size pieces—not tiny, but a good mouthful size—ensures that the broccoli will be tender through. Broccoli stems are delicious; don't throw them out, but do peel them before cooking.

BRING 3 CUPS WATER TO A BOIL IN THE bottom of a steamer. When the water is boiling, add the broccoli stems, cover, and steam until they are just beginning to turn tender, about 4 minutes. Add the florets, cover, and steam until the broccoli is tender-crisp, which will take 5 to 7 minutes.

While the broccoli is steaming, mince the zest and place it in a small bowl. Whisk in the olive oil, garlic, and the thyme leaves, along with a generous pinch of salt and several grinds of pepper. When the broccoli is steamed, transfer it directly from the steamer to the oil mixture and toss gently until the florets and stems are completely coated. Let the broccoli sit for about 10 minutes.

Light a fire in the grill, and when the coals are red and dusted with ash, put half the coals on either side of the grill. Set the grill over the coals, and set a grill pan in the center of the grill. When the grill pan is hot and after giving the broccoli a quick stir, transfer the broccoli with a slotted spoon onto the grill pan. Close the grill and grill until the broccoli is dark at the edges, and slightly crisp, and cooked to your liking, turning it often. This will take 5 to 8 minutes over a hot fire.

When the broccoli is cooked, transfer it to a serving platter, season with salt and pepper, and serve immediately.

SWEET CARROTS

CAROTTES SUCRÉES

Serves 4 to 6

Spring and early summer carrots are little sugar sticks when grilled. They need nothing but a bit of olive oil and some salt and pepper. If you can find multicolored carrots, use them here. They make a gorgeous side dish for roast chicken or pork shoulder.

And here's an idea for a great recipe for the vegans in your life: take two grilled carrots, get a fantastic hot dog bun, slather it with some vegan mayonnaise and a lot of hummus, slice up some onions very thin, and get some crisp lettuce leaves. Lay the carrot atop the hummus, close the bun, and *voila!* You've got a vegan "hot dog" (or as we say in France, *chien chaud*). See the recipe for a Grilled Carrot Dog on page 185.

SPECIAL EQUIPMENT: *Tongs, dish for rolling in olive oil, gloves*

PREPARATION AND GRILLING TIME: *25 to 30 minutes, depending on size*

DIFFICULTY LEVEL: *Simple*

1 to 2 tablespoons olive oil

Fine sea salt

½ pound (500 g) small carrots (0.75 ounce; 21 g each), scrubbed and trimmed

Freshly ground black pepper

ASTUCES: When carrots are young they don't need to be peeled, but they do need a good scrub. I leave a few of their green leaves attached, which gives them a certain *je ne sais quoi,* attracting the eye and, before you know it, the palate. Also, if you don't have small carrots, simply cut larger (not more than about 1½ ounces; 44 g) in half lengthwise. An advantage here is that they roast in half the time!

DRIZZLE THE OIL ON A FLAT PLATE OR SMALL platter and mix a generous pinch of salt into it. Roll the carrots in the oil and salt until they are coated.

Build a medium-size fire in the barbecue, or light up the gas grill using just the two outside burners. When the coals are red and dusted with ash, spread them in a tight, single layer, leaving a perimeter of grill with no coals under it; they need to emit concentrated heat. Set the grill over the coals.

When the grill is hot, set the carrots on it and cover them. After 5 minutes, turn them, and continue turning every 5 minutes until the carrots are golden and tender through, which will take a total of 20 to 25 minutes. If using a gas grill, grill the carrots in the center, moving them to the sides over the burners if they aren't browning the way you'd like them to.

When the carrots are tender, transfer them back to the plate or platter with the oil on it, roll them in the excess, then season them with freshly ground black pepper and serve immediately.

GRILLED ASPARAGUS

ASPERGES GRILLÉES

Serves 4 to 6

Here in Normandy, we know that winter is gone when the local green asparagus, spring's fleeting messenger, arrives. It's only available for a few weeks, so we eat it for just about every meal until we're sated, knowing it will be a year before it returns. Of course, we can get fat white asparagus from the Loire Valley, but honestly, there is nothing to compare with the freshly harvested, local green variety that practically melts in your mouth. You can eat the asparagus plain, serve it alongside your favorite grilled meat, or combine it with other vegetables. Here, it emerges from the grill tender through and golden on the outside. If you like your asparagus crisp, grill it for a minute or two less.

SPECIAL EQUIPMENT: *Tongs, dish for rolling in olive oil, gloves*

PREPARATION AND GRILLING TIME: *Scant 20 minutes*

DIFFICULTY LEVEL: *Simple*

---

1 to 2 tablespoons olive oil

Fine sea salt

1 pound (500 g) medium-thick green asparagus, trimmed and peeled if necessary

ASTUCES: To prepare asparagus, hold the tip with your left thumb and forefinger, and the stem end with your right thumb and forefinger, and bend the stalk; it will snap where it needs to, leaving your right thumb and forefinger holding the tough stem that will never cook to tenderness. This, you discard. If you've picked your own asparagus or gotten it fresh, the way my local farmer Baptiste sells his, you only lose the very end of the stalk. But the skin may be tough. In this case, simply peel the stalk about halfway up toward the tip.

BUILD A MEDIUM-SIZE FIRE IN THE BARBECUE, or light up the gas grill with all three burners. When the coals are dusted with ash, spread them in a tight, single layer; they need to emit concentrated heat. Set the grill over the coals.

Pour the oil on a large, flat plate or platter, and stir in some salt using a pastry brush. Place the asparagus on the plate and roll it around, or paint each stalk with the pastry brush until each is covered with oil and salt.

Place the asparagus over the coals and cook, turning them two to three times, until they are golden on the outside and tender through, which will take 7 to 9 minutes.

Transfer the asparagus back to the dish or platter with the oil and salt, roll them around a bit, and serve.

BASIC GRILLED LEEKS

POIREAUX GRILLÉS

Serves 6 to 8

The leek is *the* cornerstone of all French cooking. Its sweet, onion-like flavor enhances all dishes, from soups to stews. I love them like this, simply grilled and served with a sauce or two, or just with a touch of olive oil and a sprinkling of salt and pepper. These are particularly luscious with Romesco: Summer's Perfect Sauce (page 74), Walnut Oil Vinaigrette (page 253), or Turkish Kebab Sauce (page 275).

SPECIAL EQUIPMENT: *Long tongs, dish for rolling in olive oil, gloves*

PREPARATION AND GRILLING TIME: *8 to 10 minutes*

DIFFICULTY LEVEL: *Simple*

1 tablespoon olive oil

Fine sea salt and freshly ground black pepper

1 pound (500 g) thin leeks, trimmed of their outer leaves and roots, with about 4 inches (10 cm) green left on, cut in half lengthwise

ASTUCES: Trim a layer of tough, outer leaves from the leeks, but leave on the rest. They'll be too tough to eat, but, as you'll see, once grilled you can peel away the remaining outer layers and eat the tender insides of the leek. If you don't want your plate to be filled with charred leek leaves, then peel away all the tough outer leaves and cook the leeks a minute or so less.

BUILD A MEDIUM-SIZE FIRE IN THE BARBECUE, or light up the gas grill with all three burners.

When the coals are red and dusted with ash, spread them in a tight, single layer, leaving a perimeter of grill with no coals under it; they need to emit concentrated heat. Set the grill over the coals.

Pour 1 tablespoon of oil onto a flat plate or platter, add a generous pinch of salt, mix them together, and roll the leeks in the mixture until they are coated.

Place the leeks on the grill, cut side down, cover, and grill until the leeks are golden, about 4 minutes. Turn the leeks, cover the grill, and repeat. At this point, the leeks should be tender through. If they aren't quite tender, turn off the central burner, aggregate the leeks in the center of the grill so they aren't over direct heat, and continue cooking until they are tender, which should be a matter of a minute or two.

Transfer the leeks to a serving platter and season them with salt and pepper. Serve as is or with the sauce of your choice.

GRILLED RED BELL PEPPERS

POIVRONS ROUGES GRILLÉE

4 grilled peppers

Grilled red bell peppers are one of the culinary wonders of the world. It's worth investing in a grill just to be able to make these. They're wonderful simply dressed in olive oil and seasoned with salt and pepper. You can also use them as a base for a sauce, be it Red Pepper Sauce (page 255) or Romesco: Summer's Perfect Sauce (page 74). And once you've done all that, you'll think of 10 more uses for grilled red bell peppers.

SPECIAL EQUIPMENT: *Long tongs, gloves*

PREPARATION AND GRILLING TIME: *About 20 minutes*

DIFFICULTY LEVEL: *Simple*

**4 large red bell peppers
(about 6½ ounces; 195 g each)**

ASTUCES: I have written this recipe for four peppers, but I encourage you to grill many more. They keep in the refrigerator for several days, or you can puree and freeze them. Unlike most vegetables, you don't need to oil the peppers before grilling since the object of this exercise, besides getting a nice soft flavor from them, is to remove their skins. One more suggestion: The peppers need to sweat right after grilling, so put them in a paper bag and let them do that—it makes the skin come off more easily. Then, to remove the seeds, scrape them away using a plastic scraper. *Don't rinse the peppers*—you'll wash away all of that hard-won flavor.

BUILD A MEDIUM-SIZE FIRE IN A BARBECUE. When the coals are red and dusted with ash, divide them, putting half on each side of the barbecue. Set the grill atop them, and place the red bell peppers on the grill over the coals. Grill until they are black all over, which requires turning regularly but not often; this doesn't require close supervision and should take about 20 minutes. When they are blackened, transfer them to a paper bag, close it, and let them steam. Proceed with your recipe.

GRILLED SPRING ONIONS

LES OIGNONS NOUVEAUX GRILLÉS

Serves 4 to 6

These are fabulous. As the onions grill, their outer layers turn to crisp caramel while inside they soften into honey for a wonderful, toothsome contrast. There are a couple of ways to go about grilling these—you can leave the outer layers on and grill the onions long enough so that these turn black, then you peel them away. *Or* you can peel two layers away to begin with—the outer layers of the spring onion are surprisingly tough—then grill them carefully as suggested here so that the outer layer turns golden and is eminently edible. I recommend serving these as a side dish with Grilled Beef Chop (page 127) or with a big serving of Romesco: Summer's Perfect Sauce (page 74). They're also an integral part of the Curry Beef and Zucchini Brochettes (page 140).

SPECIAL EQUIPMENT: *Skewers, pastry brush*

PREPARATION AND GRILLING TIME: *About 15 minutes*

DIFFICULTY LEVEL: *Simple*

---

1 tablespoon olive oil

Fine sea salt and freshly ground black pepper

1 bunch (about 1 pound; 500 g) spring onions (1½ ounces; 45 g each), stems and root ends trimmed

ASTUCES: When I say spring onions, I am referring to small, round-bulbed onions with thick stalks that explode with sugar and juice from the end of May through July. If you can't find the small bulb onions called for here, use larger onions and either cut them in half or increase the grilling time. When you are trimming the root end, trim off just the hair-fine roots, leaving the onion whole so the layers stay together on the grill.

BUILD A MEDIUM-SIZE FIRE IN THE GRILL.

Skewer the onions on two to three skewers, making sure they aren't quite touching so that they will grill evenly.

Pour the oil onto a flat plate or platter. Add a pinch of salt, mix, and place the skewered onions on the oil. Rotate the skewers so the onions are evenly coated with the salt and oil.

When the coals are red and dusted with ash, spread them in a tight, single layer; they need to emit concentrated heat. Place the grill over them.

When the grill is hot, place the onions on it, cover, and grill until they are golden, 4 to 5 minutes. Turn and repeat, testing them for tenderness, for a total grilling time of 8 to 10 minutes.

When the onions are tender, transfer them to a serving plate or platter. Season them with pepper, and they're ready to go!

BULGUR

BOULGOUR

Serves 6

Traditionally, a French meal isn't worthy of the name without a grain to accompany the main course, whether that dish be made on the grill or in the oven. While rice is the main grain in the French repertoire (it's often mistakenly considered a vegetable), bulgur is easier than rice and has so much toasty flavor. This bulgur makes a wonderful accompaniment to grilled dishes.

~~~~~~~~~~~~~~~~~~~~~~~~~~~~~~~~~~~~

SPECIAL EQUIPMENT: *Medium saucepan*

PREPARATION AND COOKING TIME: *25 to 30 minutes, including resting time*

DIFFICULTY LEVEL: *Simple*

2 cups (11½ ounces; 330 g) bulgur wheat, preferably #3 size

2½ to 3 cups (625–750 ml) water or unsalted chicken broth

½ teaspoon salt

1 teaspoon olive oil

⅓ cup (7 g) fresh herbs such as tarragon, flat-leaf parsley, or basil (optional)

ASTUCES: I like the lighter taste that results from using water rather than a meat or poultry stock to cook the bulgur, but do as you prefer. Take into account that bulgur needs to "plump," so make sure you give it that extra time.

PLACE THE BULGUR, WATER, SALT, AND OIL in a medium saucepan over high heat. When the water is boiling, reduce the heat so it is simmering merrily, stir the ingredients in the pan, cover, and cook until the bulgur is tender, 10 to 12 minutes. Check the bulgur after about 8 minutes and add additional water if necessary. Remove from the heat and let the bulgur sit for at least 15 and up to 30 minutes, covered, before serving.

If you use herbs, mince them right before serving and gently stir them into the bulgur. Serve immediately.

ROOT VEGETABLE SKEWERS

BROCHETTES DE LÉGUMES RACINES

Serves 4

Root vegetables are normally considered the denizens of winter. We have them almost year-round, though: once February and March have said goodbye, it is spring, and root vegetables appear in tinier versions! This recipe is intended for the winter version of root vegetables, but can be made with them at any time of year. What makes these skewers fun and delicious are the different flavors and colors that brighten up the plate. I have chosen beets, celery root, and sweet potato. You could try turnips, potatoes, and rutabagas, but note that steaming times will differ from what is here. This is a two-step recipe. Part is done in the kitchen so that you can succeed on the grill.

SPECIAL EQUIPMENT: *Steamer with a flat steamer basket (à la All-Clad), long metal skewers, long tongs, pastry brush, gloves*

PREPARATION AND GRILLING TIME: *About 25 minutes*

DIFFICULTY LEVEL: *Simple*

---

1 to 2 tablespoons olive oil, or as needed, plus extra for oiling the steamer basket

1 medium sweet potato (7 ounces; 210 g), peeled

4 small or 2 medium beets (9 ounces; 270 g total), peeled

4 ounces (120 g) celery root, peeled

16 fresh or dried imported bay leaves

Sea salt and coarsely ground black pepper

ADD WATER TO THE BOTTOM OF A STEAMER and bring to a boil over medium-high heat. Oil the steamer basket to keep the vegetables from sticking.

Cut the sweet potato, beets, and celery root into thick (½-inch; 1.25-cm) rounds. Cut each round of each vegetable into quarters.

Arrange the slices of beets and celery root in the steamer basket, and steam them just until each vegetable is tender *but not soft,* as the slices need to hold on to the skewer: 6 minutes for the celery root, 7 minutes for the beet. Remove the celery root and beet and put the sweet potato in the steamer basket. Steam until it begins to soften, about 5 minutes.

While the vegetables are steaming, pour 1 tablespoon olive oil on a large, flat plate or platter. As the vegetables are steamed, transfer them from the steamer to the oil on the plate. Turn each slice once so it is covered with oil, and add additional oil as needed so that each slice is oiled.

Build a medium-size fire in a barbecue, or light up the gas grill with all three burners. When the coals are red and dusted with ash, divide them in the barbecue, putting half the coals on either side.

ASTUCES: I have a giant bay tree at the end of my garden that serves as both a hedge and a source of seasoning for just about everything I cook. I suggest you plant one, too. All you need to do is track one down—*Laurus nobilis*—and figure out the best place to plant it, which might be a pot that you bring inside during the winter. You will, I promise, *never* regret it. If you only have dried leaves available, Turkish are best. Soak them before use. They won't be very foldable, but they will slide onto a skewer.

Make the skewers: thread a slice of beet, a bay leaf folded in half crosswise, a slice of potato, and one of celery root, and repeat twice. Continue on three other skewers, making sure you have an equal number of slices on each skewer. Place the skewers on the plate or platter where you've oiled the vegetables. If there is additional oil on the platter, use a pastry brush to get at it and brush the vegetables on the skewers. Sprinkle them with salt and pepper, turning them as you do so they are evenly seasoned.

Set the grill over the coals. When it is hot, place the skewers over the hot coals and begin to brown on all sides, which will take about 2 minutes total. Move the skewers to the center of the grill and continue cooking them, turning occasionally, until they are golden and cooked through, about 6 additional minutes. Transfer them to the platter with the oil or another platter, adjust the seasoning, and serve.

HONEY, ROSEMARY, AND LEMON EGGPLANT

AUBERGINES AU MIEL, ROMARIN, ET CITRON

Serves 4 to 6

The flavor of a good, fat, taut-skinned eggplant fresh from the soil is nutty and rich, its texture almost silken. It is a staple from the grill in our home, and this is one of my favorite ways to prepare it, because it's just that little bit unexpected. The blend of lemon, rosemary, and garlic is great anywhere; the added sweetness of honey is an eye-popping, palate-pleasing surprise.

~~~~~~

SPECIAL EQUIPMENT: *Tongs, metal spatula, small pan, pastry brush*

PREPARATION AND GRILLING TIME: *About 15 minutes*

DIFFICULTY LEVEL: *Simple*

---

2 medium eggplants (about 1 pound; 500 g each), stem end trimmed, skinned if desired, cut lengthwise into ½-inch (1.25-cm) slices

2 to 3 generous tablespoons olive oil

Zest from half a small lemon (about 1 teaspoon minced zest)

1 large clove garlic

1 tablespoon rosemary, lightly packed

2 scant tablespoons mild honey, such as wildflower

Fine sea salt and freshly ground black pepper

BUILD A GOOD-SIZE FIRE IN THE BARBECUE, or turn on all three burners of a gas grill.

Paint the eggplant slices lightly with oil on both sides.

Mince the lemon zest, garlic, and rosemary. Place the honey in a small, heavy skillet or saucepan over low heat (you can do this on the grill if you set the pan to the side of the direct heat). Melt the honey over a low flame, then stir in the lemon zest, garlic, and rosemary. Remove from the heat.

When the coals are red and dusted with ash, divide them in the barbecue, putting half the coals on either side. Set the grill over the coals.

When the grill is hot (for the gas grill: about 500°F; 260°C), place the eggplant slices on it in the center of the grill, close the top, and cook for 2 minutes. Flip the slices and repeat.

If using a gas grill, turn off the central flame and continue to grill using the heat from the two outer flames.

continued

ASTUCES: A taut-skinned, shiny eggplant is a fresh eggplant. It won't be bitter, so there is no need to salt it before cooking. If you don't like eggplant skin, remove it. An eggplant that has been skinned will absorb more oil than an unskinned eggplant.

Stir the honey mixture, then brush each eggplant slice generously with about half the mixture. Season each slice with salt, cover the grill, and cook until the eggplant is soft through, about 5 minutes.

Transfer the slices to a platter, setting them honey side down. Brush the slices with the remaining honey mixture, season with salt and pepper, and let sit for 5 minutes before serving to give the eggplant time to absorb the flavors of the honey and the herbs.

GRILLED CARROT DOG

CHIEN CHAUD DE CAROTTE GRILLÉ

Serves 8

Fiona, my daughter, eschews eating most animal products. In a country where the cuisine is based on dairy and meat, she's made an interesting choice that leads her imagination down some very delicious paths. This carrot hot dog is one of them. We were eating grilled carrots when she said, "Mom, these would make a great vegan hot dog." I loved the idea, and I gave it a try. It's fun and delicious because carrots turn into savory little honey sticks on the grill, a perfect "hot dog" substitute. Dress this up with a Chardonnay from Les Athlètes du Vin!

SPECIAL EQUIPMENT: *Grill pan, long tongs*

PREPARATION AND GRILLING TIME: *The buns take 2 hours 45 minutes to make, the carrots 20–30 minutes to grill, depending on their size*

DIFFICULTY LEVEL: *Simple*

8 hot dog buns (made with the dough from the Hamburger (or Hot Dog) Buns (page 258)

½ to 1 cup (125 to 250 ml) Hummus (page 262), more if desired

Vegan No-Egg Mayonnaise (page 265, optional)

8 large leaves of a crisp lettuce, such as iceberg or romaine

1 small white onion, cut into very thin slices

16 small carrots (about 0.75 ounce; 21 g each), grilled (see Sweet Carrots, page 172)

TO ASSEMBLE THE HOT DOGS, SLICE THE buns down their length but not all the way through and open them like a book. Spread 1 to 2 tablespoons hummus on the bottom part of the bun. If you like, you can spread hummus on the top bun, too. Alternatively, you can spread vegan mayonnaise on the top bun, if desired. Lay a lettuce leaf atop the hummus, then top that with onions slices. Finally, lay the carrots on the onion slices. Close the bun and serve immediately.

ASTUCES: Unlike a meat hot dog, carrots aren't juicy, they're moist. This means you need to add a bit more moisture to your carrot dog than you might for a meat hot dog. I suggest using hummus and vegan mayonnaise here, but you can add yellow mustard if you like, or even ketchup. (Just don't tell me!) Allow me a little word here about making hot dog buns. The dough spreads, so the hot dog buns end up looking a little like dirigibles when they're baked. To create that classic hot dog shape, I fashion molds out of aluminum foil, which I line with parchment paper (for specific instructions see Hamburger (or Hot Dog) Buns, page 258). They won't win an industrial design competition, but this process works. Using this technique, I am able to make long, narrow hot dog buns that have a yummy, gently yeasty flavor. And finally a word about iceberg lettuce: It has much gustatory value, particularly if you can buy it freshly harvested from the producer, at a farmers' market, for instance. Just saying . . .

GARLICKY CURRIED EGGPLANT

AUBERGINES AILLÉS AU CURRY

Serves 6 to 8

The French use a surprising amount of curry in their cuisine. This use of curry dates to the silk and jewel commerce of the ninteenth century. Paris was a fashionable destination, and East Indian silk and jewel merchants made the city their home. Naturally, strains of their cuisine mingled with the local fare, which is why one now finds curry in everything from French vinaigrettes to vegetables. I love curry of every sort, and I love eggplant. The two make a harmonious combination, particularly from the grill.

SPECIAL EQUIPMENT: *Long tongs, metal spatula, pastry brush*

PREPARATION AND GRILLING TIME: *About 25 minutes*

DIFFICULTY LEVEL: *Simple*

---

1 scant tablespoon Curry Powder (page 257)

¼ teaspoon piment d'Espelette or hot paprika

1 clove garlic, minced

5 to 6 tablespoons (90 ml) olive oil

3 medium eggplant (about 6 ounces; 180 g each), peeled and cut into ½-inch-thick (1.25-cm) slices, length-wise

Fine sea salt and freshly ground black pepper

MIX THE CURRY, PIMENT D'ESPELETTE, and garlic with 2 tablespoons of the oil and reserve.

Brush the eggplant all over with some of the remaining oil.

Light a medium-size fire in the barbecue or turn on all three burners of the gas grill. When the coals are red and dusted with ash, divide them in the barbecue, putting half the coals on either side. Set the grill over the coals.

When the grill is hot, re-brush the eggplant with some of the remaining oil on one side and set them on the grill with the double-oiled side to the fire, over the coals. Brown the eggplant, which will take about 2 minutes. Flip each slice, brush each slice with oil, and brown the eggplant on the other side, which will take about 2 minutes. Move the slices to the center of the grill and brush each with the curry mixture, making sure to evenly spread it among all of the slices. Sprinkle the eggplant with salt, cover the grill, and cook until the slices are almost tender through, checking them after 5 minutes. Brush them again with any remaining turmeric mixture, and continue cooking until they are tender, which will take 5 to 8 minutes.

Remove the eggplant from the grill, season again with salt and pepper, and either serve immediately or let cool to room temperature.

ASTUCES: One of the base spices in curry is turmeric. Note that turmeric stains everything (including braces; make sure you warn anyone wearing them!). Note, too, that I call for white or striated eggplant here. I've come to prefer these over the purple variety for their mild nuttiness and deep, sweet delicacy. That said, the difference isn't staggering. So if you've got purple eggplant, please make this dish! A perfect eggplant has taut, shiny skin and no dimples or pockmarks. And of course you don't *have* to peel eggplant, but I find so many people object to the peel that I've taken to peeling it. Eggplant absorbs a bit more oil when peeled.

FRENCH FRIES

FRITES

Serves 4 to 6 (or 2 frites fanatics)

Frites, or fries, are to France what peanut butter is to the United States—immutable, part of the culture, the culinary map, the life. Making them isn't rocket science, you say. Yet there are good ones and then there are not so good ones. These here? They're perfect! I admit to making them in a little *friteuse,* an electric fryer, the kind most of my friends here in France have in their kitchens. You plug it in, you add oil, then you totally ignore the instructions because they're guaranteed to give you the soggiest frites you ever had. Instead, you follow the instructions here. I call for very hot oil, which means I crank up the temperature on my little fryer to the max—it results in perfect frites. Have your guests ready to eat as the frites come out of the oil and are seasoned. That's when they're best. You will note these frites aren't made on the grill, but because they're such a perfect accompaniment to grilled meats, particularly, they're included in this collection of recipes.

~~~~~~~~~~~~~~~~~~~~

SPECIAL EQUIPMENT: *Electric fryer (really makes this process easy), fry basket, metal "spider" or perforated spoon, brown paper bags or newspapers printed with soy ink.*

PREPARATION AND FRYING TIME: *20 to 40 minutes, including drying and sitting time*

DIFFICULTY LEVEL: *Simple*

---

1 pound (0.5 kg) potatoes, such as Yukon Gold, peeled and cut into ½-inch (1.25-cm) sticks of any length

5 cups (1.25 l) frying oil, preferably cold-pressed

Fine sea salt or fleur de sel

Piment d'Espelette (optional)

AS YOU CUT THE POTATOES, PLACE THEM IN a bowl of water. Stir them around, rinse and drain them, then put them to dry on a cotton towel that is setting on a wire cooling rack. Make sure they are entirely dry before frying.

Heat the oil to 320°F (160°C).

Prepare either brown paper bags or a good thickness of newspapers (that use soy ink) on your counter.

When the oil is at the right temperature, add a handful of the potatoes—about one-fifth the amount—you don't want to add too many or the temperature of the oil will drop too much and the potatoes will absorb it. Fry the potatoes, stirring from time to time to keep them separated, until they are softened and have a slightly translucent look, about 5 minutes. As you pull them from the oil, let them drain so the excess oil drips back into the frying pot, then turn them out onto the paper. Repeat with all the potatoes, and let them sit for at least 20 minutes.

ASTUCES: Soaking the cut potatoes in water removes some of the starch from the potatoes. This allows the frites to get crispier in the oil. When you're draining the frites after frying, do not use paper towels. They cause the potatoes to sweat and become soggy. Instead, place the frites on brown paper grocery bags or newspapers (that use soy ink).

Increase the heat of the oil to 375°F (190°C). When the oil is hot, add the pre-fried potatoes in small batches and fry until they are crisp and golden, which will take 3 to 5 minutes. Turn these out onto paper and sprinkle liberally with salt, piment d'Espelette, or your choice of flavoring. Serve immediately.

GRILLED WINTER SQUASH WITH MAPLE SYRUP

MUSQUÉE DE PROVENCE AU SIROP D'ÉRABLE

Serves 4

The French adore maple syrup, and they adore musquée de Provence squash (*Cucurbita moschata*), the pumpkin-like squash that Cinderella's chariot was modeled after.

Musquée de Provence is a majestic squash, and it's sold by the gigantic slice at farmers' markets in France. It's always exciting to watch the grower get out his or her huge, machete-like knife to cut a piece to the size that the client wants. Market gardener Baptiste holds the squash against his chest and cuts towards him with a dash of derring-do, sets the slice on the scale, and then hands it to the client. I always want to follow the piece home to see just what it will become. But I would say that nine times out of ten it turns into a thick, cream-rich soup.

Here the squash takes on a new personality as it is grilled, then drizzled with maple syrup. Maple syrup isn't French, you say. True enough; it isn't. But there is so much commerce and tourism between France and Canada that it seems like maple syrup is French, which is why it shows up in all manner of dishes, giving them the sweet touch.

~~~~~~~~~~~~~~~~~~~~~~~~~~~~~~~~~~~~

SPECIAL EQUIPMENT: *Tongs, sturdy spatula*

PREPARATION AND GRILLING TIME: *45 minutes*

DIFFICULTY LEVEL: *Moderate*

---

2 pounds (1 kg) squash, preferably musqué de Provence, but you can use the best squash you find, peeled, seeded, and cut into 1¼-inch-thick (3-cm) slices

1 to 2 teaspoons olive oil

Fine sea salt and freshly ground black pepper

6 long sprigs fresh rosemary plus 1 scant tablespoon fresh rosemary

2 tablespoons maple syrup

BUILD A FIRE IN THE GRILL, OR HEAT UP the gas grill.

Rub the squash all over with oil, then season on both sides with salt and pepper. Soak the rosemary sprigs in water.

When the coals are red and dusted with ash, divide them in the barbecue, putting half the coals on either side. Set the grill over the coals.

When the grill is hot, open it and slip the drained rosemary sprigs onto the coals. They will soon begin to smoke. When they do place the squash slices right over the coals and leave them until each slice has gold marks on it, about 4 minutes. Turn

continued

ASTUCES: If you cannot find musquée de Provence, make this with either butternut or acorn squash. As I served this pure, very French dish to an American, she said, "This would be delicious with bacon on it." So perhaps you'll take that as a suggestion!

and repeat, then place the squash slices in the center of the grill, cover, and cook until the squash is tender, about 30 additional minutes, turning them twice during the cooking process. If you want the squash very golden, move it back over the coals during the final 5 minutes of cooking.

Mince the remaining rosemary.

When the squash is cooked, transfer it to a warmed serving platter. Drizzle it evenly with the maple syrup, sprinkle the minced rosemary over it, and adjust the seasoning with salt and pepper. Serve immediately.

GRILLED SPRING PEAS

PETITS POIS SUR LE BARBECUE

Serves 4

Take each pea and push it onto a trussing skewer . . . No, that's not really what you have to do to grill fresh peas. Read the recipe and you'll find a surprising method here—it's easy, makes sense, and results in peas that are tender, sweet, and just the tiniest bit grilled-tasting. I haven't included instructions for buildling a fire in the grill because this is a side dish, one that you can cook on the same grill that you've fired up for whatever main dish you are serving.

SPECIAL EQUIPMENT: *Saucepan, "spider" or sieve or spoon with holes in it*

PREPARATION AND GRILLING TIME:
*15 minutes to shuck the peas,
10 minutes to "grill" them*

DIFFICULTY LEVEL: *Simple*

---

2 pounds (1 kg) peas in the pod, shucked, to give 2 cups fresh peas

⅓ (60 ml) cup water

Fine sea salt and freshly ground black pepper

4 fresh peppermint leaves

1 tablespoon unsalted butter

ASTUCES: Let's say you're grilling chicken, or steak, or even a big bunch of beautiful mushrooms. You can cook the peas at the same time, or over the coals when everything else has been cooked and there is still plenty of heat available.

RINSE THE SHUCKED PEAS AND PLACE THEM in a saucepan.

Bring the water to a boil in a separate pan and pour it over the peas. Add salt and pepper, and place the pan right over the coals. Cover the barbecue and cook until the peas are bright green but cooked through, about 10 minutes.

Remove the peas from the grill. Mince the peppermint.

Drain the peas and transfer them to a warmed serving bowl. Sprinkle them with peppermint, then place the butter on them and toss until they are coated with butter and mint. Season to taste and serve.

GARLIC POLENTA WITH OLIVES

POLENTA AUX OLIVES

Serves 6 to 8

The first time I ate polenta in Italy I fell in love with it, and it's an affair that has endured through all sorts of delicious iterations. Here, I take olive-studded, cheese-rich polenta and cut it into flavorful triangles, grill it to a golden crispness, and serve it as a side dish, right on the plate with either meat, like Steak with Smoky Olives (page 128), or fish—try Cod with Chermoula, from the Maghreb (page 110)—or as part of a vegetarian meal. It's even good atop a freshly made green salad or along with a plateful of sliced ripe tomatoes.

SPECIAL EQUIPMENT: *Whisk, long metal spatula*

PREPARATION AND GRILLING TIME: *About 1 hour 15 minutes, including setting time for the polenta*

DIFFICULTY LEVEL: *Simple*

---

2 tablespoons olive oil, for the countertop and for rubbing the polenta as it grills

4¼ cups (1.2 l) filtered water

1 teaspoon fine sea salt

1½ cups (240 g) instant polenta

2 large cloves garlic, minced

1 scant tablespoon fresh rosemary

Generous ¼ cup (60 g) best-quality black olives, such as Nyons, pitted and coarsely chopped

3 ounces (90 g) Parmigiano Reggiano, finely grated

Fine sea salt and freshly ground black pepper

LIGHTLY OIL A WORK SURFACE IN A rectangle (about 14-by-12 inches; 35-by-30 cm).

Bring the water and the salt to a boil in a medium saucepan.

Mince the rosemary.

When the water is boiling, whisk in the polenta, pouring it in a thin stream, then whisk in the garlic and rosemary. When the water returns to the boil, reduce the heat so it is bubbling gently and cook the polenta, whisking constantly, then switching to a wooden spoon if necessary, until it is thick, about 5 minutes. Remove from the heat and stir in the olives and the cheese, mixing until they are thoroughly combined. Pour out the polenta onto the prepared work surface into a rectangle slightly smaller than what you've oiled, about 13½-by-11 inches (33.75-by-27.5 cm). Smooth and straighten it as best you can. Let it cool until it is solid and at room temperature.

When it is cooled, brush the polenta generously with some of the remaining oil. Cut it into pieces that are about 3-by-2½ inches (7.5-by-6.25 cm), or triangles that measure 3 inches per side and 2½ inches at the base.

Build a fire in the barbecue, or light up the gas grill, using all three burners. When the coals are red and dusted with ash,

ASTUCES: Polenta bubbles and spits as it cooks if the heat is too high. So once it begins to boil, lower the heat and stay out of the hot steam's way. Before pouring the polenta from the saucepan, I suggest oiling a countertop in a rectangle slightly larger than the measurements for the polenta and pouring it onto that. This makes life easier (and makes it easier to cut the polenta) than pouring it into a pan or other receptacle. Once set and cut, you can prepare the polenta either on the gas grill or barbecue, but I find it works best on the barbecue. Finally, when I say "large" garlic clove, I don't mean gigantic like elephant garlic, but larger than average.

spread them in a tight, single layer, leaving a perimeter of grill with no coals under it; they need to emit concentrated heat. Set the grill over the coals.

When the grill is hot, place the pieces of polenta on it, oiled side down, cover, and cook them until they are golden, about 3 to 4 minutes. Brush the polenta generously with the remaining oil and turn, cover, and continue cooking until the polenta is golden and slightly firm, an additional 4 to 5 minutes.

Strew the polenta with salt and freshly ground black pepper, then transfer it to a serving platter and serve immediately.

BASIC POTATOES ON THE GRILL

POMMES DE TERRE SUR LA GRILL

Serves 6 to 8

This recipe is written for new potatoes, which are filled with moisture. They are so eager and ready to please that they cook in minutes. Once they're cooked, you can serve them as a side dish, turn them into Grilled New Potato Salad (page 199), or use them as part of a vegetable medley. There are two versions of the recipe here, one where the potatoes are left whole, another where they are cut in half, lengthwise, and get quite crisp on the outside. The cooking time is just about the same, but the uses are a bit different.

~~~~~~

SPECIAL EQUIPMENT: *Long metal skewers, pastry brush, tongs, gloves*

PREPARATION AND GRILLING TIME: *Version 1, about 9 minutes; version 2, about 8 minutes*

DIFFICULTY LEVEL: *Simple*

VERSION 1: POTATOES KEPT WHOLE

About 1 pound (500 g) potatoes (8 to 10), washed carefully

Olive oil

Fine sea salt

Freshly ground black pepper (optional)

ASTUCES: You can use less-than-new potatoes here, too, but the cooking time may be slightly longer.

LIGHT A MEDIUM-SIZE FIRE IN THE BARBECUE, or light up the gas grill using all three burners.

Place the potatoes in a bowl, drizzle them with olive oil—not too much, just enough to lightly coat them—and toss until they have a sheen of oil on them. Sprinkle with salt and toss some more. Carefully skewer the potatoes—they are slippery, so when you skewer them, keep the sharp end of the skewer away from your hand and keep the oil that has fallen to the bottom of the bowl for brushing the potatoes.

When the coals are red and dusted with ash, spread them in a tight, single layer, leaving a perimeter of grill with no coals under it; they need to emit concentrated heat. Set the grill over the coals.

Place the skewers on the grill, cover the grill, and cook until they are browned on one side, which should take 4 to 5 minutes. Turn the skewers, brush the potatoes with any oil in the bottom of the bowl, and grill until they are tender through and golden, turning them again at least once, for a total of about 9 minutes cooking time. If using a gas grill, turn off the central burner after about 6 minutes and grill until the potatoes are tender.

Remove the potatoes from the grill, shower them with pepper if desired, then either serve on the skewers or slide the potatoes from the skewers and serve.

VERSION 2: POTATOES CUT IN HALF

About 1 pound (500 g, 8 to 10)
potatoes, washed and cut in half,
lengthwise

Olive oil

Fine sea salt

Freshly ground black pepper (optional)

LIGHT A MEDIUM-SIZE FIRE IN THE BARBECUE,
or light up the gas grill using all three burners.

Place the potatoes in a bowl, drizzle them with olive oil—not
too much, just enough to lightly coat them—and toss until they
have a sheen of oil on them. Sprinkle with salt and toss some
more. Keep the oil that has fallen to the bottom of the bowl for
brushing the potatoes.

When the coals are red and dusted with ash, spread them in a
tight, single layer, leaving a perimeter of grill with no coals under
it; they need to emit concentrated heat. Set the grill over the
coals.

When the grill is hot, set the potatoes on it, cut side down.
Cover the grill and cook until the potatoes are golden, about
3 minutes. Turn the potatoes, brush them with oil, and cook
until they are tender through, about 5 more minutes. Remove
them from the grill, shower with pepper if desired, and taste!

GRILLED NEW POTATO SALAD

SALADE DE POMMES DE TERRE NOUVELLES GRILLÉES

Serves 6 to 8

This salad is so potato-ey, onion-ey, and herb-ey that you'll make it all the time during new potato season, then you'll make it after new potato season, too; I promise. As I tend to like to do, I've added a touch of maple syrup, which is a dream with potatoes. And the quantity of onions here is impressive. Don't stint on them—you'll see, it all goes together perfectly.

SPECIAL EQUIPMENT: *Long metal skewers*

PREPARATION AND GRILLING TIME: *25 to 30 minutes*

DIFFICULTY LEVEL: *Simple*

---

2 pounds (1 kg) Basic Potatoes on the Grill, Version 1: Potatoes Kept Whole (page 196), prepped but not yet grilled

1 tablespoon sherry vinegar

1 tablespoon maple syrup

Fine sea salt

¼ teaspoon piment d'Espelette or a mix of hot and sweet paprika, or to taste

¼ cup (60 ml) olive oil

⅓ cup (3 g) fresh tarragon leaves

¼ cup (2.5 g) fresh flat-leaf parsley leaves

Zest from 1 lemon, preferably organic

6 ounces (180 g) spring onions (not scallions), sliced paper-thin

1 head deep green or reddish lettuce, such as oak leaf, leaves rinsed, dried, left whole

Herb sprigs, for garnish

BUILD A GOOD-SIZE FIRE IN THE BARBECUE, or light up the gas grill using all three burners. When the coals are red and dusted with ash, spread them in a tight, single layer, leaving a space around the edge of the coals; they need to emit concentrated heat. Set the grill over the coals.

When the grill is hot, place the skewers on it, cover, and cook until they are browned on one side, which should take 4 to 5 minutes. Turn the skewers, brush the potatoes with any oil in the bottom of the bowl used for the potato recipe, and grill until they are tender through and golden, turning them again at least once, for a total of about 9 minutes cooking time. If using a gas grill, turn off the central burner after about 6 minutes and grill until the potatoes are tender.

While the potatoes are grilling, make the vinaigrette. Place the vinegar and maple syrup in a large bowl and whisk together. Whisk in the salt and the piment d'Espelette, then whisk in the olive oil.

When the potatoes are cooked through, remove them from the grill and slip them off the skewers and into the vinaigrette. Toss and let them cool.

continued

ASTUCES: Since this recipe is written for new potatoes, it's also intended for young, spring to midsummer onions, which are less hot than an aged, dried onion. Do your best to find those young onions. Also, you don't need to peel the potatoes unless you really want to . . . their peels can be bitter.

When the potatoes are cool, mince together the tarragon, parsley, and lemon zest and add to the potatoes along with the onions. Toss thoroughly. Taste for seasoning. Let the salad sit for at least 1 hour.

To serve the salad, first adjust the seasoning. Then, transfer it to a serving platter that is lined with deep green lettuce leaves. Garnish with the herbs and serve.

HONEYED TURNIPS

NAVETS AU MIEL

Serves 4

The turnip is a humble vegetable, loved by many, decried by some. Those who love them are the lucky ones, because turnips are elegant, flavorful, tender, and altogether surprising! Here, young spring turnips are rolled in honey, then grilled, which enhances their natural sweetness. This works for turnips that have some age and are slightly larger, too. You may want to cut the large ones in half before steaming.

SPECIAL EQUIPMENT: *Steamer, bowl, grill pan, long tongs*

PREPARATION AND GRILLING TIME: *About 18 minutes*

DIFFICULTY LEVEL: *Simple*

2 fresh bay leaves or dried Turkish bay leaves

12 golf ball–size turnips (about 12 ounces; 360 g total), with greens if possible

1 teaspoon olive oil

1½ tablespoons flavorful honey

½ teaspoon Szechuan pepper, slightly crushed

Fine sea salt

ASTUCES: When turnips are young enough, they don't need peeling. It's also nice to leave their stems on, because this gives the young turnips extra allure and flavor. You may want to peel older turnips, as the peel can become bitter.

BRING 3 CUPS (750 ML) WATER TO A BOIL IN the bottom of a steamer; add two bay leaves to flavor the steam. Build a charcoal fire in the barbecue.

Carefully trim the roots from the turnips, leaving them nice and round. Trim the greens, leaving about 4 inches (10 cm). Rinse them thoroughly.

Place the oil, the honey, half of the Szechuan pepper, and a generous pinch of salt in a bowl and whisk to blend.

When the water is boiling, set the steamer over it and put in the turnips. Cover and steam until the turnips are nearly tender through, which will take about 12 minutes. Remove from the steamer and turn the turnips onto a thick cotton towel and quickly pat them dry. While they are still blistering hot, turn them into the honey mixture and toss gently until they are coated with the mixture.

When the coals are red and dusted with ash, spread them in a tight, single layer, leaving a perimeter of grill with no coals under it; they need to emit concentrated heat. Set the grill over the coals and set a grill pan on the grill. When the grill pan is hot, place the turnips on it and grill, turning them frequently, until they are golden all over, which will take 5 to 7 minutes total.

When the turnips are grilled, transfer them to a serving bowl, season with additional salt and the remaining Szechuan pepper, toss gently, and serve immediately.

ZUCCHINI IN MUSTARD SAUCE

COURGETTES À LA SAUCE MOUTARDE

Serves 6

Sometimes I weep for zucchini. It's the vegetable everyone ignores, even though it can be elegant and is simply delicious. Like that forgotten kid who grows up to be a Gregory Peck look-alike and a nice guy to boot, zucchini has many, many virtues worth discovering. This recipe allows it be that gorgeous hunk, and it combines so many French flavors that, once you've tried it, you'll wonder why you didn't fall in love with zucchini before now! I like this either as a first course or a side dish. It goes well with grilled steak, grilled fish, grilled tofu, or anything else you can think of!

SPECIAL EQUIPMENT: *Tongs, spatula, 6 long metal skewers*

PREPARATION AND GRILLING TIME: *18 to 20 minutes if you've already made the mustard sauce; 23 to 25 if you haven't*

DIFFICULTY LEVEL: *Simple*

3 medium zucchini (8 ounces; 250 g each), trimmed and cut in half, lengthwise

¾ cup Mustard Sauce to Have on Hand (page 270)

Parsley or mint sprigs, for garnish (optional)

ASTUCES: There will be leftover marinade. Save it to use as part of a vinaigrette, to drizzle on Grilled Bread with Smashed Tomatoes (page 41), or to brush on a fish fillet right before you put it on the grill. It's got many uses, and it will turn into a sauce you'll always want to have on hand.

CUT THE ZUCCHINI HALVES INTO ½-INCH (1.25-cm) half-rounds.

Add the zucchini to the mustard sauce, folding the pieces into it so they are thoroughly covered. Set aside to marinate for at least 2 hours, and up to overnight.

Build a medium-size fire in the barbecue, or light up the gas grill using all three burners. When the coals are red and dusted with ash, spread them in a tight, single layer, leaving a perimeter of grill with no coals under it; they need to emit concentrated heat. Set the grill over the coals.

Thread the zucchini cubes on the skewers.

When the grill is hot, lay the skewers on it over the coals and cook them slowly, turning regularly until the zucchini is deep golden and cooked through, which will take about 18 minutes.

Remove the zucchini from the grill, and carefully transfer the zucchini from the skewers to a serving dish or platter. Drizzle with some of the leftover marinade and garnish with the herb sprigs, if desired.

WHOLE GRILLED ZUCCHINI

COURGETTES GRILLÉS ENTIÈRES

Serves 6

I get zucchini at the market from my friend Baptiste, who is the best market gardener in the region. Nice as he is, when he sees me coming during zucchini season he rolls his eyes, because he knows I'm going to ask for the tiniest he has so that I can prepare them whole and grilled, which is one of my favorite ways to eat this vegetable. Clients like me make him tear out his hair—when you're supervising an acre of zucchini plants, it is tough to pick them all when they are small, since they double in size overnight when nights are hot. I empathize, but I still ask for small zucchini because they are so tender, nutty, and flavorful. And they're fun to serve whole like this, particularly alongside grilled steak or chicken.

SPECIAL EQUIPMENT: *Plate for the olive oil and salt, tongs*

PREPARATION AND GRILLING TIME: *About 18 minutes*

DIFFICULTY LEVEL: *Simple*

1 to 2 tablespoons olive oil

Fine sea salt

6 zucchini (about 3½ ounces; 105 g each), preferably yellow, rinsed

15 fresh mint leaves

Freshly ground black pepper

ASTUCES: Choose zucchini that are firm, with shiny skins, and that are about 3½ ounces (105 g) each.

BUILD A GOOD-SIZE FIRE IN THE BARBECUE, or turn on all three burners of the gas grill.

Pour the olive oil onto a flat plate. Mix in a generous amount of salt.

Roll the zucchini in the oil and salt so that they are thoroughly covered.

When the coals are red and dusted with ash, spread them in a tight, single layer; they need to emit concentrated heat. Set the grill over the coals.

When the grill is hot, place the zucchini on it and cook until they are beginning to brown and have grill marks on them, about 3 minutes. Turn and repeat. Cover and continue to cook until the zucchini are golden on all sides and tender through, 12 to 15 additional minutes, checking them two or three times and turning them regularly so they brown easily. If they're browning too quickly, move them to the perimeter of the grill so they brown less quickly.

When the zucchini are cooked, transfer them to a platter.

Stack the mint leaves and cut them into fine strips (chiffonade). Garnish the zucchini with the chiffonade of mint and a sprinkling of pepper, and serve immediately while they're hot.

MELTED SPINACH

ÉPINARDS FONDU

Serves 4

When I'm grilling, I always like to plan menus with seasonal vegetable side dishes that make the first course sing and taste delicious on their own. Occasionally, this means I serve a dish that hasn't been prepared on the grill, and this spinach recipe is one example. It's so delicious, and it complements grilled meats, poultry, tofu, and seafood so well that I've included it here. Meaty and deep green, winter to early spring spinach is one of the best vegetables on offer.

SPECIAL EQUIPMENT: *Large saucepan, tongs, large colander*

PREPARATION AND COOKING TIME: *10 minutes*

DIFFICULTY LEVEL: *Simple*

2 pounds (1 kg) fresh spinach leaves, stems removed, washed, spun until not quite dry

1 to 2 teaspoons freshly squeezed lemon juice

Fine sea salt or fleur de sel, for garnish (optional)

ASTUCES: When you spin the spinach after rinsing, spin it just enough so that there is still some water clinging to the leaves. Don't add the lemon juice until just before you serve the spinach, as the acid in the lemon juice will yellow the leaves.

SET A LARGE COLANDER IN THE SINK.

Place the spinach in a large saucepan over medium-high heat. Cover and cook over medium-high heat until the spinach is completely wilted but still bright green, stirring and turning the spinach from time to time so it cooks evenly. This will take about 5 minutes.

When the spinach is wilted, transfer it to the colander to drain. To help the spinach drain, press on it with a potato masher or wooden spoon, and tip the colander as you press so as much liquid as possible drains away. Return the spinach to the saucepan, and set it over a pilot light or in a very low oven so it doesn't continue to cook but stays warm.

To serve, using tongs, transfer the spinach to each of four plates, letting it fall onto the plate so that it makes a lovely, light mound. Drizzle it with lemon juice, then sprinkle with salt, if using. Serve immediately.

CHAPTER 7
DESSERTS

"In everything, one must consider the ending."

—JEAN DE LA FONTAINE, POET

Finally, the chapter we've all been waiting for! I've had so much fun here, adapting dessert recipes for the grill, from chocolate cake to shortcake. I've loved grilling fruit, making cookies and cakes on the grill, and just generally having fun. The combinations here have arisen organically, based on the seasons and the weather, my mood, and requests from family and friends. Remember, when you can, make dessert first. Yes, life is uncertain, but with the dessert already completed you'll be more relaxed as you make the rest of the meal.

FLOURLESS CHOCOLATE CAKE ON THE GRILL

GÂTEAU AU CHOCOLAT SUR LE GRIL

Serves 8 to 10

Yes, this lovely cake is baked on the grill, over a charcoal fire. It is tender and moist, without a hint of smoke. Why then, you say, bake it on the grill? Because the grill is already hot from grilling supper. So, you sit down and enjoy your grilled meal while dessert bakes in the residual—and not insignificant—heat of the barbecue. It makes life simple, easy, and delicious.

SPECIAL EQUIPMENT: *9½-inch (24-cm) heavy cake pan, gloves, stand mixer or whisk and large bowl, wire cooling rack, small pan*

PREPARATION AND GRILLING TIME: *About 40 minutes*

DIFFICULTY LEVEL: *Simple*

6½ ounces (200 g) semisweet (52 to 60%) chocolate, coarsely chopped

3½ ounces (105 g) unsalted butter, cut in pieces

Generous pinch of fine sea salt

4 large eggs, at room temperature

½ cup plus 1 tablespoon (120 g) Vanilla Sugar (page 281)

1 tablespooon confectioners' sugar, for garnish

Fresh edible flower blossoms, for garnish

PREHEAT THE GRILL TO 350°F (180°C) OR LIGHT a fire in the barbecue. Butter and flour a 9½-inch (24-cm) round cake pan.

Place the chocolate, butter, and salt in a small pan over low heat and melt them, stirring occasionally to be sure the chocolate isn't sticking. (You can do this on the grill if there is room.) When the mixture is melted, remove it from the heat to let cool slightly.

In a large bowl or the bowl of an electric mixer, whisk the eggs until they are combined. Add the sugar and continue whisking until they are pale yellow and slightly foamy, which will take several minutes.

When the chocolate mixture is cooled to lukewarm, fold it into the eggs and sugar until thoroughly combined. Pour the batter into the prepared pan, holding the bowl low over the pan so that the mixture doesn't have to "fall" too far.

When the coals are red and dusted with ash, divide them in the barbecue, putting half the coals on either side. Set the grill over the coals.

Set the pan in the center of the grill. Cover and bake until the cake is puffed and slightly firm to the touch on top, which will take 25 to 30 minutes. Remove the cake from the grill and let cool to lukewarm before slicing

ASTUCES: You can mix up the cake and put it in the pan well before you bake it, so it's easy to put it on the grill while you're having dinner. The cake will puff up nicely and look gorgeous, and then it will deflate and look less gorgeous. Don't worry, you can make it lovely on the plate. When the cake has cooled to lukewarm, place a serving plate atop it and flip it. The cake will gently fall onto the plate. Decorate it with confectioners' sugar and flower blossoms, and all will be well. Note: I recommend using a heavy, nonstick pan for this cake.

GRILLED PISTACHIO, ALMOND, AND HONEY STUFFED APRICOTS

ABRICOTS FARCIS AUX PISTACHES, AMANDES, ET MIEL SUR LE BARBECUE

Serves 6 to 8

When apricots are in season I love to prepare and serve them this way. Apricots turn to honey on the grill, though they retain a certain tartness that complements the exotic filling here. I serve these with the Sablés: Normandy Sand Cookies (page 230) and Vanilla Ice Cream (page 243), for a sort of deconstructed tart.

These apricots are also wonderful as a side dish for Duck Breast à l'Orange (page 93) or Lemony, Garlicky, Rosemary Lamb Shoulder Over the Coals (page 143).

SPECIAL EQUIPMENT: *Food processor*

PREPARATION AND GRILLING TIME: *About 20 minutes*

DIFFICULTY LEVEL: *Medium*

---

12 medium apricots (about 1.25 ounces; 40 g each)

⅓ cup (45 g) pistachio meats

2 tablespoons (22 g) raw almonds

Pinch of fleur de sel or fine sea salt

3 tablespoons very thick (not runny) medium-flavored honey, such as wildflower

Large pinch ground cinnamon, preferably Vietnamese, or to taste

Sablés: Normandy Sand Cookies (page 230)

Mint leaves, for garnish

CUT THE APRICOTS DOWN ONE SIDE JUST far enough that you can work out the pit.

To make the filling, grind the pistachios and the almonds with the pinch of salt in the work bowl of a food processor until they are finely ground, but not so much that they begin to form a paste. Add the honey and cinnamon and grind, using pulses, until the mixture is homogeneous. Taste for seasoning.

Stuff each apricot with an equal amount of the filling, which should be about 1 teaspoon per apricot. Close the apricot over the filling, place them on a plate or in a dish, cut side up, and refrigerate for at least 30 minutes (you can also make these up to 2 hours in advance).

Build a medium-size fire in the barbecue. When the coals are red and dusted with ash, divide them in the barbecue, putting half the coals on either side. Set the grill over the coals. Set a grill pan on the grill.

When the grill pan is hot, place the apricots on it with the cut to the side and grill them, turning two or three times, until they are soft through, which will take a total of 6 to 7 minutes.

ASTUCES: Be sure to use apricots that aren't soft in this recipe. If they are too soft, they dissolve on the grill. They need to be "just" ripe. Make the shortest possible slit in the apricot, just big enough to work out the pit and slip in the filling. Note that you place the apricots on the grill with the cut to the side so the filling doesn't run out. Finally, the salt in the filling adds great contrast; you should be able to distinguish that there is salt in it.

Transfer the apricots to a serving platter. Let them sit for at least 10 minutes before serving them, for they are blistering hot at this point. To serve, place two sablés on a plate, and top each with an apricot and a mint leaf or two. Alternatively, serve the cookies alongside the apricots.

GLORIOUS APRICOT, CREAM, AND BASIL TART

TARTE AUX ABRICOTS À LA CRÈME ET AU BASILIC GLORIEUSE

Serves 8 to 10

I host a wine tasting in my home once a month with a group of wine enthusiasts who have been assembling together for more than 15 years. My friend and colleague Hervé Lestage drives to Louviers from Honfleur, where he is the owner of La Feuille de Vigne, a wine shop, and the pocket-size wine bar Bacaretto, a destination for wine buffs in the know.

Sometimes I cook for the tasting, sometimes I don't. Hervé and I consult before he comes, and if I've cooked, he tends to lean toward wines that will complement what I made. This would seem obvious, *n'est-ce pas?* But it's not, because one of the fundaments of Hervé's philosophy is that a wonderful wine will go with everything and anything if it's a wine you love. Having tasted wine with Hervé for so many years, I can only agree.

I digress. For a recent wine tasting, I had a case of apricots on hand and a big desire to make a dessert for the wine tasting. This tart is the result. I stuck my neck out with it because I rarely make a cream-filled tart, and my friends know it. As does Fiona, my daughter, who took one bite, looked at me, and said, "Mom, this is so not you. But it's fabulous." When I served it to the group, silence fell. I have to admit that everyone swooned over it. So it's a keeper, and here it is for you. Try a Vin de Paille from the Jura here, or a lightly sweet Muscat, such as the one from Domaine de Barroubio.

SPECIAL EQUIPMENT: *Gas grill, long tongs, metal spatula, platter*

PREPARATION AND GRILLING TIME: *About 1½ hours, including the making of the pastry and cream*

DIFFICULTY LEVEL: *Moderate*

FOR THE APRICOTS:

2 pounds (1 kg) apricots, just under-ripe, pitted

2 tablespoons unsalted butter, melted

2 tablespoons Vanilla Sugar (page 281)

LIGHT THE GAS GRILL, USING ALL THREE burners. Place a grill pan on the grill.

Place the apricot halves in a large bowl, pour over the melted butter, and toss the apricots so that they are covered with a light layer of the butter.

When the grill pan is hot, place the apricots on it, cut side down, and grill until they are golden, which will take about 2 minutes. Turn them, close the grill, and grill until they are tender, which will take from 4 minutes to 12 minutes, depending on the variety and the ripeness of the apricots. You want the apricots tender

continued

2 ¼ cups Lighter Than Air Pastry Cream (page 280)

1 Sweet Pie Pastry (page 279), pre-baked

¼ cup fresh, tiny basil leaves, preferably from the *Ocimum minimum* species

ASTUCES: Be sure to use apricots that aren't soft in this recipe. If they are too soft, they dissolve on the grill. They need to be "just" ripe. Even so, grilling time varies wildly, from 4 to 12 minutes, so be sure to stand by and watch while they are grilling. As you assemble the tart, you will be faced with a sweet dilemma: to use or not to use all of the pastry cream. If you use it all (usually my choice), you have to accept that when you cut the pieces, the cream will spill over the edges of the cut pieces, giving a deliciously blowsy look. If you use two-thirds of the pastry cream, the tart will be more orderly but not quite so opulent.

but not mushy, and some will soften right before your eyes when exposed to the heat, while others will take longer.

Transfer the apricots to a platter, and sprinkle them with the sugar while they are hot. Let them cool. They will give up some juice.

To assemble the tart, pour the amount of pastry cream you decide to use into the prebaked tart pastry, and spread it into an even layer. Top with the apricot halves, cut side down. Drizzle with a tablespoon or two of the juices that are on the platter. Let the tart sit for at least 30 minutes and up to 2 hours.

Just before serving, garnish the tart with the basil leaves.

SUGAR~GRILLED PEARS WITH POUND CAKE AND CARAMEL

POIRES AU SUCRE GRILLÉES AVEC QUATRE-QUARTS ET CARAMEL

Serves 4

Pears love to be grilled over the coals (or on a gas grill). It's a cooking method that turns them into a translucent, honeyed confection. Once they are grilled, I like to serve them either plain, with Vanilla Ice Cream (page 243) or, better yet, as here with slices of grilled pound cake and a drizzle of salted caramel sauce. You can serve the pears as a "vegetable" with either lamb or poultry, too—they're delicious disguised this way!

SPECIAL EQUIPMENT: *Melon baller for coring, vegetable peeler*

PREPARATION AND GRILLING TIME: *About 25 minutes if you've already made the pound cake and caramel sauce; about 1 hour 35 minutes if you haven't*

DIFFICULTY LEVEL: *Simple*

4 medium pears (8–10 ounces; 250–300 g each), Anjou variety suggested, not too ripe, cored, peeled, and halved

2 teaspoons brown sugar

1 teaspoon freshly squeezed lemon juice

Nutmeg, freshly ground, to taste

4 thick (1-inch; 2.5-cm) slices Golden Vanilla Pound Cake with Orange Marmalade (page 246)

Salted Caramel Sauce (page 277)

BUILD A FIRE IN THE BARBECUE AND WHEN
the coals are red and dusted with ash, divide them in the barbecue, putting half the coals on either side. Set the grill over the coals.

When the grill is hot, place the pears on it right over the coals, cut side up. Leave them there just long enough that they get golden grill marks, which will take a matter of seconds. Turn the pears and let them get grill marks on the other side, again a matter of seconds. Move the pears to the center of the grill, keeping them cut side down. Cover and grill until they are nearly soft through, about 6 minutes. The temperature of the grill will be about 375°F (190°C). Turn them, cut side up, cover, and cook until they are completely tender through, an additional 3 minutes.

Divide the sugar evenly among the pears, mounding it in the indentation left by the core. Drizzle each mound of sugar with an equal amount of lemon juice. Cover the grill and let cook for an additional 2 minutes so the sugar begins to bubble. Transfer

continued

ASTUCES: The most difficult thing here is to give you exact weights and cooking times, because pears aren't standard and no one's palate is the same. These ideas come about, are tested and quantified, and then the variations begin. So I give times that give me the result I want, and I list amounts that suit my palate and make my family and guests happy. I trust that you'll experiment to see what suits you. It's very important to note that the pears should be underripe, not soft. They shouldn't be hard like bullets, but they should be good and firm.

the pears to a warmed serving platter. Dust them with nutmeg to taste.

To toast the pound cake, place the slices on the grill over the coals and turn them regularly until they are golden on both sides, which will take a total of 5 minutes. Quickly, and using a bread knife, cut the slices of cake in half on the diagonal.

Serve the pears and the toasted pound cake either hot, warm, or at room temperature, drizzled liberally with the caramel sauce.

GRILLED PEACHES WITH LITTLE SPICE COOKIES AND SPARKLING JELLY

PÊCHES GRILLÉS AVEC PETITS PAINS D'ÉPICES ET GELÉE ETINCELANTE

Serves 6

This is a perfect summer dessert, but beware! Every element is so addictive that you'll want more cookies, more peaches, more *gelée*. The cookies resemble French *pain d'épices* (spice bread), and the ripe peaches are so fragrant they turn the whole house into a peachery. The cookies are easy to make and they keep well, so I tend to have them on hand. The same goes for the sparkling red currant jelly, which I make by the pint every summer—it's my favorite thing to put on toast in the mornings or use in desserts. With these two ingredients at hand, you're always ready for dessert!

SPECIAL EQUIPMENT: *Grill pan, long tongs, long metal spatula*

PREPARATION AND GRILLING TIME: *About 15 minutes if the cookies are already made; about 35 minutes if they're not*

DIFFICULTY LEVEL: *Simple to moderate*

6 medium peaches (4 to 5 ounces; 120 to 150 g each), not too ripe, pits removed, cut in half

½ teaspoon olive oil

12 Little Spice Cookies (page 244)

2 to 4 tablespoons red currant jelly, or to taste

Tarragon leaves, for garnish (optional)

PLACE THE PEACHES IN A LARGE BOWL.
Drizzle with the oil and, using your hands, toss them gently until they are coated.

Light the gas grill using all three burners, and place the grill pan on it.

When the grill pan is hot, place the peaches on it, skin side down. Cover and grill until the skin is golden, about 4 minutes. Flip the peaches and cook until they are tender, an additional 4 minutes. If you are working with quartered peaches, grill them about 2 minutes per side, until the peaches are soft but not at all mushy. Transfer them to a plate or platter and let them cool to room temperature.

When the peaches are cool, you can easily remove the skin (if desired—this isn't necessary).

To assemble the dessert, place two cookies on each of six plates. Set a half peach atop each cookie. Put a small dollop of jelly in the indentation of each peach. If your peaches are in quarters, arrange them on the cookies and drizzle with equal amounts of red currant jelly. Garnish with the tarragon leaves, if desired, and serve.

ASTUCES: The peaches in France tend to be clingstone, which means they give up their pit with reluctance. If you have the same sort of peaches, you may find yourself with peach quarters instead of peach halves. It doesn't really matter; you just have to be more vigilant at the grill, as the cooking time differs slightly. Also, I love "deconstructed" recipes, so I've given such a suggestion for the presentation of this dessert. But, you know, it's all up to you!

GRILLED PEACHES WITH ORANGE FLOWER WATER

LES PÊCHES À LA FLEUR D'ORANGER GRILLÉE

Serves 4 to 6

A lot of orange flower water makes its way into French cuisine, thanks to the Maghreb and its residents, many who make France their home. I love the flavor so much I planted an orange tree in my garden just to have the aroma for a few weeks a year; I also love its exotic perfume in both sweet and savory dishes. Here it enhances peaches in the simplest way possible. You can purchase orange flower water at any Middle Eastern grocery store and at many upscale supermarkets.

SPECIAL EQUIPMENT: *Gas grill, grill pan, long tongs, pastry brush*

PREPARATION AND GRILLING TIME: *About 15 minutes*

DIFFICULTY LEVEL: *Simple*

6 medium freestone peaches (5 ounces; 150 g each), either white or red, stone removed, cut in half

1 teaspoon olive oil

1 tablespoon Vanilla Sugar (page 281, optional)

1 tablespoon orange flower water

A small handful of red currants, for garnish (optional)

About 1 tablespoon small, fresh mint leaves, for garnish (optional)

BRUSH THE PEACHES ALL OVER WITH THE OIL.

Light the gas grill on all burners. Place the perforated grill pan on the grill.

When the grill pan is hot, place the peaches on it, skin side down. Brown them for 3 minutes, turn and brown them for 2 minutes, then return them to the skin side, cover the grill, and cook until the peaches are tender but still hold their shape, about 5 more minutes.

Transfer the peaches to a serving platter. Immediately sprinkle them with the sugar, if desired.

Just before serving, drizzle the peaches with the orange flower water and swirl them on the platter so it is well mixed among them. Garnish with the red currants and mint leaves, if using, and serve immediately.

ASTUCES: Choose peaches that are fragrant and slightly firm. Softer peaches will work, but they tend to melt on the grill. I like to use a perforated grill pan, and I prefer to grill these on a gas grill. Note that white peaches are generally sweeter than their yellow counterparts. I've suggested garnishing this dessert with red currants, though it really won't need beautifying if your peaches are blushing red. Finally, the sugar is optional, optional, optional.

GRILLED SUMMER FRUIT SALAD

SALADE DE FRUITS D'ÉTÉ GRILLÉES

Serves 6 to 8

I rejoice when summer fruits like nectarines, apricots, peaches, and berries are finally in season. It signals everything wonderful: long, warm days, vacations with friends and family, lots of outdoor grilling, and relaxed meals in the garden. It also makes way for luscious recipes like this one, where fruits are grilled to optimize their perfumed flavors and succulent textures. This is a simple dessert that can be either elegant or rustic, and you'll find yourself making it all the time!

SPECIAL EQUIPMENT: *Mesh grill basket, spatula, long tongs, platter*

PREPARATION AND GRILLING TIME: *About 20 minutes*

DIFFICULTY LEVEL: *Simple*

---

2 pounds (1 kg) peaches, a mix of white and yellow if possible, pit removed, cut in quarters

1 pound (500 g) apricots, halved, pits removed

4 teaspoons olive oil

1 generous tablespoon mild (all flower) honey

2 tablespoons freshly squeezed lemon juice

1 heaping teaspoon lemon thyme leaves

At least 1 cup (½ pint; 120 g) blueberries or raspberries, more if desired

LIGHT UP THE GAS GRILL USING ALL THREE burners. Set the mesh grill basket on the grill.

Place the peaches in a bowl and the apricots in a separate bowl. Divide the oil between the fruits, using slightly more for the peaches because they have more surface area. Gently but thoroughly toss with your hands until the fruit is lightly coated with the oil.

When the grill is hot, place the peaches on it, skin side down. Cover and grill until the skin is golden, about 4 minutes. Turn the peaches onto one side and grill until that side is golden, which will take about 2 minutes. Turn the peaches on their other side and continue grilling until the peaches are soft but not at all mushy. Transfer them as they are cooked to a serving platter. If the peaches have stuck at all to the grill, quickly brush it to remove anything sticking to it, then wipe it quickly with a damp cloth.

Place the apricots on the grill, skin side down, cover, and grill until the skin is golden, about 3 minutes. Turn the apricots and grill them cut side down until they are tender through, which will take 1 to 2 additional minutes. Transfer them to the platter with the peaches, arranging them prettily atop them.

ASTUCES: Use slightly underripe fruit, which holds up better to grilling. You may be surprised at the call for olive oil—it is surprisingly delicious with summer fruits. You won't want to set fruits atop the apricots, as they almost melt when grilled. Instead use the apricots as a garnish.

If the honey is solid, not runny, put it in a heatproof pan and set the pan on the grill just long enough for it to liquefy but not boil. Remove it from the grill and stir in the lemon juice. Pour this mixture evenly over the fruit. Strew the fruit with the lemon thyme. Right before serving, strew the berries over the salad.

STRAWBERRY SHORTCAKE FROM THE GRILL WITH COCONUT WHIPPED CREAM

PETITS GÂTEAUX AUX FRAISES SUR LE BARBECUE
À LA CRÈME DE COCO

Serves 8

So what to do when your darling daughter decides that animals are for loving, not eating? You go to your tried-and-true recipes and see how to adapt them so she—and all the other eaters like her—can enjoy them. I did that with this favorite recipe, and it's gorgeous. And then I went a step further, since I was developing recipes for this amazing book, and baked it over the coals. It works so well you won't believe it. But you need a nonstick grilling mesh (something that's very easy to find). So grill your supper, then grill your dessert! You may serve this with strawberries, raspberries, peaches, nectarines, or even lush and ripe apricots. Adding a bit of sugar to the fruit—not too much—encourages it to give up some juice so you have a sauce without doing any extra work.

SPECIAL EQUIPMENT: *Sieve for sifting, parchment paper, food processor (not essential but very handy), nonstick grilling mesh, pastry brush, handheld or stand mixer, metal pastry scraper, wire cooling rack*

PREPARATION AND GRILLING TIME: *About 25 minutes*

DIFFICULTY LEVEL: *Simple*

BUILD A MEDIUM-SIZE FIRE IN THE BARBECUE.

Combine the berries with 1 tablespoon of the vanilla sugar and toss. Set them aside at room temperature, covered.

Sift together the flour, salt, and baking powder onto a piece of parchment paper. Transfer the dry mixture to the bowl of a food processor fit with the knife blade. Add all but 1 tablespoon of the remaining vanilla sugar and pulse once or twice. Then add the chilled coconut oil and pulse until the mixture is about the size of coarse cornmeal, about five or six times.

Whisk together the soy cream and the almond milk in a small bowl.

continued

3 pints (1½ kg) ripe strawberries, hulled and thickly sliced lengthwise

6 tablespoons (75 g) Vanilla Sugar (page 281)

1¾ cups (270 g) all-purpose flour

½ teaspoon fine sea salt

2½ teaspoons baking powder

7 tablespoons (90 g) solid coconut oil

½ cup (125 ml) soy cream

½ cup (125 ml) almond milk

FOR THE GARNISH:

About ½ cup (125 ml) coconut cream (from one 13.5-ounce; 400-ml can of coconut milk), refrigerated

1 tablespoon confectioners' sugar, or to taste

Mint leaves, for garnish

ASTUCES: To bake over the coals, just make sure half the amount of coals are pushed to each side of the grill. The grill temperature, when covered, should be 425°F; 220°C. You can also bake this on a gas grill with the middle burner turned off; the concept is the same.

If you love the flavor of coconut, use flavored coconut oil here. Otherwise, use a good, organic, unflavored coconut oil. Whichever type you choose, *put it in the refrigerator* so that it's solid when you add it to the dry ingredients. Measure or weigh out the coconut oil, and then refrigerate it until right before you add it.

Transfer the dry mixture to a large bowl and fold in two-thirds of the soy cream mixture. If the dough doesn't hold together, fold in the remaining liquid. (The amount of liquid you use depends on the ambient humidity; flour absorbs moisture from the air, which means it absorbs less liquid when the air is damp. Trust me, I live in Normandy and I know.) The dough will not be wet but will hold together.

Brush the grilling mesh with coconut or other unflavored oil. Press the dough into a 9-inch (22.5-cm) circle on the grilling mesh. Cut the dough into eight equal pieces, being careful not to cut through the grilling mesh. I use a metal pastry scraper, which works perfectly. Sprinkle the remaining 1 tablespoon of vanilla sugar in an even layer on top of the dough.

When the coals are red and dusted with ash, divide them in the barbecue, putting half the coals on either side. Set the grill over the coals.

When the grill is hot, transfer the grilling mesh with the dough on it carefully to the grill, setting it in the center. Cover and bake the shortbread until it is puffed and golden, which will take 12 to 18 minutes. The baking time depends on the grill you are using; check the shortcakes after 12 minutes.

When the shortcake is baked, transfer the grilling mesh immediately to a wire cooling rack. After about 10 minutes, remove the shortcake from the grilling mesh and return it to the rack to cool completely.

Right before you serve the shortcake, place the chilled coconut cream into the bowl of an electric mixer or a large metal bowl. Whisk the cream until it is thickened, then whisk in the 1 tablespoon confectioners' sugar and continue whisking until the cream holds soft points.

To serve, divide the shortcake among eight plates. Top each with an equal amount of the berries, then garnish with the whipped cream and mint leaves.

SABLÉS: NORMANDY SAND COOKIES

LES SABLÉS DE NORMANDIE

Makes about 10 dozen sablés

These tender, melt-in-your mouth cookies will become a staple in your repertoire. They go wonderfully with a fruit dessert after dinner, and they make a perfect afternoon snack with tea or coffee. Make and freeze the dough in logs—it will keep well for several months. Remove the dough from the freezer about 30 minutes before you plan to bake the cookies, which will give it time to thaw enough so that you can cut the dough. Cookies in the barbecue? Yes, it's true: You bake them in the residual heat of a charcoal fire. Serve them to your guests warm, with a fresh fruit salad or a Grilled Summer Fruit Salad (page xx).

SPECIAL EQUIPMENT: *Parchment paper, stand mixer, baking sheets, wire cooling racks*

PREPARATION AND GRILLING TIME: *30 to 33 minutes without chilling time; 2½ hours with chilling time*

DIFFICULTY LEVEL: *Simple*

FOR THE SABLÉS:

3¾ cups (500 g) all-purpose flour

Pinch of fine sea salt

½ teaspoon baking powder

1½ cups plus 2 tablespoons (13 ounces; 400 g) unsalted butter, at room temperature

1 cup plus 3 tablespoons (140 g) vanilla confectioners' sugar

1 large egg, lightly beaten

USING A SIEVE, SIFT THE FLOUR, SALT, and baking powder onto a piece of parchment paper.

In a large bowl or the bowl of an electric mixer using the paddle attachment, mix the butter until it is soft and pale yellow. Add the confectioners' sugar and mix until it is thoroughly blended into the butter, then add the egg and mix until it is thoroughly blended into the butter and sugar.

Add the sifted dry ingredients to the butter and sugar mixture and mix well. Refrigerate the dough for about 15 minutes to make it easier to handle, as it is very soft.

Turn the dough out onto a lightly floured surface and divide it into six pieces. Roll each piece into a log that measures 1 inch (2.5 cm) in diameter. Sprinkle the vanilla sugar on a flat work surface, and roll each log in the sugar to coat it evenly. Wrap each log and refrigerate for at least 2 hours and up to 24 hours so the dough firms up enough to slice.

Just before slicing, preheat the grill to 425°F (220°C). Line two baking sheets with parchment paper.

FOR ROLLING THE SABLÉS:

All-purpose flour

½ cup (100 g) Vanilla Sugar (page 281)

ASTUCES: If you find that the dough sticks to your countertop, dust it *very lightly* with flour; though, if you can avoid this, so much the better. If you like larger cookies, make larger logs! And put them on baking sheets that have the air cushion in them. Depending on the temperature of your grill, your baking time should be about the same as listed here. You can also bake these in the oven if your grill is busy and you want to get these baked. The baking temperature is the same.

Cut the logs into ¼-inch (0.75-cm) thick rounds and set them on the prepared baking sheets, leaving about ½ inch (1.25 cm) between each sablé. Bake one sheet at a time in the center of the grill until they are golden at the edges but pale in the center, 7 to 8 minutes. Remove from the grill and transfer them to wire cooling racks. Repeat with the remaining dough.

FIGS AND CHOCOLATE

FIGUES AU CHOCOLAT

Serves 6

You'll swoon with pleasure when you try this handsome dessert. Seriously, handsome it is, and handsome it tastes. (If you think that handsome is delicious, which I do, then you know exactly what I mean.) Figs are ephemeral, and when they're in season I try to serve them often. My usual is to braise them in red wine, or simply sauté them and serve them as a vegetable. Here, though, they caramelize on the grill, are set in a bed of rich chocolate sauce, and then get a squeeze of lime juice over the top. Oh my, what a dessert.

~~~~~~~~~~~~~~~~~~~~~~~~~~~~~~~

SPECIAL EQUIPMENT: *Grill pan, long tongs*

PREPARATION AND GRILLING TIME: *About 10 minutes*

DIFFICULTY LEVEL: *Simple*

---

12 medium figs, firm but ripe, rubbed clean, stem end trimmed

1 tablespoon almond, sesame, or olive oil

6 ounces (180 g) bittersweet (70%) chocolate, Valrhona or Lindt brand suggested, coarsely chopped

7 tablespoons (105 ml) water

2 tablespoons Vanilla Sugar (page 281)

Sweet and Salty Grilled Almonds (page 31, optional)

1 lime (preferably organic) cut into wedges

ASTUCES: You need a good, hot fire for this because you want to cook the figs fast so the sugar caramelizes nicely on their skin and they turn tender and hot through but don't get too soft. Their skin will stick to the grill in spots, but don't worry, they still look gorgeous.

PLACE THE FIGS IN A LARGE BOWL.

Pour the oil over them and toss gently until they are coated.

Build a medium-size fire in the barbecue, or light the gas grill with all three burners. When the coals are red and dusted with ash, spread them in a tight, single layer, leaving a perimeter of grill with no coals under it; they need to emit concentrated heat. Set the grill over the coals and set the grill pan on the grill.

While the coals are heating, make the sauce. Place the chocolate and the water in a small saucepan over medium heat, and as the chocolate melts into the water, whisk it until it is smooth. Remove from the heat and keep warm.

When the grill pan is hot, brush or rub it with oil. Sprinkle the sugar over the figs, toss them so they are coated with it, and place them on the grill pan. Cook the figs until they are golden and caramelized, turning them often, closing the cover of the barbecue from time to time if necessary to calm the coals if the flames leap up, until the figs are golden all over and softened. This will take about 3 minutes total.

Transfer the figs to a platter.

To serve, divide the chocolate sauce among six dessert plates, placing a round in the center of the plate. Place two figs atop the chocolate, sprinkle several almonds on top (if desired), garnish with a lime wedge, and serve immediately.

TANGY BASIL SORBET

SORBET AU BASILIC ACIDULÉ

Serves 4 (small portions)

Chef Frédéric Anton guides the fine kitchen at Le Pré Catelan, which is located in the heart of Bois de Boulogne, a lush public park in Paris. He is responsible for the idea behind this truly amazing basil and lime sorbet. Its intense flavors pop and zing all over as the sorbet melts on your tongue.

I've classified this as a dessert, and I often serve it at the end of the meal. But you can think about different ways to serve it: as an *amuse-bouche* (you won't want to serve wine with it, as the lime juice isn't compatible), right before the cheese as a palate freshener, or with freshly sliced peaches, strawberries, or a big bowl of just-picked raspberries. It's versatile and a crowd pleaser, and its bright and refreshing flavor makes it a perfect foil for grilled dishes.

SPECIAL EQUIPMENT: *Citrus press*

PREPARATION AND COOKING TIME: *Sitting time of 1 hour; preparation and turning time, about 20 minutes*

DIFFICULTY LEVEL: *Simple*

½ cup (100 g) sugar

2 scant tablespoons water

Juice from 4 freshly squeezed limes (to give a scant ⅔ cup; 160 ml)

2 cups (20 g) lightly packed, fresh basil leaves

ASTUCES: Note that portions are small. This is purposeful, because the flavors are intense. You don't have to cool the sugar syrup in ice, but doing so makes the process much quicker.

FILL A LARGE, HEATPROOF BOWL TWO-THIRDS full of ice cubes.

Place the sugar and water in a saucepan, whisk them together, and bring to a boil over medium-high heat, occasionally shaking the pan gently. Not all the sugar will dissolve, but don't be concerned.

Place the pan in the bowl of ice to cool quickly. By the time the syrup cools, all but just the tiniest bit of sugar will have dissolved.

When the syrup is cool, whisk in the lime juice—the two liquids won't willingly combine at first, but mix them as best you can. Add the basil leaves, pushing them gently under the surface of the syrup. Cover and let sit at room temperature for 1 hour.

Blend the mixture either with an immersion blender or in a food processor until it is deep green with flecks of basil. Freeze it in an ice cream freezer according to the manufacturer's instructions.

VEGAN COCONUT ICE CREAM

GLACE À LA NOIX DE COCO VEGAN

Makes 1 quart (about 1 liter)

This is super, ultra simple, and absolutely delicious. I like to serve it either plain or with ripe peach or nectarine slices. Or with lime zest sprinkled on top. Or with some toasted, unsweetened coconut on top. Or alongside a flourless chocolate cake. Or . . . well, you'll think of plenty of ways to serve it! The chill of ice cream and the pure flavor of this particular recipe create an ideal finish to a grilled meal any time of year.

SPECIAL EQUIPMENT: *Immersion blender or mixer, ice cream maker*

PREPARATION AND FREEZING TIME: *15 to 20 minutes, including freezing time*

DIFFICULTY LEVEL: *Simple*

---

2 cans coconut milk (15 ounces; 450 ml each), preferably organic

½ cup (100 g) Vanilla Sugar (page 281)

½ to 1 teaspoon vanilla extract

Pinch fine sea salt

Zest from 1 lime, for garnish (optional)

ASTUCES: Contrary to the process used to make most ice creams, don't chill this coconut mixture before you freeze it. This is because the fat in the coconut hardens in the refrigerator, blocking the ice cream maker. Also, this ice cream is best the day it is made. You can refreeze it, of course, but it loses a bit in translation. If you have some left over, though, and you want to freeze and then serve it, I suggest putting it in the microwave for 15 seconds to soften it enough to serve.

PLACE THE COCONUT MILK IN A LARGE BOWL with the sugar, vanilla extract, and salt. Using an immersion blender, blend the mixture until it is smooth, then freeze according to the manufacturer's instructions.

Mince the lime zest, if using, sprinkle it over the ice cream, and serve immediately.

ARABICA ICE CREAM

GLACE À L'ARABICA

Makes about 3½ cups (875 ml) ice cream

Many French cooks make their own ice cream and sorbets, and they have a way with flavors that are always pure and simple. I follow their flavor lead and infuse milk with everything delicious and edible I can think of. Here, I've used the best possible Arabica coffee, ground fine, because one of my favorite desserts is . . . coffee ice cream! I serve this plain. It is also not bad at all with Salted Caramel Sauce (page 277). Ice cream is a natural finish to any meal, but particularly one prepared on the grill. And what's even better than the rich, deep flavor of this recipe is that you can make it ahead of time.

SPECIAL EQUIPMENT: *Heavy saucepan, heatproof spatula, sieve, cheesecloth, ice cream maker*

PREPARATION AND COOKING TIME:
30 minutes to make the custard; several hours chilling; churning time 20 minutes

DIFFICULTY LEVEL: *Simple to moderate*

---

2 cups (500 ml) whole milk

1 cup (250 ml) heavy cream, preferably not ultra-pasteurized

½ cup (20 g) finely ground, best quality coffee

5 large egg yolks

¾ cup (150 g) Vanilla Sugar (page 281)

Small pinch sea salt

MIX THE MILK AND CREAM IN A MEDIUM heavy-bottomed saucepan and whisk in the coffee. Place the mixture over medium heat and scald. Remove from the heat, cover, and let infuse for 20 minutes.

Once the milk and cream have infused, whisk together the egg yolks with the sugar and salt in a large bowl until they are pale yellow and light. Set a sieve lined with cheesecloth over the egg yolks and sugar, and slowly pour the infused milk and cream through it. You may have to encourage the liquid to move past the coffee into the bowl by rubbing it back and forth, gently, through the cheesecloth with a spoon or rubber scraper (if some coffee grains get through, don't be concerned). Remove the sieve and whisk the liquid into the eggs and sugar.

Set a large bowl near the stove and set a clean sieve in it. No cheesecloth this time.

Wash the pan you used to scald the milk and cream, then pour the coffee mixture into it and set it over medium heat. Cook the mixture, stirring constantly but slowly in a figure-eight motion, until it is thickened. There are many ways to test the proper thickness, but the best one is just to "feel" it—it will feel quite thick, then will feel thinner, then it will thicken up again and you'll feel a slight resistance as you stir. If it takes

ASTUCES: Stirring the custard in a figure eight is essential so that all of the liquid moves evenly across the bottom of the pan, allowing the emulsion of yolks, sugar, and heavy cream to cook evenly. Don't leave the custard for one minute, and glue your eyes and your stirring hand to it as it thickens—suddenly, it will be just right, and 1 minute later it will go all wrong and curdle. The minute it's thick, pour it through a sieve into a bowl. This way, in case the mixture has begun to curdle, you'll catch any bits that have solidified.

forever and the mixture isn't thickening, you'll have to brave it and turn up the heat, then stir and watch like a hawk. The second you feel it thicken, pour it through the sieve and into the bowl.

Let the custard cool to room temperature, then refrigerate it until it is chilled through. Make the ice cream according to the ice cream maker's instructions.

VEGAN HAZELNUT ICE CREAM

GLACE AUX NOISETTES VEGAN

Makes 3 generous cups (750 ml)

It takes a village to raise a child, or at least to find luscious foods that they will eat as they meander down the lanes of dietary trends. My dear friend and neighbor Lena is very empathetic to my daughter Fiona's vegan proclivity. Lena loves everything hazelnut, and she accidentally came up with a recipe that was very similar to this. She was so surprised at how good it was that she called to have me come taste it. I did, was bowled over by its flavor and texture, and started making it myself. Everyone who has tasted it can't believe how good it is, and they're not vegans. They just love great ice cream! I love serving this after any meal, but particularly after one from the grill.

SPECIAL EQUIPMENT: *Whisk, ice cream maker*

PREPARATION TIME: *About 15 minutes*

DIFFICULTY LEVEL: *Simple*

⅔ cup (150 ml) pure hazelnut butter or paste

½ cup (100 g) Vanilla Sugar (page 281)

2½ cups (625 ml) oat or other grain milk

1 teaspoon vanilla extract

Pinch sea salt

WHISK TOGETHER ALL OF THE INGREDIENTS in a large bowl until they are thoroughly combined. Pour them into your ice cream maker and proceed according to the manufacturer's instructions. The mixture will freeze hard enough that you can make great scoops, but you'll need to ask your guests to eat it immediately, as it melts quickly.

ASTUCES: Don't chill the mixture before you put it into the ice cream maker, as it will freeze too quickly to the sides of the ice cream maker, and the rest of the mixture won't freeze. Just whisk and pour it into the running ice cream maker while the mixture is at room temperature. A few minutes later, you will have an amazing ice cream. Note that oat milk is best here, as it doesn't have much flavor of its own to interfere with the hazelnut paste. Note, too, that the hazelnut paste called for here is just ground hazelnuts, without any additives at all. I recommend Damiano brand hazelnut butter, but use what you find at your grocery, or get hazelnut butter online from retailers like Prana Organic (www.prana.bio). Finally, this ice cream is best the day it is made.

HAZELNUT ICE CREAM

GLACE AUX NOISETTES

Makes 3 generous cups (750 ml)

This is for the nonvegans. There is something about the flavor of toasted hazelnuts that appeals to all ages at almost any moment of the day or night. I have memories of tasting my first hazelnut ice cream in Piedmont, in northern Italy. There, the gorgeous Tonda Gentile hazelnut has brought the region fame, first as an addition to pastries and cookies, and second as a major ingredient of Nutella, that famed chocolate hazelnut paste that began life in loaf form, to be sliced and inserted between slices of bread for a nutritious sandwich. Needless to say, my first taste of Piemonte ice cream (gelato) was life changing.

Here, I make a traditional vanilla crème anglaise, and then whisk hazelnut paste into it while it's still hot so that the paste and the crème anglaise meld together perfectly. You'll love this, and your guests will sign up for seconds.

SPECIAL EQUIPMENT: *Sieve, large bowl, whisk, ice cream maker*

PREPARATION AND COOKING TIME: *30 minutes to make; chilling time several hours; churning time 20 minutes*

DIFFICULTY LEVEL: *Simple to moderate*

3 cups (750 ml) half-and-half

1 vanilla bean, slit down the center

7 large egg yolks

1 cup (200 g) Vanilla Sugar (page 281)

Small pinch sea salt

⅔ cup (150 ml) hazelnut paste, Damiano brand preferred

SCALD THE HALF-AND-HALF WITH THE vanilla bean in a large, heavy-bottomed saucepan over medium heat. Remove from the heat, cover, and infuse for 20 minutes.

In a large bowl, whisk together the egg yolks with the sugar and salt until they are pale yellow and light. Slowly whisk in the warm infused half-and-half, then return the mixture to the pan that held the half-and-half and vanilla beans, after rinsing it first.

Prepare a bowl with a sieve resting on it, right next to where you are working.

Cook the custard mixture over medium heat, stirring slowly but constantly in a figure-eight motion, until it is thickened. There are many ways to test the proper thickness, but the best one is just to "feel" it—it will feel quite thick, then will feel thinner, then it will thicken up again and you'll feel a slight resistance as you stir. If it takes forever and the mixture isn't thickening,

continued

ASTUCES: The best hazelnut paste I've had is the Damiano brand. If you can't find it, use what you find in your local grocery. You can also order hazelnut butter online from retailers like Prana Organic (www.prana.bio). Stir the egg yolk, sugar, and infused mixture in a figure-eight motion so that it moves evenly and regularly across the bottom of the pan and doesn't curdle. Be sure to thoroughly chill the ice cream mixture before you freeze it. This ice cream keeps well in the freezer. To soften it before serving, transfer it from the freezer to the refrigerator about an hour in advance.

you'll have to brave it and turn up the heat, then stir and watch like a hawk. The second you feel it thicken, pour it through the sieve and into the bowl.

Whisk the hazelnut paste into the hot custard, take the vanilla bean from the sieve, and return it to the custard. Let the mixture cool, then chill it thoroughly. After removing the vanilla bean, make the ice cream according to the ice cream maker's instructions.

VANILLA ICE CREAM

GLACE À LA VANILLE

Makes 3¾ cups (930 ml) ice cream

This is the best vanilla ice cream anytime, anywhere. Simple and rich, it is flecked with vanilla seeds that you scrape from the vanilla bean. This gives a true vanilla flavor, which is heightened by the use of vanilla sugar. Once you've made this, you'll never buy vanilla ice cream again!

Note that when making the custard for the ice cream, you must bring it very close to the curdling point in order for it to cook properly. The purpose of the strainer over the bowl is to strain out any beginnings of curdled custard. I suggest making the custard the night before you want to serve the ice cream. This way it will be chilled through before you churn it.

SPECIAL EQUIPMENT: *Sieve, whisk, ice cream maker*

PREPARATION AND COOKING TIME: *30 minutes to make; chilling time several hours; churning time 20 minutes*

DIFFICULTY LEVEL: *Simple to moderate*

3½ cups (750 ml) half-and-half

1 vanilla bean, split lengthwise, seeds removed

9 large egg yolks

1 cup plus 2 tablespoons (230 g) Vanilla Sugar (page 281)

Small pinch fine sea salt

PLACE THE HALF-AND-HALF IN A LARGE, heavy-bottomed saucepan. Scrape in the seeds from the vanilla bean, and add the whole bean as well. Stir and scald over medium heat. Remove from the heat, cover, and infuse for 20 minutes.

In a large bowl, whisk the egg yolks with the sugar and salt until they are pale yellow and light. Slowly whisk in the warm half-and-half with the vanilla bean, then return it to the pan.

Prepare a bowl with a sieve resting in it.

Cook the custard mixture over medium heat, stirring constantly in a figure-eight pattern, until it is thickened. There are many ways to test the proper thickness, but the best one is just to "feel" it—it will feel quite thick, then will feel thinner, then it will thicken up again and you'll feel a slight resistance as you stir. If it takes forever and the mixture isn't thickening, you'll have to brave it and turn up the heat, then stir and watch like a hawk. The second you feel it thicken, pour it through the sieve and into the bowl.

Remove the vanilla bean from the strainer, rinse, pat dry, and return it to the custard.

Let the custard cool to room temperature, then refrigerate it until it is chilled through. Remove the vanilla bean and make the ice cream according to the ice cream maker's instructions.

LITTLE SPICE COOKIES

PETITS PAINS D'ÉPICES

Makes 4 dozen cookies

Pain d'épice, literally "spice bread," is found in almost every region of France. It's a cross between bread and cake, sweetened with honey and sometimes fruit compote, and spiced with anise, but also with ginger, cloves, and occasionally nutmeg. Pain d'épice didn't always belong to the French; the Chinese are thought to have invented a long-lasting, spiced honey cake. Genghis Khan fed his soldiers an early version of this simple bread; he believed in good nutrition, and the combination of honey and rye flour in a bread indeed made for a healthy snack. Today the home of pain d'épice is considered to be the Alsace region, though each region of France tends to have its own version.

These little cookies here are based on pain d'épice without the rye flour. Sweetened with sugar that is deepened with honey, they provide a spiced backdrop to grilled peaches and red currant jelly. And there is nothing quite like one of these cookies with afternoon coffee.

SPECIAL TOOLS: *Sieve, stand mixer, baking sheets, parchment paper, spatula, spice or coffee grinder, wire cooling rack*

PREPARATION AND BAKING TIME: *20 minutes maximum*

DIFFICULTY LEVEL: *Simple*

ASTUCES: You can easily bake these cookies on the grill using the residual heat from the dinner preparation! To do so, all you need to verify is that the temperature of the grill is at 400°F (200°C). Place the cookies on an air cushion baking sheet or on a mesh grill pan, then put them on the grill, cover the grill, and bake away!

I use star anise here, a spice that is used in southwestern France. Spice traders roamed through that territory and, as they went, star anise dropped from their bags into the regional cuisine. It is the only French region that incorporates this flavor, and I prefer it to regular anise. To grind star anise, you need a lot of perseverance and a great spice or coffee grinder. Persist, because it works.

¾ cup (1½ sticks; 180 g) unsalted butter, at room temperature

1 cup (200 g) brown sugar

¼ cup (60 ml) honey, medium flavor, such as blackberry, at room temperature so that it is liquid

1 large egg

2¼ cups (295 g) all-purpose flour

2 teaspoons baking soda

½ teaspoon fine sea salt

1 heaping teaspoon ground ginger

½ teaspoon ground cloves

1 teaspoon ground star anise

½ cup (100 g) Vanilla Sugar (page 281)

PREHEAT THE OVEN TO 400°F (200°C).

Line two baking sheets with parchment paper.

Cream together the butter and brown sugar in a large mixing bowl or the bowl of an electric mixer until light and fluffy. Add the honey, then the egg, mixing well after each addition.

Using a sieve, sift together the flour, baking soda, salt, and spices onto a piece of parchment paper. With the electric mixer working, or by hand, stir the dry ingredients into the honey mixture. The resulting dough will be quite stiff.

Pour the vanilla sugar into a shallow bowl. Form the dough into ¾-inch (about 2-cm) balls, and roll each in the sugar. Place them on the prepared baking sheets, about 2 inches (5 cm) apart and bake until they are puffed and golden, about 10 minutes (you can do this on the grill in the residual heat!). Transfer the cookies to a wire cooling rack, and when they are cool, store in an airtight container. The cookies will keep for 1 week, but they will never last that long!

GOLDEN VANILLA POUND CAKE WITH ORANGE MARMALADE

QUATRE QUARTS À L'ORANGE AMÈRE

Serves 10

Simple, tender, moist, and delicious, this cake can be served at any meal and all those moments in between when you want a cup of tea or coffee with a little something buttery and delicious! Here, I put marmalade on top. You can put anything you like or nothing at all over the cake—it stands on its own. I find the deliciously bitter tang of orange marmalade to be a perfect foil for the cake. The slices grill beautifully, and they take on a toasty, caramel flavor. I serve this cake with grilled pears (see the recipe for Sugar-Grilled Pears with Pound Cake and Caramel, page 217) and a drizzle of Salted Caramel Sauce (page 277). Oh, so good!

SPECIAL EQUIPMENT: *Sieve, parchment paper, loaf pan*

PREPARATION AND COOKING TIME: *About 1 hour 10 minutes*

DIFFICULTY LEVEL: *Simple*

FOR THE CAKE:

1¼ cups (200 g) all-purpose flour

Generous ¼ teaspoon fine sea salt

¾ cup (1½ sticks; 180 g) unsalted butter, softened

¾ cup plus 2 tablespoons (180 g) Vanilla Sugar (page 281)

3 large (180 g) eggs

2 teaspoons vanilla extract

FOR THE ORANGE GLAZE:

¼ cup (60 ml) orange marmalade

PREHEAT THE OVEN TO 350°F (180°C).
Line a 9-by-5-by-3-inch (23-by-13-by-7.5-cm) loaf pan with parchment paper (alternatively, you can butter and flour the pan).

Using a sieve, sift the flour and salt onto a piece of parchment paper.

To soften the butter, place it in a large, heatproof bowl, and place the bowl in the oven as it heats. When the butter is about one-third melted, remove it from the oven and, if using an electric mixer, transfer it to the mixer bowl and whisk the butter until it is light, almost mousse-like. If making the cake by hand, whisk it right in the warm bowl. Add the sugar and continue whisking at high speed (or very vigorously if mixing by hand) until the mixture is very light and fluffy.

ASTUCES: If your marmalade is very thick, heat it slightly with a teaspoon or two of water before pouring it over the cake. You'll note there isn't baking powder in this cake. There are times when baking powder gives a bitterness to cake like this, and if you whisk the butter, eggs, and sugar to a light enough consistency, as indicated here, you don't need baking powder.

Reduce the speed to medium (or mix with less vigor) and add two of the eggs, one at a time, mixing after each addition until they are thoroughly incorporated into the butter and sugar. If the mixture "breaks" and becomes liquid with bits of solid butter, don't be concerned. Add half the flour and salt. Mix at medium speed (with the same vigor) until it is blended into the mixture. Add the vanilla, mix, and then add the additional egg and mix well. Then add the remaining flour and salt.

Pour the batter right down the middle of the prepared baking pan to avoid getting batter on the sides—the batter will spread to fill the pan evenly. Using a sharp knife, slice right down the length of the batter in the center, which will help the cake rise evenly. Place the cake in the center of the oven and bake until it has risen and is golden, 50 to 55 minutes. To test for doneness, stick a metal skewer into the middle of the cake, and if it comes out clean, it's baked. Transfer the cake to a wire cooling rack.

While the cake is baking, place the marmalade in a small pan and heat it over low heat just to liquefy it.

While the cake is still hot, poke several holes on the top with a metal skewer, then pour the marmalade over the top. You may need to *gently* spread the marmalade over the top to even it out.

Let the cake cool for about 10 minutes, then remove it from the pan by pulling on the edges of the parchment paper. Set it on the cooling rack and let cool entirely; remove the parchment paper and serve.

RHUBARB AND APRICOT TORTE

TOURTE À LA RHUBARBE ET AUX ABRICOTS

Serves 6 to 8

What would summer be without rhubarb? Summer? Yes, depending on the variety, rhubarb provides several crops from spring through summer, and as I write this in August, I will soon be stepping into the garden to harvest stalks that I'll turn into this tourte. This year, rhubarb and apricots have overlapped, so I'll slather the pastry with apricot jam. I highly recommend the combination! If you don't have apricot jam on hand and you do have rhubarb, follow the recipe and use a bit more sugar than called for here. You're in for a treat.

~~~~~~

SPECIAL EQUIPMENT: *Removable-bottom tart tin measuring 9½-inches (24 cm) across, rolling pin, baking sheet, parchment paper, wire cooling rack*

PREPARATION AND BAKING TIME: *If you're making the pastry, 1 hour 20 minutes, including baking time*

DIFFICULTY LEVEL: *Simple*

FOR THE TORTE:

1 small egg

2 teaspoons water

1 Sweet Pie Pastry (page 279)

½ cup (100 g) Vanilla Sugar (page 281)

2 generous tablespoons fine tapioca

1½ pounds (750 g) rhubarb, cut in large dice

½ pound (250 g) grilled apricots (see method in Grilled Summer Fruit Salad, page 224)

TO FINISH THE TORTE:

1 tablespoon Vanilla Sugar (page 281)

PREHEAT THE OVEN TO 425°F (220°C).

In a small bowl, whisk together the egg and water. Line a baking sheet with parchment paper.

Roll out the pie pastry to a 13-inch (32.5-cm) circle. Fit it gently into a 9½-inch (24-cm), removable-bottom tart tin, leaving the pastry to hang over the edge of the tin. Brush the bottom of the pastry with half the egg glaze.

Combine the sugar and the tapioca in a large bowl. Add the rhubarb and mix until it thoroughly combines with the mixture, then turn half of it into the prepared pastry. Top with the grilled apricots, laying them out as evenly as possible, then cover with the remaining rhubarb mixture. Carefully fold the edges of the pastry over the fruit—they will be ragged, but don't be concerned; this adds charm! Quickly and thoroughly brush the pastry with the remaining egg glaze. Sprinkle the tablespoon of vanilla sugar lightly over the pastry, then place the tart tin on the prepared baking sheet. Bake it in the bottom third of the preheated oven until the fruit and the pastry are golden and cooked through, about 50 minutes.

Remove from the oven and immediately remove the torte from the edge of the mold. Let cool on a wire cooling rack, then serve.

ASTUCES: You can bake this on the grill if you have a grill that keeps a consistent 425°F (220°C) temperature for the length of time required for it to bake through. Should rhubarb be red or green? There is no right answer to that, nor is there much of a flavor difference. Flavor depends on *terroir* (that is, soil and climate). My rhubarb is green and it's wonderful; I get red stalks at the market occasionally, and they're wonderful, too.

And now, what is a tourte versus a tart? A tourte is a double-crusted tart. Here, I fold the pastry over the filling so it is almost double-crusted, though some of the filling shows, so this is a tourte. Finally, I use a baking sheet lined with parchment for two reasons: setting the tourte on the baking sheet makes it easier to handle; and if juices run out, they are caught by the paper and the baking sheet rather than falling on the bottom of the oven to burn. To remove the tourte from the tart tin, set it on a bowl with a diameter smaller than the bottom of the tart tin, and let the sides fall away. Quickly transfer the tourte to a wire cooling rack.

CHAPTER 8

BASICS: THE BUILDING BLOCKS

*"Basically, it takes as much intelligence to create a successful pantry
as to write a good piece of literature."*

—JULES RENARD, WRITER AND PLAYWRIGHT

B asic recipes are the pantry of French cuisine, the building blocks that make all other dishes taste so good. Using the basic recipes here you can make all of your dishes—grilled and nongrilled—extra flavorful, extra French. I suggest having many of these basic items on hand, such as Herbes de Provence, Curry Powder, Syrian Spice Mix, and Mustard Sauce, so that you can sprinkle them over and blend them into dishes at the drop of a hat. Bon appétit!

CLASSIC VINAIGRETTE

VINAIGRETTE CLASSIQUE

Makes ⅓ cup (80 ml), enough for about 14 cups (350 g) greens

This vinaigrette is terrific to have on hand. I mix up a triple batch (without the chives), pour it into a pretty old wavy glass wine bottle, and have it on hand. As needed, I add chives, minced shallot or garlic, minced fresh herbs, lemon zest and juice, or cracked black pepper. This base makes life so easy. You can use this vinaigrette with a medley of grilled vegetables, grated carrots or beets, fresh tomatoes, or lettuce. It is also great on grilled fish or pork chops.

SPECIAL EQUIPMENT: *Whisk, bowl*

PREPARATION TIME: *5 minutes*

DIFFICULTY LEVEL: *Simple*

---

2 teaspoons Dijon mustard

4 teaspoons red wine vinegar

Sea salt

3 tablespoons (45 ml) mild oil, such as peanut oil

1 tablespoon olive oil

Freshly ground black pepper

1 small bunch chives, to add right before you plan to use the vinaigrette

ASTUCES: If the vinaigrette is too thick for your liking, add a bit of warm water to thin it out (not too much—you don't want it watery). The basic vinaigrette mixture keeps well at room temperature, sealed and in a cool spot, for a month. Remember to shake the bottle vigorously before you use the vinaigrette.

WHISK THE MUSTARD, RED WINE VINEGAR, and a pinch of sea salt together in a small bowl. Slowly whisk in the mild oil until the mixture has emulsified, then whisk in the olive oil. Add pepper and more salt to taste.

Right before you plan to use the vinaigrette, mince the chives and stir them into it. Adjust the seasoning.

WALNUT OIL VINAIGRETTE

VINAIGRETTE Á L'HUILE DE NOIX

Makes ¼ cup (80 ml), enough for about 8 cups (210 g) greens

Walnut Oil is a classic addition to vinaigrettes in the southwest, and in the region around Grenoble, both regions where walnut trees grow with abandon. In both regions, the nuts are grilled before being pressed, to give a toasty oil that improves all it touches.

~~~~~~

SPECIAL EQUIPMENT: *Whisk, bowl*

PREPARATION TIME: *5 minutes*

DIFFICULTY LEVEL: *Simple*

1 tablespoon best quality red wine vinegar

1 shallot, sliced paper thin

Fine sea salt and freshly ground black pepper

⅓ cup (80 ml) walnut oil

ASTUCES: Keep walnut oil—and all nut oils—in the refrigerator between uses, as they're volatile and will spoil quickly.

WHISK THE RED WINE VINEGAR, SHALLOT, a pinch of sea salt, and a grind of pepper together in a small bowl. Slowly whisk in the walnut oil until the mixture has emulsified, then whisk in the olive oil. Add pepper and more salt to taste.

RED PEPPER SAUCE

LA SAUCE POIVRONS ROUGE

Makes about 2 cups (500 ml)

When I say this sauce is good on or with just about everything, I am serious. Roasted red peppers are gorgeous, and this sauce is double-gorgeous because it's gently but intensely flavored with steamed garlic, which adds a hauntingly sweet dimension. Sometimes I season this sauce with cumin, whisk in yogurt, and use it as a dip for crudités. Or I add crème fraîche and a lot of minced parsley and basil to use on grilled potatoes, turkey, chicken . . . the sky is the limit. With this basic sauce on hand, you have dinner in a thrice.

SPECIAL EQUIPMENT: *Tongs, paper bag, plastic scraper, food processor*

PREPARATION TIME: *25 minutes (if using preroasted peppers)*

DIFFICULTY LEVEL: *Simple*

---

8 fat cloves garlic, with skin

4 Grilled Red Bell Peppers (page 177), skin and seeds removed

Fine sea salt

Piment d'Espelette, or a blend of hot and sweet paprika (optional, but advised)

ASTUCES: I encourage you to double or triple the amount of sauce you make here, then freeze what you don't use. Also, once the sauce is ready you can add a tablespoon or two of crème fraîche to dress it up a bit and make it elegant.

BRING 3 CUPS (750 ML) WATER TO A BOIL IN the bottom half of a steamer. Place the garlic in the steamer, cover, and steam until the garlic is completely soft, which will take 15 to 20 minutes. Remove from the heat. When the cloves are cool enough to handle, remove the skin.

Puree the peppers and the garlic in a food processor, then transfer the puree to a medium heavy-bottomed saucepan and bring it to a simmer over low heat. Cook just until all of the pepper liquid has evaporated and the sauce has thickened, 8 to 10 minutes. Remove from the heat and season to taste with salt and piment d'Espelette. The sauce will keep for several days in the refrigerator and for up to three months in the freezer.

CUMIN SALT

SEL AU CUMIN

Makes 3 mounded tablespoons

I like to have seasoning mixtures on hand to dress up a meal, and this is a favorite. I strew it over strips of leftover pastry that I've previously brushed with milk to make it stick, I sprinkle it on freshly sliced cucumbers or avocados. It's great on roast chicken, grilled fish . . . you'll find lots of ways to use this wonderful salt.

SPECIAL EQUIPMENT: *Small, heavy skillet, mortar and pestle or spice (coffee) grinder, jar*

PREPARATION TIME: *5 minutes*

DIFFICULTY LEVEL: *Simple*

---

2 tablespoons very fresh cumin seeds

4 teaspoons fleur de sel

ASTUCES: I keep this mixture in an airtight jar in my spice drawer, but it still doesn't last forever, which is why I make it in small quantities. This way it is always fresh and sprightly with flavor.

I prefer to grind the cumin and the salt in a mortar and pestle, because it results in a mixture that is nicely combined but still has much of its delicate "crunch." If you don't have a mortar and pestle, you can use a spice or coffee grinder. But be gentle about it—you don't want fine dust, but a full-textured mixture.

PLACE THE CUMIN SEEDS IN A SMALL, HEAVY skillet over low heat and toast them until they turn golden and begin to emit a fragrant aroma, which will take 3 to 4 minutes. Remove them from the heat and transfer them to a mortar, or a spice or coffee grinder. Add the fleur de sel and grind the spices together until they are uniformly but coarsely ground. It should be very "sprinkle-able."

Place the mixture in an airtight jar and keep in a dark place.

CURRY POWDER

POUDRE DE CURRY

Makes about ⅓ cup (80 g)

Make this in small batches and use it up, or make it in a larger quantity and keep it in an airtight container in a cool, dark place. Once you've made this curry powder, you may want to adapt this recipe to your own taste, or simply make a variety of powders for a variety of dishes.

~~~~~~~~~~~~~~~~~~~~~~~~

SPECIAL EQUIPMENT: *Small, heavy skillet, spice or coffee grinder, whisk, jar*

PREPARATION TIME: *5 minutes*

DIFFICULTY LEVEL: *Simple*

---

2 small, dried hot peppers

1 tablespoon coriander seed

1 generous tablespoon cumin seed

½ teaspoon red mustard seed

½ teaspoon yellow mustard seed

1 generous teaspoon fennel seed

10 cardamom seeds

2 whole cloves

½ teaspoon ground ginger

¾ teaspoon turmeric

ASTUCES: I have a coffee grinder that I reserve only for grinding spices. I suggest you do the same, because it's impossible to remove the aroma of all the spices I grind, and I'm not wild about curry-flavored coffee.

PLACE EVERYTHING BUT THE GINGER AND the turmeric in a small skillet over medium heat and toast until you can smell the seeds and they begin to turn golden. This will take just a few minutes, 3 to 4, so be vigilant! You can do this on the grill while you're heating it up for something else, by the way!

Transfer the peppers and seeds to a bowl to cool, then grind them to a fine powder in a spice grinder.

In a small bowl, whisk together all of the ingredients so that your powder is homogeneous. Use it up, or store it carefully!

HAMBURGER (OR HOT DOG) BUNS

DES PETITS PAINS POUR L'HAMBURGER (OU HOT DOG)

Makes 8 large buns

For the first many years I lived in France I couldn't find commercially made hamburger buns. That wasn't such a problem, because I love to make bread and have always made my own hamburger and hot dog buns. Now they're easy to find, but I still insist on making my own. As for hot dog buns, I think it will take a while for the French to put a *saucisse de Strasbourg,* which is the French equivalent of a hot dog, into a bun and slather it with neon mustard. So I make these, too. I urge you to do the same—these buns are so much better than anything you can buy.

SPECIAL EQUIPMENT: *Stand mixer (I love my KitchenAid), baking sheets, parchment paper, heavy-duty aluminum foil, wire cooling racks*

PREPARATION TIME: *2 hours 45 minutes, including rising times*

DIFFICULTY LEVEL: *Simple if you're accustomed to making bread; simple to moderate if not*

---

1 cup (250 ml) very warm water (hot water if you use SAF yeast)

1 teaspoon dry baker's yeast, SAF brand recommended

3 tablespoons sugar

3 to 3½ cups (508 g) bleached all-purpose flour

1¼ teaspoons salt

1 large egg

1 tablespoon (15 g) unsalted butter, more if needed

2 teaspoons white or black or both sesame seeds, for garnish (optional)

PLACE THE WATER IN A LARGE BOWL OR THE bowl of an electric mixer. It should be hot enough that when you put a drop on the inside of your wrist you feel it's hot. Using the paddle (not the dough hook) mixer attachment, or a large wooden spoon, stir in the yeast and 1 tablespoon of the sugar and let the yeast proof. It should begin to bubble in less than 5 minutes. When you see bubbles on the surface of the water, stir in 1 cup (145 g) of the flour, the salt, the egg, and the remaining sugar, and mix well. Gradually add 2 cups (290 g) flour, mixing slowly and thoroughly until you have a soft dough. If the dough is still very sticky, slowly add the remaining ½ cup (73 g) of flour. Either knead or mix the dough until it is satiny, for 3 to 4 minutes, then remove the paddle. Cover the dough with a damp towel and let it rise until it is doubled in bulk. This should take about 1½ hours.

Prepare a baking sheet by lining it with parchment paper or make molds for the hot dog buns (see Astuces).

Gently deflate the dough by punching it down and kneading it a few times, and divide it into eight equal pieces. Shape each piece into a round ball (or a log shape if making hot dog buns) by rolling it on an unfloured surface (unless it is very sticky; then, lightly dust the surface and your hands). To make the circle, roll the dough around in your hand, cupping your hand around it without really touching it. Transfer the buns to the prepared

ASTUCES: You may be tempted to use more yeast, but don't. This recipe calls for just the right amount, which results in deliciously puffy, tender bread. I recommend foolproof SAF brand yeast. It requires hot, not lukewarm, water. Don't use quick-acting yeast—it gives a dry result. Note that the flour called for is bleached, all-purpose, which most closely resembles French flour. If you use unbleached flour, you can expect to use a bit less than called for. Also note that the amount of flour called for varies, depending on the ambient humidity. The dough should be very soft and moist, but it shouldn't stick to your hands. You may be tempted to add extra flour, but don't; if the dough is sticky, simply dust your hands and the work surface with a very light dusting of flour. If making these for a vegan, omit the egg and the butter (the buns are still delicious). Finally, if you want to make hot dog buns, simply shape the dough into 5½- to 6-inch (14- to 15-cm) by about 1¾-inch (4.5-cm) logs rather than rounds. You will, however, need to make molds to hold the dough into place. Take aluminum foil and bend it to make narrow molds to help hold the shape of the buns, then fit these molds into a baking pan. Line the individual molds with parchment paper, and you've got hot dog bun molds. (This is so much easier than it sounds, by the way.)

baking sheet, leaving about 3 inches (7.5 cm) between them. If making the hot dog buns, divide the dough into eight pieces and roll each piece into 1-inch (2.5-cm) cylinders. Put them in the molds that you've made. Let the buns rise until they are nearly doubled in bulk, which will take about 45 minutes.

Toward the end of the rising time, heat the oven to 375°F (180°C). Place the butter in a heatproof pan and place the pan in the oven so the butter can melt. When it's melted, brush the buns on the top and sides with the butter.

Bake the buns until they are puffed and golden, which will take 15 to 18 minutes. Remove them from the oven and brush each bun with more butter. Sprinkle with the sesame seeds if desired, then transfer them to a metal cooling rack.

SOME LORE ABOUT HERBES DE PROVENCE

"A year is a crown made of flowers, sheaves, fruits, and dried herbs."
—JOSEPH JOUBERT, MORALIST AND ESSAYIST

Herbes de Provence include the plants that grow wild in the maquis (the landscape of the Mediterranean shores): rosemary, oregano, savory, and thyme. The proportions of herb leaves used in the classic mixture are as follows: just less than one-third rosemary, oregano, and savory, with the complement made up of fresh thyme. Mince the herbs right before you plan to use them. One-half cup of fresh herb leaves will give about 1 tablespoon finely minced herbs. Don't mince them in advance of using them; wait until the last possible minute.

Contrary to popular opinion, classic herbes de Provence, the well-loved mixture that takes you to Provence in a single little pinch, doesn't include lavender. Everyone wants it to have this ingredient, since images of Provence abound with tidy, rounded rows of lavender. But lavender isn't for putting in your herbs; it's for making oil to rub on achy joints, or for sprinkling on your pillow to ensure a calm and peaceful sleep.

HERBES DE PROVENCE

Makes about 1 cup plus 2 tablespoons herbs (11 g);
7 tablespoons (4 g) minced; ½ cup (5 g) dried

This is an almost mythical mix traditionally made with herbs that grow wild throughout Provence. It echoes the landscape, evoking the delicate villages perched atop rugged hills, the twisted vines that produce gorgeous wines. There, this herb mixture is added to everything from soup to fresh goat cheese to the crisp, flat pizzas that come from the many pizza trucks parked in village squares and marketplaces. I use these fresh during the summer and dried in the winter, when I want the sun on my palate.

SPECIAL TOOLS: *Clippers, sun and shade*

PREPARATION TIME: *15 minutes*

DIFFICULTY LEVEL: *Simple*

⅓ cup (3 generous g) fresh rosemary

⅓ cup (3 generous g) fresh savory leaves

⅓ cup (3 generous g) fresh oregano leaves

2 tablespoons fresh thyme leaves

ASTUCES: To dry these herbs, put them outside *in the shade* so that they dry with the hot breeze of summer. Once dried, store them in an airtight container in a dark, cool spot.

MIX THESE TOGETHER AND EITHER USE them as is, or mince just before using.

HUMMUS

Makes about 2⅓ cups (580 ml) hummus

Hummus is an element of the Mediterranean pantry that has made its way to France. While not as common as it is in the United States, it still has its place on the French table. It's easily available at any organic grocery and at some of the more upscale groceries here, too. I like to make my own with organic chickpeas and serve it either as a dip for grilled vegetables or to complement grilled carrots (see Grilled Carrot Dog, page 185).

SPECIAL EQUIPMENT: *Food processor, sieve, plastic scraper or spatula for pushing the hummus through the sieve*

PREPARATION AND COOKING TIME: *About 2½ hours, including resting time for the chickpeas*

DIFFICULTY LEVEL: *Simple*

1 cup (6½ ounces; 195 g) dried chickpeas, or 1 can (1 pound, 500 g) cooked chickpeas

½ teaspoon baking soda

2 teaspoons cumin seeds

2 large cloves garlic

3 tablespoons tahini (sesame paste)

2 tablespoons freshly squeezed lemon juice, more if needed

2 to 3 tablespoons olive oil

Fine sea salt to taste

Piment d'Espelette or hot paprika

ASTUCES: The fresher the dried chickpeas, the more quickly they'll cook and the more flavor they'll have. The soda used here tenderizes the chickpea. As for putting the hummus through a sieve, you don't need to do this, but you'll add a level of refinement to the finished dish if you do.

PLACE THE DRIED CHICKPEAS IN A LARGE, heavy-bottomed saucepan and cover them with about 3 inches (7.5 cm) of water. Place the saucepan over medium-high heat, stir in the baking soda, and bring the water to a rolling boil. Remove the saucepan from the heat and let the chickpeas sit for at least an hour, then drain them. Return them to the saucepan, add water to cover by about 3 inches (7.5 cm), stir in the cumin seeds, and set the pan over medium-high heat. When the water comes to a boil, reduce the heat to medium so that the water is at a relaxed boil and cook the chickpeas, partially covered, until they are very tender, which will take from about 45 minutes to more than an hour.

When the chickpeas are tender, drain them, reserving the cooking liquid. Cool the chickpeas to room temperature.

Place the chickpeas in the work bowl of a food processor and process to a chunky puree. If you're going to sieve the puree, process the chickpeas to as smooth as you can get them, sieve them, and proceed with the recipe. Add the garlic and pulse a couple of times, then add the tahini, lemon juice, and 2 tablespoons of the oil and process until the mixture is light and smooth. At this point, you may add some of the cooking liquid, if you like, to make a softer hummus.

Season the hummus to taste with additional lemon juice if desired, salt, and the piment d'Espelette. To serve, transfer this to a bowl and drizzle with any remaining oil. Either serve this as is, or reserve it for Grilled Carrot Dog (page 185).

LEMON AND GINGER RICE

LE RIZ AU CITRON ET GINGEMBRE

Serves 6

In France, many cooks consider rice a vegetable, and it is routinely served alongside fish, poultry, meat, and vegetables. So I follow suit from time to time, and this is one of my favorite ways to season it. Try this rice with everything, from Lemony Tofu Skewers (page 120) to Grilled, Stuffed Turkey Not Like Thanksgiving (page 96). And if there are leftovers, it's great for breakfast, warmed with a bit of brown sugar on top!

SPECIAL EQUIPMENT: *Fine mesh sieve, medium saucepan*

PREPARATION AND COOKING TIME: *30 minutes, including resting time*

DIFFICULTY LEVEL: *Simple*

2 cups (325 g) white basmati rice

3½ cups (875 ml) filtered water

½ teaspoon fine sea salt

1 inch (2.5 cm) of ginger, peeled and diced

Zest from ½ lemon, preferably organic, minced

ASTUCES: Rinsing the rice removes excess starch, which allows the grains to separate better as they cook. I always call for organic citrus when the zest is to be used. Much citrus is coated with a fungicide wax, which makes it shiny but unhealthy.

RINSE THE RICE IN A FINE MESH SIEVE

under cold water until the water flows clear from it. Place the rice with the other ingredients in a medium saucepan and bring the water to a boil over medium-high heat. Boil until the rice has absorbed most of the water and there are bubble holes on top of the rice, about 10 minutes.

Cover the rice and reduce the heat to medium-low. Cook for 10 minutes.

Turn off the heat under the rice, but leave it covered and let it sit for 10 minutes. Just before serving, stir the rice with a fork to make sure the ginger and the lemon are thoroughly mixed into it. Serve immediately.

MAYONNAISE

Makes about 1¼ cups (310 ml)

Mayonnaise is a fundamental sauce in the French repertoire, and most cooks make it at the drop of a hat. I'm serious. Need mayonnaise? No problem. Five minutes later, there is mayonnaise. You can do that, too, with this basic recipe. Always begin with a neutral oil and finish off with a flavored oil, such as a nut oil or olive oil. The proportions given here are based on my taste and my palate—you may want to adjust them according to your own.

SPECIAL EQUIPMENT: *Wet towel, whisk, blender (optional—this is so easy to make with a whisk)*

PREPARATION TIME: *5 minutes*

DIFFICULTY LEVEL: *Simple*

---

1 teaspoon fine sea salt

1 teaspoon Dijon mustard

1 tablespoon red or white wine vinegar, or freshly squeezed lemon juice

2 large egg yolks

1 cup (250 ml) untoasted peanut or other neutral oil

¼ cup (60 ml) fine quality, extra virgin olive oil

PLACE A WET TOWEL UNDER A MEDIUM nonreactive (such as stainless or pottery) bowl to keep it from sliding around.

Place the salt, mustard, and vinegar in the bowl and whisk them together. Whisk in the egg yolks. Then, *very slowly* and in a fine, fine stream, whisk in the oils. The mixture will thicken as you whisk. You may stop adding oil when it gets to the thickness you desire.

ASTUCES: There are many myths wrapped around mayonnaise. One of the best known is that all the ingredients need to be at the same temperature. This is not true. The only thing that will guarantee the success (i.e., emulsion) of a mayonnaise is the speed with which you add the oil. That speed is *slow,* as in drip by drip. Another note: Although you can make mayonnaise in a blender or food processor, it will not be as tender as the mayonnaise you make by hand. Finally, this recipe makes a very thick mayonnaise; if you want your mayonnaise thinner, begin by adding ¾ cup (185 ml) of the neutral oil and 2 tablespoons of the olive oil, and then proceed with the remaining oils if necessary.

VEGAN NO~EGG MAYONNAISE

MAYONNAISE SANS OEUFS VEGAN

Makes a generous ½ cup (125 ml)

This mayonnaise is for the non-egg eaters in your life. It is rich and thick and, well, tastes just like mayonnaise!

SPECIAL EQUIPMENT: *Whisk*

PREPARATION TIME: *5 minutes*

DIFFICULTY LEVEL: *Simple*

1 tablespoon Dijon mustard

1 tablespoon best-quality, neutral soy cream

¼ teaspoon fine sea salt, or to taste

½ cup (125 ml) neutral vegetable oil, such as peanut or sunflower

1 teaspoon freshly squeezed lemon juice

1 to 2 tablespoons olive oil

ASTUCES: If you like your mayonnaise less thick, simply cut back on the amount of oil that you add. Always remember to leave some room for at least a tablespoon of olive oil, for flavor. Some soy creams have the flavor of cardboard. What you want here is a neutrally flavored soy cream. Once you've got this made, you can season it with flavors like lemon zest, minced garlic, and fresh herbs.

IN A MEDIUM NONREACTIVE BOWL, WHISK together the mustard and the soy cream. Whisk in the salt and, pouring very slowly, whisk in half of the vegetable oil. Whisk in the lemon juice, then whisk in the remaining oils. Season to taste with salt and additional lemon juice, if desired. If you don't use up all of the mayonnaise, it keeps well in the refrigerator, tightly covered, for at least one week and up to two.

AIOLI

Serves 6 (1 ¾ cups; 435 ml)

This sauce is a cornerstone of Provençale cuisine, evocative of sunny climes and the warmth of the Provençale character. Hot with garlic and tender with oil, it goes with so many things in so many situations. I suggest it alongside any grilled vegetables or Rotisserie Chicken (page 99). You can dollop it on Grilled Bread with Smashed Tomatoes (page 41) or tofu. You'll find all sorts of uses for aioli, and you'll be amazed at how easy it is to make.

You may wonder why I call for neutral oil here. I've learned through experience that aioli made with 100 percent olive oil can end up bitter. What's more, it can "break" with no warning, becoming thin and oily. Traditionally it was made with olive oil. Perhaps an oily, slightly bitter aioli pleased the ancient palate, but it won't please yours. My preference is to begin with a pure, neutral, preferably cold-pressed oil such as sunflower or untoasted peanut oil, then finish off with olive oil. Since I've started doing this, "breaking" and bitter aioli are problems of the past!

SPECIAL EQUIPMENT: *Whisk, mortar and pestle or food processor, pitcher for pouring oil*

PREPARATION TIME: *10 to 15 minutes*

DIFFICULTY LEVEL: *Simple*

---

3 medium cloves garlic, the freshest you can find

1 teaspoon sea salt

1 teaspoon Dijon mustard

2 large egg yolks

¾ to 1 cup (185 to 250 ml) neutral oil, preferably cold-pressed sunflower or untoasted peanut oil

1 to 2 teaspoons freshly squeezed lemon juice, or to taste

¼ to ½ cup (60 to 125 ml) fine quality, extra virgin olive oil

MAKE A PASTE OF THE GARLIC AND SALT IN a mortar and pestle by working the pestle around slowly in the mortar. If you don't have a mortar and pestle, either finely mince the garlic with the salt, transfer it to a medium bowl, and press on it with a wooden spoon until it makes a rough paste, or simply mince the garlic and salt together in a food processor.

If you are making the aioli in a mortar, add the mustard and egg yolks and mix until they are blended with the garlic and salt, then using either the pestle or a whisk, slowly add the neutral oil, beginning with ½ cup (125 ml). Add the lemon juice, then add enough of the neutral oil to make a loose emulsion. If you like a very thick aioli, add the entire amount of neutral oil, always finishing off with the olive oil, which gives a gorgeous taste to the aioli. Remember as you add the oil, *slow* is the operative word. If you are using a food processor or blender, keep the machine

continued

ASTUCES: What makes the emulsification here possible is the slow suspension of the oil in the acid and the egg yolks, so when adding the oil to the aioli think *slow, slow, slow.* Should your aioli "break" and become oily and like a thin sauce, there is a simple remedy: Put an egg yolk in another bowl and *slowly* whisk the separated aioli into it. Another thing to note: There is a large variable in the amount of oil used here because the amount you use determines the thickness of the sauce. Finally, I make aioli in a mortar and pestle because I love to do it. I realize not everyone is in love with their tools the way I am, so please, use your food processor or blender if that suits you better. You can keep aioli in the refrigerator for up to a week, but know that when you bring it to room temperature it may "break" and become oily. If it does and you want to "repair" it, whisk the broken sauce into an egg yolk. Garlic is most fresh in the early summer through about November. It is perfectly good after that, but will gradually become less pungent as the year progresses.

running and slowly add the oil. You can also whisk this mixture together in a bowl. If you're using a bowl, put a damp towel under it so it doesn't dance around on the work surface.

If you've used all the oil called for in the recipe and you decide that your aioli is too thick, you can use warm water to loosen it up, a teaspoon at a time. You can also use lemon juice, but you don't want the aioli to be too acidic, so judge accordingly.

Taste for seasoning, and adjust with salt if necessary. Aioli will keep for at least a week in the refrigerator in an airtight container, but it is best served within 24 hours of being made.

MUSTARD CREAM

CRÈME À LA MOUTARDE

Makes about ¾ cup (185 ml)

This is a quick, simple, and elegant appetizer to use as a dip for grilled seasonal vegetables. Think about asparagus, carrots, broccoli, or even potatoes straight from the grill. As for raw vegetables, the sky is the limit. This is wonderful with grilled fish and chicken, too.

SPECIAL EQUIPMENT: *Whisk and bowl*

PREPARATION TIME: *5 minutes*

DIFFICULTY LEVEL: *Simple*

⅔ cup (160 ml) crème fraîche

2 to 3 tablespoons Dijon-style mustard, to your taste

ASTUCES: If you make this ahead of time and chill it, the cream will be very solid. So I recommend chilling it but then removing it from the refrigerator about 15 minutes before you plan to serve.

WHISK THE CRÈME FRAÎCHE UNTIL IT IS thickened. Whisk in 2 tablespoons of the mustard until combined. Taste, and add the additional mustard if desired. Refrigerate until ready to use.

MUSTARD SAUCE TO HAVE ON HAND

SAUCE À LA MOUTARDE POUR L'ÉPICERIE

Makes about ¾ cup (185 ml), enough to season a rabbit, a chicken, several batches of zucchini . . .

As you probably know, the French have "mustard love" in their DNA. If you live here long enough, you will too because not only is French mustard gorgeously delicious, but it makes everything better. I always have at least two kinds in the refrigerator, both smooth and grainy. I put it in every vinaigrette I make, rub it on rabbit, serve it with pork or beef, spread it on bread, and use it in sauces such as this one.

I like to have this sauce on hand for marinating poultry, fish, or pork, and it's also excellent for vegetables. You'll find more uses for it, too. If you make it to have on hand, then don't add the chives; they go in right before you use it. If you're using leftover sauce, add more chives right before you use it.

SPECIAL EQUIPMENT: *Whisk*

PREPARATION TIME: *5 minutes*

DIFFICULTY LEVEL: *Simple*

2 shallots, cut in half and peeled

4 cloves garlic

6 tablespoons Dijon mustard

2 tablespoons grainy mustard

½ cup (125 ml) olive oil

Pinch sea salt (optional)

Freshly ground black pepper

1 bunch chives

ASTUCES: Keep all mustard in the refrigerator, as it loses its kick if kept at room temperature. Mince the chives at the last minute, right before you plan to use them.

MINCE THE SHALLOT AND THE GARLIC

together and place in a medium bowl. Whisk in the mustards, then whisk in the olive oil. Season with salt, if necessary, and a generous grind of black pepper.

Just before you use the sauce, mince the chives and add them. Keep the sauce in the refrigerator if you don't use it immediately.

CILANTRO OIL

L'HUILE DE CORIANDRE

Makes 1 cup (250 ml)

Here, the lemony grassiness of cilantro is softened by being blanched and then blended with top-quality olive oil. Its flavor emerges gently, but its color is a blast of green that brightens every dish it touches. When a new ingredient comes to France, as cilantro did from North Africa, French chefs co-opt it with their special artfulness, as is the case here. I predict you'll make this oil often. You can use this on its own; add it to a vinaigrette, a soup, or a stew; or drizzle it over any meat or fish straight from the grill.

SPECIAL EQUIPMENT: *Food processor, linen or cotton towel, wire cooling rack*

PREPARATION AND COOKING TIME: *25 minutes*

DIFFICULTY LEVEL: *Simple*

Large pinch of salt, for boiling water

4 cups cilantro leaves, gently packed

1 cup (250 ml) olive oil

ASTUCES: This oil is the very best the day it is made, though you can stretch it a day or two if you keep it refrigerated.

TO MAKE THE CILANTRO OIL, FIRST PREPARE a medium bowl of ice water. Cover a cooling rack with a cotton or linen tea towel.

Bring a large pot of lightly salted water to a boil. Place the cilantro leaves in a mesh sieve, and lower the sieve into the boiling water, stirring the leaves gently once they're in the water so they don't clump together. The minute the water returns to the boil, remove the sieve with the cilantro from the boiling water and plunge it into the ice water to cool. As soon as the cilantro leaves are chilled, transfer them to the prepared cooling rack to drain for about 5 minutes. Then, wrap them in the towel and twist the towel as tightly as you can to remove any excess water from the cilantro. The cilantro will feel almost dry when you are finished.

Place the leaves in the work bowl of a food processor fit with the steel blade. Add ¼ cup (60 ml) of the olive oil and process to make a thick paste. With the processor running, add the remaining oil. Transfer the oil to a container and reserve, covered, at room temperature. The oil keeps its intense flavor for a day or two if refrigerated.

PARSLEY OIL

L'HUILE DE PERSIL

Makes 1¼ cups (310 ml)

Parsley has an intense, almost mineral flavor that sings with sunshine when it's fresh. I always use flat-leaf (Italian) parsley because its texture is almost meaty and it is intensely flavorful. Here it gets tamed by blanching, and then it is added to oil to give a fine flavor and color. You can use this on its own; add it to a vinaigrette, a soup, or a stew; or drizzle it over any meat or fish straight from the grill.

SPECIAL EQUIPMENT: *Food processor, linen or cotton towel, cooling rack*

PREPARATION AND COOKING TIME: *25 minutes*

DIFFICULTY LEVEL: *Simple*

Large pinch of salt, for boiling water

4 cups flat-leaf parsley leaves, gently packed

1¼ cups (310 ml) olive oil

ASTUCES: This oil is the very best the day it is made, though you can stretch it a day or two if you keep it refrigerated.

TO MAKE THE PARSLEY OIL, FIRST PREPARE A medium bowl of ice water. Cover a cooling rack with a cotton or linen tea towel.

Bring a large pot of lightly salted water to a boil. Place the parsley leaves in a mesh sieve, and lower the sieve into the boiling water, stirring the leaves gently once they're in the water so they don't clump together. Let the water boil for 2 minutes, then remove the sieve with the parsley from the boiling water and plunge it into the ice water to cool. As soon as the parsley leaves are chilled, transfer them to the prepared cooling rack to drain for about 5 minutes. Then, wrap them in the towel and twist the towel as tightly as you can to remove any excess water from the parsley. The parsley will feel almost dry when you are finished.

Place the parsley leaves in the work bowl of a food processor fit with the steel blade. Add ¼ cup (60 ml) of the olive oil and process to make a thick paste. With the processor running, add the remaining oil. Transfer the oil to a container and reserve, covered, at room temperature. The oil keeps its intense flavor for a day or two if refrigerated.

GARLIC AND PARSLEY SAUCE

PERSILLADE

Makes about ⅔ cup (150 ml)

This is an almost permanent sauce in the French summer kitchen, when parsley is at its "meatiest" and best. Try it with lamb chops, fish fillets, or even steak. It will keep well in the refrigerator for up to one week.

~~~~~~

SPECIAL EQUIPMENT: *Sharp chef's knife*

PREPARATION TIME: *5 to 7 minutes*

DIFFICULTY LEVEL: *Simple*

9 cloves garlic

3 cups (30 g) flat-leaf parsley leaves

⅔ cup (150 ml) olive oil

Fine sea salt

Freshly ground black pepper

ASTUCES: The minute you mince the garlic and parsley, put them in a bowl and cover them with oil to trap the flavors; otherwise they dissipate into the air. Note that you can mince the garlic and parsley in a food processor, but the result is more of a mash than a mince, and it will not be as precise or as flavorful as if you had used a very sharp knife.

DICE THE GARLIC CLOVES, THEN COMBINE them with the parsley and mince them together. Place the garlic and parsley in a small bowl and whisk in the oil. Season to taste with salt and pepper.

TURKISH KEBAB SAUCE

SAUCE POUR KEBAB TURQUE

Makes 1¼ cups (310 ml)

This sauce is intended for the Mediterranean Burgers (page 138), which are inspired by the succulent kebabs that are found on every street corner in cities and towns throughout France. A gift from the Turks, the kebab was first served with flatbread in the nineteenth century, before restaurants appeared in the Ottoman Empire. Traditionally the kebab is lamb; today, though, because there are so many kebab shops and the price of a hearty kebab is kept low, the kebab is often made with turkey. With this sauce, even a turkey kebab is yummy! You can make lamb burgers as a variation of the kebab, or doner kebab as it's sometimes called. Douse your burger liberally with this sauce. You can also use it as a dip for your French Fries (page 188) or on Grilled Asparagus (page 174) or Basic Potatoes on the Grill (page 196).

SPECIAL EQUIPMENT: *Small, heavy skillet, spice grinder, whisk*

PREPARATION TIME: *10 minutes*

DIFFICULTY LEVEL: *Simple*

1 cup (250 ml) Greek yogurt

1 tablespoon Mayonnaise (page 264)

1 tablespoon freshly squeezed juice, more if needed

1 shallot, minced

1 clove garlic, minced

1 bunch chives (¼ cup, when minced)

½ teaspoon toasted cumin seeds, finely ground, or to taste

½ teaspoon piment d'Espelette or a blend of mild and hot paprika, or to taste

Fine sea salt, to taste

PLACE THE YOGURT AND THE MAYONNAISE in a medium bowl and whisk them together. Whisk in the lemon juice, shallot, and garlic.

Mince the chives and whisk them into the sauce along with the cumin and piment d'Espelette.

Season to taste with salt, and add additional lemon juice and/or spices to your taste. This sauce keeps well in the refrigerator for about 5 days.

ASTUCES: I suggest toasting cumin seeds in a small skillet on the grill, alongside your burgers or other foods that are grilling, and then grinding them in a spice grinder or in a mortar and pestle. Also, if you want your sauce more spicy, you know what to do (hint: add more spices!).

SYRIAN SPICE MIX

MÉLANGE D'ÉPICES SYRIENNE

Makes ⅓ cup (80 g)

Once you have this spice in your pantry, I predict you will use it all the time. I use it on everything from lamb chops to grilled vegetables. I also use it on morning toast (after drizzling some olive oil on it!). You, too, will find many uses for this spice mix—like sprinkling it over grilled chicken (or rubbing it under the skin before grilling), adding it to melted butter or olive oil for garnishing popcorn, and blending it with Turkish yogurt as a dip for vegetables. Okay, I'll stop. The point is that this spice mix is the kind of thing you will love to have on hand.

SPECIAL EQUIPMENT: *Whisk, airtight container*

PREPARATION TIME: *Less than 5 minutes*

DIFFICULTY LEVEL: *Simple*

¼ cup Aleppo pepper or pepper flakes, or a mix of piment d'Espelette and Hungarian sweet pepper

4 teaspoons freshly ground black pepper (I like to use voatsiperifery)

2 teaspoons ground allspice

1 teaspoon ground cinnamon (I like Vietnamese)

ASTUCES: If you can, use Aleppo pepper, which has its own rich, smoky flavor that really sets this blend apart. You can easily get it from online retailers such as Penzeys Spices (www.penzeys.com).

PLACE ALL THE INGREDIENTS IN A BOWL and whisk to mix. Store this mixture in an airtight container in a dark, cool spot. It will keep for several months.

SALTED CARAMEL SAUCE

SAUCE CARAMEL SALÉE

Makes 1½ cups (375 ml)

This is a dessert sauce everyone swoons over. It is rich with caramel flavor, bright with salt, and so good you'll want to lap it up from a teacup. I love to use it with grilled pears and pound cake, or over just about any ice cream. You'll find many uses for it, too; and since it keeps in the refrigerator for at least a week, you can take your time!

SPECIAL EQUIPMENT: *Wooden chopstick; whisk; medium, heavy-bottomed saucepan*

PREPARATION AND COOKING TIME: *10 minutes*

DIFFICULTY LEVEL: *Moderate (well, simple but intimidating)*

1¼ cups (310 ml) heavy cream, not ultra-pasteurized

1 cup (200 g) Vanilla Sugar (page 281)

¼ teaspoon fleur de sel

ASTUCES: Don't move one inch from the pan while the sugar is caramelizing! It can burn in the blink of an eye, so you must keep a close watch over it. When you whisk in the warm cream, the mixture will boil up; be brave and just keep whisking until it calms down. I use a chopstick to stir the sugar and break up clumps, if this is necessary.

PLACE THE CREAM IN A SMALL SAUCEPAN over medium heat and heat it so that it is hot to the touch but nowhere near boiling. Keep it hot over low heat.

Place the sugar in a medium, heavy-bottomed saucepan in an even layer over medium heat. When it begins to liquefy and darken at the edges, tilt the pan and stir gently so the sugar is melted and the caramel begins to smoke and turn a deep amber color. If the sugar clumps at any point along the way, you can break up the clumps with the chopstick. Immediately remove the saucepan from the heat and slowly whisk in half the hot cream—slowly but thoroughly. The mixture will bubble up. Be brave and continue to whisk until the cream is incorporated.

Replace the pan over the heat and slowly whisk in the remaining hot cream. If there are any hard bits of sugar in the sauce or at the edges of the pan, just keep whisking over medium heat and the caramel will melt into the sauce

Season the sauce with the fleur de sel to taste, and use it warm or cooled.

ON RUE TATIN'S TENDER TART PASTRY

LA PÂTE TENDRE D'ON RUE TATIN

Makes one pastry for a 10½-inch (26.5-cm) to 12½-inch (31.5-cm) tart, with a bit leftover

Tender, buttery, almost like puff pastry, this simple recipe will change your life. It's very quick to make, and the trick to its success is handling it as little as possible.

~~~~~~~~~~~~~~~~~~~~~~~~~~~~~~

SPECIAL EQUIPMENT: *Food processor*

PREPARATION TIME: *8 minutes*

DIFFICULTY LEVEL: *Simple*

1½ cups (205 g) unbleached all-purpose flour

¼ teaspoon sea salt

¾ cup (180 g) unsalted butter, chilled and cut into 12 pieces

5 to 6 tablespoons ice water

ASTUCES: This is made in a food processor so that the ingredients stay cold while they're being put together. Once the pastry is made, it needs to sit at room temperature before rolling out. If your kitchen is very warm, you may need to put the pastry in the refrigerator for 10-ish minutes, just to firm it up enough to roll out.

For the leftovers: don't reroll the pastry, because rerolling makes it tough. Lightly paint the scraps with milk, then sprinkle them with Cumin Salt (page 256). Cut them into ½-inch-wide (1.25-cm) strips and bake in a preheated 400°F (200°C) oven until they are golden. You'll have the best appetizer you've ever tasted!

PLACE THE FLOUR AND THE SALT IN A FOOD processor and pulse once to mix. Add the butter and process until the mixture resembles coarse meal. Add 5 tablespoons of the ice water and pulse just until the pastry begins to hold together. If the pastry seems dry and dusty, add the remaining 1 tablespoon water.

Transfer the pastry from the food processor to your work surface and form it into a flat round. Let it rest on a work surface, covered with a bowl, for at least 30 minutes. The pastry can sit several hours at room temperature, as long as the room isn't warmer than 68°F (20°C). The pastry is ready to use as desired.

SWEET PIE PASTRY

PÂTE SUCRÉE

Makes one pastry for a 10½-inch (22.5-cm) tart; 36 cookies

This is a wonderful French pastry recipe that results in a cookie-like crust for tarts. I use it when I want the sweet crispness of pastry that will hold a cream filling. It also makes terrific cookies.

SPECIAL EQUIPMENT: *Food processor, rolling pin, baking sheet, 10½-inch (22.5-cm) removable-bottom tart tin, pastry weights, wire cooling rack*

PREPARATION TIME: *About 25 minutes*

DIFFICULTY: *Simple*

1¾ cups (230 g) all-purpose flour

½ teaspoon fine sea salt

½ cup Vanilla Sugar (page 281)

½ cup (125 g) unsalted butter, at room temperature

4 large egg yolks

ASTUCES: You can either press the dough into your tart pan or you can do as I do and roll it out first. Dust a work surface lightly with flour, dust the pastry lightly with flour, and then roll out the dough as far as possible. Roll it over the rolling pin, unroll it out into the tart pan, and then gently press it the rest of the way so as to fit the pan. There is always just enough left over to make a 5-inch (12.5-cm) roll of pastry to chill. (That pastry roll can be cut into rounds and baked into a batch of delightful cookies.)

PLACE THE FLOUR, SALT, AND SUGAR IN THE work bowl of a food processor and pulse a couple of times to mix. Add the butter and pulse until the mixture is pebbled, like coarse cornmeal. Add the egg yolks all at once and pulse to begin to mix them into the rest of the ingredients, then process until the pastry almost holds together.

Turn the pastry out onto a work surface. If it doesn't quite hold together when you press it into a flat round, using the heel of your hand, smear the dough against the work surface to completely mix it until it holds together.

Lightly dust the work surface and the surface of the pastry with flour, and roll it out as far as you can. If you can't roll it out to fit the tart pan, don't be concerned. To transfer it to the tart pan, roll it loosely around the rolling pin and unroll it over the tart pan, then press it into the tart pan so that it lines it evenly.

To prebake the pastry, preheat the oven to 375°F (190°C).

Line the pastry with aluminum foil, then a single layer of pastry weights, making sure the weights evenly cover the bottom of the tart tin, all the way to the edges. Bake the pastry until the rim is golden, 12 to 15 minutes, then remove the foil and weights and continue to bake until the bottom of the pastry is pale golden, about 8 additional minutes.

Remove from the oven and proceed with your recipe. If making cookies, store them in an airtight container. They'll keep for about 1 week.

LIGHTER THAN AIR PASTRY CREAM

CRÈME PÂTISSIÈRE ALLÉGÉE

Makes about 2¼ cups (560 ml)

This is so delicious and so easy to make that you'll wonder why you don't make it all the time. It is also versatile. I use it as a base for banana cream pie, for the Glorious Apricot, Cream, and Basil Tart (page 215), for a trifle, and . . . you'll find lots of uses for it, too.

SPECIAL EQUIPMENT: *Heavy-bottomed saucepan, whisk*

PREPARATION AND COOKING TIME: *30 minutes*

DIFFICULTY LEVEL: *Simple*

FOR THE PASTRY CREAM:

1¼ cups (310 ml) milk

1 vanilla bean, cut in half

5 large egg yolks

⅓ cup (75 ml) Vanilla Sugar (page 281)

1 tablespoon bleached, all-purpose flour

Pinch sea salt

FOR THE WHIPPED CREAM:

¼ cup (60 ml) heavy, not ultra-pasteurized cream, chilled

2 tablespoons Vanilla Sugar (page 281)

SCALD THE MILK WITH THE VANILLA BEAN in a medium saucepan over medium heat. Remove from the heat, cover, and let sit until it cools to lukewarm, about 20 minutes.

When the milk is lukewarm, whisk the egg yolks and the ⅓ cup sugar in a medium bowl until they are pale yellow and fluffy. Whisk in the flour and slowly whisk in the warm milk to make a smooth mixture.

Clean the pan you used to scald the milk, then pour the milk mixture back into it.

Place the pan over medium heat and bring the mixture to a boil, whisking constantly. Whisk in the salt and cook until the sauce thickens, 5 to 8 minutes. Continue cooking until the sauce thins just slightly and becomes glossy, then remove from the heat and let cool slightly.

When the pastry cream is cooled, whip the cream with the 2 tablespoons sugar in a large bowl until the cream holds soft points, and fold it into the pastry cream. Proceed with your recipe.

ASTUCES: The pastry cream will thicken as it cooks, then when the flour is fully absorbed it will thin just slightly. That's when it is ready. If you prefer a thicker pastry cream, double the amount of flour in the recipe. If you're going to make it in advance, rub the surface of the cream with butter while it's hot. This will prevent a skin from forming on top.

VANILLA SUGAR

SUCRE VANILLÉ

Makes 8 cups (3½ pounds; 1¾ kg)

Every baked good is better with vanilla sugar. And every cup of coffee is, too—if my friends who sugar their coffee are to be believed. You don't need to search the grocery store for vanilla sugar; it's easy to make your own. Just follow the recipe, and in about a week you'll have an ample supply.

SPECIAL EQUIPMENT: *Large, airtight jar*

PREPARATION TIME: *5 minutes or less*

DIFFICULTY LEVEL: *None*

---

8 cups (3½ pounds; 1¾ kg) sugar

2 fresh vanilla beans or 4 used vanilla beans

ASTUCES: If you make anything using a vanilla bean, such as Vanilla Ice Cream (page 243) or crème anglaise, rinse and dry the vanilla bean you've used and stick it into your sugar pot. It's got plenty of flavor left to make vanilla sugar. Each time you use a vanilla bean, recycle it this way.

POUR THE SUGAR INTO AN AIRTIGHT container, and push the vanilla beans down into the sugar. Cover and let "ripen" for at least 1 week. Replenish the sugar as you use it, pouring out the sugar that is already flavored, adding new sugar to the container, and topping it with the flavored sugar. Replace the vanilla beans once every 3 to 4 months.

INDEX

* Italics are used to indicate illustrations.